DESTROYERS ON THE ROCKS:

SEVEN SHIPS LOST

Spencer Duckworth

Cypress House

Destroyers on the Rocks: ***Seven Ships Lost***

Cypress House
155 Cypress Street
Fort Bragg, CA 95437
(800) 773-7782
www.cypresshouse.com

Cover and book design: Michael Brechner / Cypress House

Library of Congress Cataloging-in-Publication Data

Duckworth, Spencer, 1923-
Destroyers on the rocks : seven ships lost / by Spencer Duckworth.-- 1st ed.
p. cm.
Includes bibliographical references and index.
ISBN 1-879384-55-8 (pbk. : alk. paper)
1. United States. Navy. Destroyer Squadron 11--History. 2. Shipwrecks--California--Honda, Point--History--20th century. 3. Honda, Point (Calif.)--History, Naval. 4. Destroyers (Warships)--United States--History--20th century. I. Title.
VA63.D4D83 2004
910'.9164'32--dc22 2004008058

Printed in the USA
2 4 6 8 9 7 5 3 1

Dedication

To all those who have served on the destroyers of the United States Navy, and especially to those who, in 1923, lost their lives in the disaster on the coast of California just north of Pt. Arguello, this book is respectfully dedicated.

Foreword

Spencer Duckworth approaches the tragic wreck of seven United States Navy destroyers at Point Honda from a different perspective than other authors do. He describes the background of Destroyer Squadron 11, the reason for its having sailed from San Francisco to San Diego, the wreck itself, the rescue, with its attendant survivals and losses, and the court martial that followed, but goes on to help us answer the question, "Why did it happen?" This book not only fixes blame for the tragedy, as have others, but also shows precisely how the decision-making process was flawed and where it broke down.

On the night of September 9, 1923, the nearby small town of Lompoc was preparing for a big Saturday-night pageant, which was interrupted when nearly everyone went to see the destroyers on the rocks and offer assistance. The most spectacular event in the town's fifty-year history, it even relegated to the position of a back-page story the great Einstein Theory-proving solar eclipse at its peak totality at Point Conception on September 10. Now, eighty years later, there are still Lompoc residents who went to the coast to see the ill-fated ships, and the story is told of how eerie it was to see the scene of the previous day's disaster grow dark during the midday eclipse.

In 2023, just nineteen years from now, one hundred years after the collision with the rocks and reefs near the mouth of Honda Canyon, none of the surviving seamen and no one in Lompoc who saw the ships aground will be here to remember. Spencer Duckworth's *Destroyers on the Rocks* will sustain, for their descendants and for the reading public, the memory of this disturbing peacetime disaster.

—Vance Newcomb, editor, *Legacy,*
Lompoc Valley Historical Society

Contents

Illustrations

Displayed between Chapters 7 and 8

Preface

On the morning of 8 September 1923, Destroyer Squadron 11, U.S. Battle Fleet Pacific, left San Francisco for its home port of San Diego. Before 9 P.M., the squadron's commanding officer, Capt Edward Watson, and his navigator on the flagship USS *Delphy,* mistakenly determined that the squadron was clear of Pt. Conception and positioned for a safe turn eastward into the Santa Barbara Channel. The *Delphy,* followed by its column of thirteen destroyers, turned eastward, but *Delphy* was not in the approach to the Santa Barbara Channel—she was three miles north of Pt. Arguello and less than two miles from shore. Thus *Delphy* led her ships directly into the rocky coast of central California at Pt. Pedernales, west of the town of Lompoc. By 9:06 P.M., seven of the destroyers were stranded on the rocks, and 600 men were in peril. The only buildings in this area were the Southern Pacific's railroad section quarters at Honda, which became the center of the rescue effort and the popular name for Pt. Pedernales. An hour later, the railway telegrapher at nearby Surf touched his key, and *The Los Angeles Times* headline soon appeared: DESTROYERS ON THE ROCKS.

This, the story of the U.S. Navy's record-breaking peacetime disaster, is a story of the major errors by the command of Destroyer Squadron 11. Reduced to its simplest, the reason for this disaster is "navigational error." The question is how could this have happened to ships under the command of experienced officers and manned by outstanding naval crews? In contrast, Destroyer Squadron 12 and the balance of the U. S. Battle Fleet Pacific successfully passed southward to San Diego on the same day.

At the center of the story are the three officers aboard the squadron flagship *Delphy* who were involved in the navigational mess: Squadron Commander Captain Edward Watson; the *Delphy*'s captain, Lieutenant Commander Donald Hunter; and the *Delphy*'s executive officer and navigator, Lieutenant junior grade Lawrence Blodgett.

The disaster occurred while the squadron was making a twenty-knot endurance run from San Francisco to San Diego—a run ordered by RAdm Kittelle, Commanding Officer, Destroyer Squadrons, to test the destroyers' cruising turbines.

Typical summer weather prevailed at the time the ships were lost: low clouds, variable fog, and a brisk westerly wind. The casualty rate was low because the ships became stranded on land, survival efforts by the navy crews were heroic, and rescues by the local people—fishermen, railroad section hands, and train crews—were outstanding.

Complications arose before the squadron left San Francisco. Mr. Eugene Dooman, Capt Watson's invited guest for the voyage, came aboard the *Delphy*, and the two men discussed their diplomatic experiences in Japan. Capt Watson ruled that the desired 20-knot order from Radm Kittelle would be maintained at all times, an interpretation at odds with the usual understanding that such an order is permissive; that is, the stated speed must be maintained unless, in the commander's judgment, seagoing conditions become adverse.

Before the voyage began, Capt Watson changed the squadron's navigational arrangement: he gave responsibility for navigation to LCdr Hunter, his flagship commander. Thus from the start of the voyage, LCdr Hunter took over the responsibilities of the *Delphy*'s regular navigator, Ltjg Blodgett. Later, Capt Watson issued an order prohibiting his ship commanders from requesting radio compass bearings from the U.S. Navy's Radio Compass (RC) Station at Pt. Arguello. As the voyage progressed, the command aboard the flagship *Delphy* led the squadron, yet failed to share its navigational data with its squadron commanders.

During the voyage southward, LCdr Hunter neither foresaw nor understood the potential consequences of his continual dead-reckoning (DR) navigation. At 9 P.M., The *Delphy*, with its ships in column behind it, turned eastward without giving notice. Two of the division commanders blindly followed; the third, relying on his own navigator, steamed westward.

The survival, loss, and rescue of the destroyer men on the seven stranded ships was a story of courage and discipline. Many naval personnel were given official commendations. The quality of the squadron's senior officers was also evident in the rescue effort. (Years later, more than a dozen Squadron 11 officers would achieve flag rank. H. G. Rickover, a young ensign in Squadron 12, would become Admiral Hyman Rickover, and lead the development of the navy's nuclear submarine program. Fifty of the "four-stacker" destroyers would play heroic roles in escorting transports to Britain—the Lend-Lease program of World War II.)

The 10 September 1923 headline from The Los Angeles Times is shown in Illustration **1**, and two of the wrecked destroyers are shown in Illustration **2**. The names of all the men lost are on the memorial plaque shown in Illustration **29**; the plaque is now on display in the Museum of the Lompoc Historical Society. A map of the squadron's route is shown in Illustration **3**. The illustrations are identified in the text to call attention to their story location. A list of Illustrations (**1–31**) is given in the table of contents, and the illustrations are presented with captions and credits between Chapters 7–8.

My experience over the North Pacific Ocean began in 1944 when I became a weather officer in the U. S. Army Air Corps, with responsibilities for predicting flight times (gas loads) for aircraft flying long distances over the Pacific. I have been thrilled to approach the California coast at the end of a fifteen-hour flight over the North Pacific in a propeller-driven airplane, and fortunate to recognize the first major landfall I saw.

I started sailing along the coast of California in 1968. One day, I approached San Francisco from the open sea in a thirty-foot sailboat in zero-visibility fog, with diesel engine, depth sounder, and radio direction finder operating. Since then I have "motor-sailed" in five northern California storms—and one when I was headed home from Victoria, B.C.—with wind gusts of more than fifty knots recorded at nearby airports. I held a U.S. Coast Guard License for fifteen years, and spent a fair number of weeks observing California coastal weather from my sailboat, mountaintops, and airplanes. Notes about my career may be found at the end of this book.

In 1987, the National Weather Association published "Storm in the Gulf of the Farallones: A Sailing Disaster," my technical paper about the April 1982 storm off the coast of San Francisco. Seven sailboats and six sailors were lost in that storm. Sailors who survived it suggested that I study the weather that caused the great 1923 naval disaster on the central California coast. Studying, I learned that there had been no storm, only normal coastal summer weather. My initial search yielded several books about what happened in 1923, but little about why.

To answer that question, I have spent much of the last ten years pondering a wealth of historical data about the disaster, and the important scenes where human strength and frailties played out against a background of error and crisis. One key question is: Why did the competent Capt Edward Watson, the man with the control over Destroyer Squadron 11, and a man aware of the hazards of turning eastward around the coastal elbow of California at Pt. Conception, attempt that turn without exchanging navigational information with his talented commanders?

Certainly, Capt Watson was no fool, so why did he approve his navigator's decision to turn eastward without knowing the flagship's actual position? Why did the flagship's navigator never confer with the squadron's other navigators? Why did Watson fail to order one of his commanders to slow down and take depth soundings? Why did the navigator, LCdr Hunter, fail to request the navy's Pt. Arguello Radio Compass Station confirm one of its RC bearings—when he feared the station had reversed one of the compass bearings it sent to the squadron flagship?

I adopted a factual approach to tell this story without burying it in technical detail. I have taken some latitude in describing the meetings between the sailors and officers on the land, on the sea, and during Fleet Week in San Francisco. In setting those scenes, I relied on the available references, news accounts, people who were there, and my experiences during several Fleet Weeks. Except where otherwise indicated, throughout the book, I have recreated conversations as I believe they were likely to have taken place.

Acknowledgments

Cited references are given in the bibliography. The primary documents are the court of inquiry's "Twentieth Day Report," court martial record, nautical charts, ship's deck logs, court of inquiry's exhibit—the Radio Compass Bearing Sheet of the U. S. Naval Compass Station at Pt. Arguello, California State Surface Wind Climatology, and U. S. Weather Bureau's Weather Maps and Records for September 1923. The assistance of the National Archives and the other agencies that provided copies of the key documents is acknowledged and greatly appreciated.

The background for this story comes from the material cited in the bibliography, and in *Destroyers-60 Years* (Capt W. Schofield); *The Last Hours of Seven Four-Stackers* (Charles Hice); *Tragedy at Honda* (C. Lockwood and H. Adamson); *Course 095 to Eternity* (E. Overshiner); *Marine Weather Handbook* (Cdr K.E. Lilly, Jr.); *Honda Left Turn 095* (J. and M. Silva); *History of the United States* (J. T. Adams); the 1923 articles in the *Lompoc Record* (R. Adam, ed.); and "Rescue by the Men of the Southern Pacific Railroad" (L. Mullaly). The contributions of these authors and those in the bibliography are gratefully acknowledged.

I am grateful to people from the following organizations who contributed to this story: the *Lompoc Record;* Lompoc Valley Historical Society; Lompoc Museum; Vandenberg AFB; U. S. Lighthouse Society; California State Library; U. C. Davis Library; National Archives; Historian-Mare Island Naval Shipyard; Staff-California Railroad Museum; California Air Resources Board; *The Los Angeles Times* and other cited newspapers, and to those who helped obtain historical photographs and writings.

Illustrations **1–31**—maps, charts, and photographs of the ships and monuments—are grouped between Chapters 7 and 8. The memorial plaque is shown in Illustration **29**; St. Peter's Chapel is shown in Illustration **30**; and a classic flush-deck-class destroyer, the *Sumner*, DD 333, is shown in Illustration **31**.

The author appreciates the photographic and artistic skills that contributed to the book; the captions carry specific credits. Special thanks to artists Marilyn Judson and Bill Jackman of Davis, and photographer Janet D. Wilson of Sacramento. Janet Gift and Karen Morriss of Davis helped type and copyedit the first draft of the manuscript, and Joe Shaw of Cypress House did the final copyedit.

Special appreciation is given to Stuart Wilson of Sacramento for obtaining copies of documents on file in the National Archives; Larry Mullaly of Central Point, Oregon, who reviewed an early draft of the book and who wrote Chapter 6; to Robert Cooper of Davis for publication guidance; Mark Franke of Davis, who converted the graphic art into computer format and commented on the final manuscript, and to David Denkers of Davis, who made editorial recommendations on Part II.

Congratulations are due Larry Mullaly on the recent publication of his book, *The Southern Pacific in Los Angeles, 1873–1996,* and to Robert Floyd Cooper on his fine book, *Serenade to the Blue Lady,* the story of Bert Stiles, a heroic young B-17 copilot in WWII.

Thanks to the *Lompoc Record* for the 1923 Ronald Adams articles (Chapter 5), and to the Lompoc Historical Society for Vance Newcomb's editorial comments in the society's *Legacy* articles. Thanks to Vance for permission to use his father's photographs, Vance's photographs (Illustrations **10** and **29**), and his discussions with me about the first draft of the text.

The historical record was incomplete, and I could not obtain all the deck logs from the National Archives. (The logs from the *Delphy* and the *Young* were apparently lost when the ships went down, and the logs from the other five lost ships—according to chronicler Elwyn Overshiner—"are missing from the Master Files." The key document, the court of inquiry's "Twentieth Day Report," is presented in Part III.

Of the many meetings that took place among the people of Squadron 11, only a few were documented. Major references are indented in the text. Only a few of the day-to-day exchanges were written down. For example, Cdr Roper, Commander, Destroyer Division 32, made a radio request of Capt Watson to go to the aid of his division ship, the *Reno*. Capt Watson refused to approve that request, and the two men used some salty language in the tart exchange between them, none of which was written down. Hence, here and elsewhere, much of the dialogue is generalized, and the technical material simplified to show the essence of the encounters and the nature of the command's failure.

The reader is alerted to the nature of the story, most of which doesn't take place in a courtroom; the characters are seldom in the same place at the same time, and the real-life drama is difficult to portray. These destroyer men do what they do, and it is not always explainable; sometimes, what they do is mysterious and may seem contradictory.

A sense of unreality pervades at key moments in the story, and it is often difficult to figure out what is happening, even though the characters are clearly identified and are engaged in distinct activities. Every speech has a known speaker, and the strong emotions of envy, suspicion, falsehood, and self-importance prevail. The squadron's captain and its flagship commander-navigator proceed in isolation from the rest of the squadron.

The lead characters, Capt Watson and LCdr Hunter, are determined, strong-willed officers who move about confidently in their clear-cut world. They walk firmly through their roles, even though they are technically confused on occasion. By the end of the court martial, a part of the audience understands and appreciates what Watson and Hunter tried to do, but remain amazed at the incompetence with which they did it.

PART ONE

Steaming Southward

Chapter 1

1923

I completed my apprentice training at Goat Island in San Francisco Bay, and was given a rating of Seaman 2nd with a pay increase to $36 a month. I was fifteen years old.

—Casey M. Bass, USS *Fuller*

Introduction

The theme of the 1920 election was "a return to normalcy." Most people wanted to avoid responsibility and get back to the days before the First World War, the days before the nation had plunged into the maelstrom of the outside world. Those who desired the impossible return to prewar life and policies argued with those who realized that America was entering a new era of international relations.

Warren G. Harding, a man unprepared to deal with the country's dominant role in world economics, was elected president in 1920. By 1923, it was clear that most of the officials Harding had appointed were corrupt. One of the worst scandals to surface on the national government scene—The Teapot Dome—was created when Secretary of the Interior Albert Fall induced Harding to sign an order transferring the U. S. Navy's oil reserves to the Department of the Interior. Harding's order was without constitutional authority, and Secretary of the Navy Edwin Denby had no right to comply with it. Harding summed up his situation and complained, "It's Hell! No other word to describe it."

The following "signs of the times" are from the chapter "Mad Decade" in *History of the United States,* by James T. Adam:

> One cannot but feel a certain sense of pity for the man (President Harding) who, somewhat against his will and judgment, allowed himself to be elevated to a position for which he was wholly unfitted and who let himself become surrounded by and dependent upon the worst gang of ruffians and grafters that have disgraced any administration in our history.
>
> The radio, which had been used to some extent before the war for transmission of messages only, began to revolutionize the lives of the people with the erection of the first broadcast station in 1921.
>
> Like the old legend of the Fountain of Youth, a new belief arose that we had discovered the way to eternal prosperity... Why wait until one had saved money for anything one wanted? The introduc-

> tion—on a great scale and in new fields—of the installment-purchase idea became another forced draft underpinning the rise in production and apparent prosperity.
>
> There is good evidence that by the summer of 1923 Harding was becoming greatly worried over the situation of both his administration and himself, including his former relationship to a certain Nan Britton... The results of Harding's easy handing over of his responsibility to others, and his own personal habits and weakness, were beginning to involve him in a situation from which there was no escape... when he started a trip to Alaska in June 1923... Returning from Alaska to San Francisco, he was said to be suffering from ptomaine poisoning... the mystery of his death has never been cleared up, and as all his papers were destroyed by Mrs. Harding... there was evidently much that may now be never known.

Another sign of the times was the land-boom hysteria that swept over parts of the country. According to the article "The Madness that Swept Miami" by D. Stewart, a carnival atmosphere prevailed in south Florida. One photograph shows a huge gathering of workers, tractors, steam shovels, motorcycles, horse-drawn wagons, automobiles, and a wagon pulled by a small elephant. The location for this publicity shot was a remote intersection in Miami Beach that was about to be converted into a housing tract. The scene before the crowd arrived showed only a few lampposts and two unpaved roads.

President Harding Goes to Alaska

The president's advisers decided that something had to be done to diffuse the Senate's investigation of the various national scandals. It was decided that the President would visit Alaska and inspect its oil reserves. The U. S. Navy offered its large transport, USS *Henderson,* to take the president and his official party on the round-trip to Alaska. A massive return ceremony was planned for late July—a

Presidential Review of the U. S. Battle Fleet Pacific in Puget Sound. The navy soon ordered the battle fleet—battleships, destroyers, and other ships—to move northward from San Diego for the review.

The *Henderson* returned to Seattle on schedule. On July 27, on a somewhat foggy morning, the *Henderson* steamed into Puget Sound escorted by the destroyers USS *Corry* and USS *Hull* (two of the newer ships in Squadron 12). Later, the other destroyer escort approached: the USS *Zeilin* (the newest ship in Squadron 11). The President, Mrs. Harding, Mr. and Mrs. Hoover, and other officials were asleep aboard the *Henderson*. At 7:55 A.M., the *Henderson* rammed the portside of the *Zeilin,* which was flooded and listing badly by 8:15. The crews of all the nearby ships worked to save the *Zeilin,* but the crew had to quickly abandon ship. *Corry* and *Hull* aided the *Zeilin*'s crew. An army tug and a navy tug led the rescue, and managed to beach the *Zeilin*'s bent hull. The captain of the *Henderson* took no rescue action, but he got favorable reviews in the newspaper for maneuvering the *Henderson* so it did not cut the *Zeilin* in half. The president and the official party were not disturbed. There was some doubt as to how the *Zeilin* managed to get in front of, and across the bow of, the *Henderson*.

The fog thinned as the day progressed, and the greatest peacetime Presidential Review of the U. S. Battle Fleet got underway. The fleet included three divisions of battleships, two squadrons of destroyers, the fleet flagship, the armored cruiser USS *Seattle*, the destroyer squadron's flagship, USS *Melville,* and various support ships. The president was ill, and stood with help from Mrs. Harding and an aide. When the review ended, Mrs. Harding quickly put the president on a train for San Francisco. There, on August 2, the president died in the Palace Hotel.

On August 24, a month after the review, Squadron 11 headed for San Francisco. The destroyers arrived in foggy weather off the Golden Gate in the early morning of August 31. The crew dressed for liberty, as it was Fleet Week in San Francisco. The fog thickened, and Squadron 11 anchored to sea several miles from the San Francisco Lightship. At 10 A.M. the visibility improved and the "tin cans," flags flying, were impressive as they steamed into San Francisco Bay.

Navy crews always looked forward to the party called Fleet Week. On the business side, however, the navy brass looked at a grim budget, with the battleship men in control of its distribution. The destroyer men were distressed when they saw their scant allowance for buying fuel oil and such necessary new gear as depth-sounding instruments.

Destroyer History

The history of the Flush Deck Class of destroyers is exceptional. It began in 1918 and continued through its combat role in World War II. Fifty of these destroyers protected the Atlantic route to Britain and played a major role in combating the Atlantic submarine threat. While carrying refugees to Australia, the destroyer *Pillsbury* (Illustration **20**), with only a frigate and a gunboat by its side, fought the Japanese Navy and lost.

From the construction of the first one, the destroyer was a special vessel. In his book, *The People's Navy,* historian Kenneth Hagan put it this way:

> When John Paul Jones pleaded for a fast-sailing ship because he intended 'to go in harms way,' he set the tone for the first hundred years of naval history. The navy in the age of sail and in the early years of steam was built around "fast ships skippered by bold captains, officered by ambitious lieutenants, and manned by individualistic seamen." The navy in the era of the sailing frigate was designed to hit and run, to attack enemy merchant vessels, small warships—but flee if faced with a stronger naval opponent. This strategy, which the French call guerre de course, reached its apogee ... when Captain Semmes set a world-class standard for commerce raiding as skipper of the famed Confederate raider *Alabama* .

The first destroyer in the U. S. Navy was the *Bainbridge,* DD-1. Built in 1902, it was a direct descendant of the original torpedo boats. At 420 tons it was one-third the weight of the destroyers in this story. Coal-fired from a supply of 180 tons, it had the destroyer characteristics: long, narrow, and fast (215 ft., 23.5 ft., and a trial speed of 28 knots). It proved itself beyond equal in versatility, reliability, and readiness to answer any emergency call upon the world's sea-lanes. It had a smoky profile from burning coal.

The second destroyer to carry the name *Bainbridge* was a flush-deck destroyer launched in June 1920. In December 1922 it was in the Sea of Marmara (between European and Asian Turkey and between the Bosporus and Dardanelles) when it received an emergency call for help for the French military transport *Vinh-Long.* As described by Capt William Schofield, USNR, in his book *Destroyers–60 Years:*

> The *Bainbridge* fought her way alongside the burning transport and attempted to remove passengers and crew trapped by a raging blaze. Ammunition explosions twice blasted the *Bainbridge* away from the side of the flaming French ship, but the *Bainbridge* struggled back to keep the rescue operation in hand. To hold her position, *Bainbridge* finally rammed her bow into the doomed French ship. Thereupon her crew, working under a rain of exploding munitions, saved the lives of 482 of the 495 men and women who had been trapped aboard the blazing transport.

The third *Bainbridge* was DD 246, a "Flush Deck Class" (also known as "Clemson") destroyer, slightly older but nearly identical to the *Delphy* of Squadron 11. All the destroyers at sea in 1923 were in that class, the first of which was built in 1918. This was the largest class of destroyers ever built, and the class eventually carried the hull numbers DD 185–347. They were kindly called "flush-deckers," "cavalry of the sea" (because of their mobility), "four-stackers" (design profile), "greyhounds of the sea" (speed), and "tin-cans" (thin steel construction). The battleship men called them "small boys," and the naval strategists called them "spearheads of sea power." To the enemy, they were instant signals to flee or fight.

Many of the flush-decker destroyers afloat in 1923 were built in the San Francisco Bay area. USS *Trever,* DD 339 (Illustration **4**) and USS *Litchfield,* DD 336 (Illustration **6**) were built in the Mare Island Naval Shipyard in Vallejo. The head-on view of the *Trever* and the profile of the *Litchfield* give a feeling of these ships. They look like the ⅜-inch ½ steel they were made of: cold, tough, wet, and uncomfortable. Both were sister ships of Squadron 11's *Young,* DD 312. The ships of Squadron 11 and 12 mentioned in this story—*Corry, Reno, Selfridge, Sloat, Somers, Thompson,* and *Zeilin*—were built in the Bethlehem Steel Shipyard at South San Francisco. (A technical description of the class is given in Appendix VI.) The heart of each destroyer was its engine and boiler rooms. It was here that the engine men sweated, labored, observed steam, water, air, vacuum, hydraulic and fuel gages—turned valves, carefully gauged the revolutions per minute of the straining steam turbines, and made the countless motions necessary to maintain the squadron's standard speed.

These sleek men-of-war destroyers were built just after World War I and suffered from the wave of military economy in its aftermath. They were sorely undermanned, and in some cases carried only two-thirds of their required complement of officers and men. Most ships carried two radiomen instead of the normal crew of three. Double watches were often the order of the day, particularly for men carrying titles as Fireman, Watertender, Engineman, and Machinist. Although many of the crew were recruits fresh out of a naval training station, they were quick to pick up the necessary skills. Illustration **31** shows the USS *Sumner,* DD 333, steaming in the open ocean.

These destroyers were noted for their speed, maneuverability, and armament. The space inside was crowded. The ships' power was evident, and the captain's curtains rustled with the ship's vibration. The rumble of the turbines and the roar of the air blowers echoed throughout the ships, which pitched, rolled, and yawed in different combinations as they knifed the waves. A novice moving about had to be alert and have a keen eye for the next grab rail.

In 1923, the battleship men in charge of the higher echelons of the navy viewed destroyers somewhat disparagingly. They were concerned with fixing the tonnage ratio between the U.S., Great Britain, and Japan, and had little concern for the development of new destroyer, submarine, or air capability. This attitude contributed to the lack of budget for destroyer operations, and new equipment such as the "sonic depth finders" that were already on British destroyers. According to the historian Hagan, the battleship attitude followed the theories of battleship importance set down by Alfred T. Mahan, at the turn of the century, in the doctrines of naval conflict. Capt Edward L. Beach, a navy historian and one of its greatest submariners, put it this way:

> The minds of the battleship men in control were not attuned to the changes being wrought by advancing technology. Mahan's near mystical pronouncements had taken the place of reality for men who did not understand, but were comfortable in not understanding.

As a result of attitude and politics, the navy's destroyers were operating under a budget crunch that gave scant funds for fuel oil. The result was a speed limit of 15 knots for a ship that had a top speed of 35. According to newspaper accounts, better times for the fleet appeared ahead, and naval appropriations proposed for 1923–24 would be increased. This would bring the short-handed crews up to strength and permit increased fuel allowances.

Chapter 1: 1923

Living on a "Four-Stacker"; Excerpts from Seamen's Letters

A glimpse of how the seamen viewed their lives aboard those destroyers is in Hice's 1967 book, *The Last Hours of Seven Four-Stackers*. Here are a few excerpts from the seamen's letters. The entry about Casey Bass is from Joe Silva's 1986 book, *Honda Left Turn 095*.

These letters give a picture of what it was like to be a youthful seaman, perhaps fifteen years old, with many duties. Try to envision a young sailor with seasickness that lasted for days as his ship pitched (bow up, bow down), rolled (portside up, portside down), and yawed (bow swings to port, bow swings to starboard). Imagine trying to sleep in a bunk or hammock while listening to the nonstop vibrations and rumblings of the ship's huge power plant. Think about going for days without vegetables, learning to steer a course, take depth soundings by hand, send a message with signal flags, cook, launch and row a whaleboat, chip paint, and climb to the crow's nest. Try to imagine being one of a hundred men squeezed into a narrow, pointed steel ship designed to operate at high speed, engage the enemy, drop depth charges, fire torpedoes, fire deck guns, and hit the target.

R. J. Bernier, a seaman just turned eighteen

The crew had a fierce pride in our ship. The *Somers* was always near the top in all competitions. I received $5 extra every month for being a sharpshooter on our four-inchers. A seaman's pay was $48 per month. I also remember the whaleboat races in the fleet and the preparation we spent on them ... The guinea Pullman contained four tiers of three bunks each. Our messing and berthing compartment was below the wardroom and above the magazines. The wardroom was below the main flush deck and opened up into the well deck section, just aft of the bridge structure. The starboard well deck, outside of that of the radio shack was where we had so many enjoyable bull sessions. Our boatswain's mate first class kept us younger men entranced for hours with sea stories. He was a good man and clever enough to teach us sea lore and was another one of those who made the ship's spirit so good...

Otto A. Phelps, Radioman 3rd, *Kennedy*

Navy men lived pretty much as they do now on small ships. We were close to the water and liked it. It was more of a dungaree navy than the battle wagons. There were times we worked harder with less comfort. We were always shorthanded and our job was not a specialty. I have had something to do with almost every job on the ship, except throttle watch, and I'm a radioman. I have scrubbed decks, stood boiler watches, generator watches, bridge watches, acted as coxswain for the Captain's boat, took a crew of seamen out in the whaleboat at sea. I repaired radio antennas at sea, cleaned the bottom of the boat in dry dock, painted the sides in port, manned the aircraft gun (we had one three inch) and was #1 leader on the four-inch guns. We didn't say, "That ain't my job."

Our officers were for the most part reasonable men who used what they had to the best advantage. All we had to do was keep our noses clean and be willing to do our share of the things we could do best. We were given every consideration... If there were only two radiomen at sea we just stayed on watch until we got tired and called the other man. We copied the press news... from a long wave receiver, while we listened for local signals from another receiver. If we traveled... in formation, a press ship would be picked and one man would stand watch, the other copy press... We would all get the press later on the inter-squadron frequency.

The fleet generally went to Panama in the winter and Puget Sound in the summer. We ate good and played hard when we had the chance... I got $60 a month... In 1924 I made 2nd class and got a $1 raise. I now work for Air Force Procurement. We have a few Gemini products to watch. From the Old spark set in the early 20s to the space capsules of the future. I am a retired CWO–USN.

Paul Buckly, Ship's Cook, *Chauncey*

She was scheduled to go to China in 1922, but was canceled... Fresh supplies were all that we could carry... (I loaded until we had no more storage room.) Lots of time our icebox was out of ice. They were set on deck outside of the galley. The scuttlebutt was too warm most of the time. And at times our fresh meat would spoil before we could use it. We had oil ranges to cook on. We had two forty-gallon coffee urns, and two oil ranges. They burned the same fuel that the ship did. We fed three meals a day. Pie and cake were a luxury. We got them in port only. They were supplied by shore boats, which arrived just before the noon meal. This was stopped by the Division Commander because that is all the sailors would eat. The noon meal was ignored... We had baked beans, corn bread twice a week for breakfast. The rest of the meals consisted of beef, pork, veal, ham etc. Also any fresh vegetables by season... Bread was bought ashore. Ten-day store for sea is what we carried. Bread was moldy in three days. After 4 to 5 days we ate smoked meats till we reached port. For longer trips we provisioned at sea sometimes...

Navy blues, whites and dungarees for dirty work were the uniforms. Regulations were more relaxed than on larger ships. We would have movie parties to the Battleships and other places when possible. Fresh water was not wasted and often rationed. Often we had to take a bath and wash clothes in 2½ gallons of fresh water... They had a time after working hours to get or draw water rations. Be there or do without!

J. W. Donovan, Chief Electrician's Mate, *Thompson*

I was only 24 when I reported on board... She made the cruise to Australia in 1925 and had a fine gunnery record for several years... Yes, things were different in those days. But we loved it and stayed with it. We had a fine bunch of chiefs... I think *Thompson* was the best, and I served 30 years with the Navy.

Casey M. Bass, Seaman 2nd, *Fuller*

Casey was fifteen years old and anxious to enlist in the U. S. Navy when his father agreed to sign him up in Greenville, TX. After his enlistment he was given six dollars for food and a ticket to San Francisco. He completed his apprentice training at Goat Island in San Francisco Bay and given a rating of Seaman 2nd Class with a pay increase from twenty-one to thirty-six dollars per month. He had a rough time on his first ship, the battleship *Pennsylvania,* and he was relieved when he was assigned to the destroyer *Fuller* in San Diego.

Prior to Squadron 11's departure for its fateful voyage southward on September 8, the *Fuller* was tied to the docks at Oakland. He recounts, "The night before we left Oakland we were sitting on forecastle, smoking and telling tales that sailors tell in their moments of ease, when one of the boys noticed that rats were leaving the ship. He made the remark in a joking way that when rats leave a ship she is doomed. Of course we all laughed, but nevertheless we all felt a bit uneasy, even if none of us wanted the others to notice it…The boys started talking about their wives and sweethearts in San Diego, our home port. Such scenes as this were going on the other destroyers that were heading for home in the morning.

Frank Brandenstein, Baker 1st on the old Squadron's Flagship, *Charleston,* in San Diego

The tin-cans had bunks with lockers beneath. On most ships the enlisted men lived out of sea bags and used hammocks. They were issued ditty boxes for their toilet articles, stationery, sewing kits etc.

Earl A. Buck, Quartermaster, who served on the *Alabama,* and later served on the *Henly* in World War I

Officers in those days wore "choker" style collars, winter and summer. They acted and looked like officers…

James Coward, Chief Warrant Officer, retired
I was stationed on the *Mahan,* a destroyer four-piper attached to the old mine force on the east coast... Those old pipers were rough in those days. At sea, they seemed to be under water... as much as they were on top.

George T. Mann, Chief Radioman, *Delphy*
We got ashore hand over hand—on a rope rigged from ship to shore—and just saved the clothes we had on... When the ship struck, all the lights went out. It was pitch dark. All I had on was a pair of dungarees and an undershirt... It was cold and wet. We built a fire of driftwood and dried ourselves as best we could. Capt Watson took it extremely hard. He sat by the fire and cried... One of the stewards jumped overboard and was crushed between the ship and the rocks.

Chapter 2

Men and Ships; RAdm Kittelle's Order to Test the Cruising Turbines

It was September 4, Fleet Week was in full swing, and afternoon temperatures reached 80 degrees. San Francisco welcomed the sailors, and they enjoyed the food, entertainment and hospitality that the city offered.

—Ens J. A. Morrow, USS *Delphy*

Welcome to San Francisco

San Francisco is a wonderful place. It was during WW II when I arrived. Sailors were everywhere, the morning sky overcast, the temperature cool, and the City's profile softened by a light fog. The ferry's horn announced its arrival after passing under the Oakland-San Francisco Bay Bridge. The views of the skyline and the harbor from the water, and the ships seen from the docks, were outstanding. It was a busy place. My navy friend had to get to his ship, so he climbed on a ship at the dock and sent a blinker-light signal to his ship. His mates came and picked him up, and off he went onto his ship and into the Pacific Ocean. It seemed impossible that we were the same people who had been civilians together in college in 1942.

Later, I was on an army bus headed out of San Francisco over the Golden Gate Bridge, and I looked back at the City. It was inspiring. Airborne a short time later, the C-54 transport left Hamilton Army Air Field and passed over San Francisco Bay. I looked north and saw the field, home of the C-54s. Their summer flying time to Hawaii was twelve hours, but on a headwind day in winter, they might carry enough gas for as many as fifteen hours. To the northeast was the Kaiser Shipyard at Richmond, and at a distance the great Mare Island Naval Shipyard at Vallejo. Farther northeast was the Fairfield-Suisun Army Airfield, favored by the B-29 pilots because of its long runways, cool temperatures, and headwinds. To the east was view of the Alameda Naval Air Station, the Oakland Airport, and the Kaiser Steel Shipyard at Oakland. All were busy.

Navy ships of all kinds were anchored in the bay, and young seamen were hauling supplies and crews to and fro. To the south were the Bethlehem Steel Shipyard and San Francisco Airport, and in the distance to the southeast the Navy's Moffett Field, home to the lighter-than-air patrol blimps.

In sailing San Francisco Bay and the coastal waters offshore between 1968 and 1995, I favored the summer season, because that's when the afternoon winds are brisk. Summer sailing offshore was typically cool and windy. During mid-afternoon the wind was 30 knots, with an uncomfortable amount of sea spray everywhere. By evening, the docks, anchorage, boats, sails, and sailors were wet and cool. At night it was common to see hardy sailors outside, dressed in comfortable jackets, boots, hats, and gloves. On high-pressure days the sailing winds were miserably light. Few people went out on stormy days, but I vividly recall sailing a couple of storms with peak winds of 50 knots. That was the time when each sailor attached their harness to a steel anchor bolted to the boat's hull. Once, Mary and I aided a sailor in the water, and once we had a beautiful Dacron jib torn in half. On a stormy day in April 1982, the winds at Pt. Bonita, outside the San Francisco Entrance, gusted to 70 knots. Seven boats and six sailors were lost. Two survivors of that storm suggested I write about the 1923 California storm that sank seven destroyers.

The Ships and Men of Destroyer Squadron 11

Shipboard life had been difficult while the squadron was headed from San Diego to Seattle—the headwinds quartered on the bow, and the northwest waves produced a mixture of cold wetness, pitching, rolling, and yawing. Careful, steady steering was the rule. In the City of San Francisco, a sailor's town during Fleet Week in September 1923, the sailors looked forward to a happy week on land, a routine downwind run home, and a comfortable shipboard life after they tuned the corner at Pt. Conception and entered the Santa Barbara Channel. The map in Illustration **3**, "Pt. Reyes to San Miguel Island," shows Squadron 11's planned route.

Destroyer Squadron 11 was organized into three divisions. When the squadron started south, it was in "Cruising Formation Five," as shown in Table 1.

Table 1: Formation Five
***Squadron Flagship* Delphy**

Div. 33 Flag	Div. 32 Flag	Div. 31 Flag
S. P. Lee	***Kennedy***	***Farragut***
(3 ships following)	(3 ships following)	(4 ships following)

About 4:30 P.M., the *Delphy* put up the flag signal for "Formation Eighteen," the order for the squadron to form in column after her. (The ships' locations in the column, names, DD numbers, and commanders are given in Table 2; this destroyer class is described in Appendix VI.)

Capt Edward H. Watson, Commander, Destroyer Squadron 11, the son of RAdm John C. Watson, was born in 1874 in Frankfort, Kentucky. He was competent and moved steadily upward in rank. He served in the Atlantic during World War I and won the Navy Cross for meritorious service. He was given command of Destroyer Squadron Eleven in July 1922.

LCdr Donald T. Hunter, Commander, Squadron Eleven Flagship *Delphy*, was born in 1887 in Elgin, Illinois. He was known for his consummate confidence on the bridge, and his cordial manner off of it. As a young officer in World War I, he served with distinction as a navigator aboard an American destroyer based in Queenstown, Ireland. He came to the squadron after teaching navigation for two years at the U. S. Naval Academy.

Ltjg Lawrence Blodgett, Navigator and Executive Officer, Flagship *Delphy*, was born in Stoneham, Massachusetts, and served as an enlisted man during World War I. Following commendable service, he was promoted to ensign and served as assistant navigator on the destroyers *Belknap* and *Case*. He was promoted to Ltjg in early 1920, and joined the *Delphy* as navigator and executive officer later that year.

Table 2—Formation Eighteen

DesRon 11 - Capt Edward H. Watson
1. *Delphy,* DD 261 - LCdr Donald T. Hunter

DesDiv 33 - Capt Robert Morris
2. *S. P. Lee,* DD 310 - Cdr W. H. Toaz
3. *Young,* DD 312 - Cdr W.L. Calhoun
4. *Woodbury,* DD 309 - Cdr L. P. Davis
5. *Nicholas,* DD 311 - LCdr H. O. Roesch
[USS *William Jones* & USS *Zeilin*]

DesDiv 31 - Cdr William S. Pye
6. *Farragut,* DD 300 - LCdr J. F. McClain
7. *Fuller,* DD 297 - LCdr W. D. Seed
8. *Percival,* DD 298 - LCdr C. H. Cobb
9. *Somers,* DD 301 - Cdr W. P. Gaddis
10. *Chauncey,* DD 296 - Cdr R. H. Booth
[USS *John Francis Burns*]

DesDiv 32 - Cdr Walter G. Roper
11. *Kennedy,* DD 306 - LCdr R. E. Bell
12. *Paul Hamilton,* DD 307 - Cdr T. L. McCauley
13. *Stoddert,* DD 302 - LCdr L. E. Bratton
14. *Thompson,* DD 305 - LCdr T. A. Symington
[USS *Farquhar* and USS *Reno*]

Chief Quartermaster Harry Cummings of the *Delphy* was twenty-seven. He spent his hours as the lookout, signalman, visibility observer, and standby emergency man. His brisk, matter-of-fact manner had a calming influence on everyone.

Capt Robert Morris, Commander, Division 33, was born in Atlantic, Iowa in 1878, and his division was the squadron's premiere division: it had the newest squadron ships, was always first in line when in column formation, and had the greatest number of ship commanders with the rank of commander. The *S. P. Lee* was Capt Morris' flagship. Morris was experienced, and was described as indefatigable in dealing with emergencies. In the command hierarchy, his subordinates knew him as competent and direct. In dealing with Capt Watson, however, Capt Morris was deferential.

The new skipper of Division 33's *Young*, Cdr William Calhoun, was known for his role as navigator of the battleship *Maryland*, his commander's role at the Mare Island Naval Shipyard, and his great-grandfather, the marathon legislative orator Senator John C. Calhoun.

The youngest division commander, Cdr William Pye, Commanding Officer, Division 31, was an excellent officer and was well qualified in technical and command skills. Capt Watson described him as one who "never failed to use proper initiative and who always handled his division well in tactical maneuvers." Cdr Pye was known by his flagship staff, on *Farragut,* for being interested in the ship's navigation and for spending most of his time on the bridge.

Cdr Walter Roper, Commanding Officer, Division 32, was the senior division commander when Cdr Morris was promoted to captain. Cdr Roper was known for his close relationships with his bridge staff aboard the Division 32 flagship, *Kennedy;* and the division's Lt MacNally was one of the few navigators described as "excellent." He and the *Kennedy*'s young OODs were known for their skill. Cdr Roper was known for his presence on the bridge, his forthright speech, and for allowing his junior officers to speak freely. Roper's men admired his honesty, but Capt Watson thought Roper argumentative. Roper's officers of the deck were alert, in touch with their ship captains, had ship safety on their minds, and were ready to recommend needed actions.

Chronology of Events: August 31 to Morning of September 8

The fleet was in the port of San Francisco on the typically warm autumn week known as Fleet Week, when San Francisco welcomes all sailors. Everyone had a chance to enjoy fine food, great entertainment, and widespread hospitality that this famous city offered. The warm weather started when the offshore winds decreased on Sunday, and Pt. Reyes (Illustration **3**) came in with a daily average wind speed of only 10 knots. As shown in Appendix IV, the less-than-usual wind speed lasted through Thursday, Sept. 6, with the max temperature reaching 80–87 degrees on Tuesday, Sept. 4, Wednesday, Sept. 5, and Thursday, Sept. 6. Coastal weather was also warm on those days, with the San Luis Obispo max temperature running 93–96 degrees. This warm weather pattern is characterized by a decrease in coastal fog, improved visibility, and improved cruising condition along the coast from San Francisco to Pt. Arguello.

Friday, August 31, Afternoon

It was a typical San Francisco day, cool with high fog. RAdm Sumner E. W. Kittelle's flagship, *Melville,* lay at anchor in Berth 2. Capt Edward M. Watson's flagship, *Delphy,* was moored alongside. Capt Watson, the son of an admiral, was near the top of the promotion list and looked forward to being promoted soon. Capt James H. Tomb's Squadron 12 flagship, *McDermut,* was berthed down the dock with his squadron's ships.

RAdm Kittelle was proud of his destroyer command, but he was concerned about the engineering troubles the ships had experienced on the voyage to and from Seattle. To help shake out problems, he signed an order for the two squadrons to make a 20-knot endurance run to San Diego on September 8. The order was not formally presented to Squadrons 11 and 12 until September 7.

Monday, September 3, Afternoon

Fleet Week in San Francisco was in full swing, and the expected warm weather arrived. The sailors found it pleasant as the max temperature went up to 74 degrees, and the average wind at Pt. Reyes—Illustration **3**—stayed at a low 13 mph.

The crew of each ship was primed to disembark, enjoy each other, see the sights, be entertained, and eat well. Three months out of the U. S. Naval Academy, Ens J. A. Morrow of the *Delphy* had an acute interest in navigation, meteorology, and the history of determining longitude on ships at sea. He had been assisting on the bridge for several months, and the command agreed he was ready to serve as an OOD. He spent the morning walking downtown and visiting Corday Counts, the U. S. Weather Bureau's friendly young meteorologist.

Morrow was now on the dock, seated on a canvas cushion, and waiting to talk and eat with his friend, Harry Cummings, chief quartermaster. As soon as Harry appeared, Morrow greeted him warmly. Cummings was in a Fleet-Week mood and greeted Morrow with, "Hello, you look sleepy."

With mock assurance, Morrow replied, "I'm wide awake."

"Glad to hear that," the chief said, and sat down. "Let's finish our talk about steering and estimating speed on our voyage south next week. Then, let's look for the best food in town."

"I'm eager, let's go," Morrow said.

Cummings began: "The ship will be bathed in northwest winds, and waves will quarter over her starboard stern. She'll yaw as the bow swings from side to side, and you and the helmsman will have a job keeping the course heading as the bow goes to starboard and he tries to correct back to the course heading. He will likely let the bow swing slightly to port. This will produce an endless back-and-forth S-shaped image over the bottom. It will be difficult for the helmsman to steer that prescribed course, and your OOD's job will be to watch for any tendency the helmsman may have to oversteer to one side. That can end up with the course made good being different from the one prescribed."

Having already been sensitized to this situation, Morrow now called out, "Helmsmen, mind your rudder."

The chief emphasized the importance of the ship's speed over the bottom. Morrow knew the engineer estimated the ship's hourly speed through the water by reading the counter that showed the number of propeller revolutions. Its accuracy depended on the marine growth on the hull, and a periodic calibration of revolutions over a measured mile. But the chief emphasized another point: "A yawing ship seldom makes its estimated speed. The side-to-side yawing motion of the bow makes the steering difficult." They agreed it would improve their estimate of distance traveled if they had a patent log to drag over the stern.

The chief then focused on the need for the navigator to get a periodic position fix to verify the ship's estimated course and speed over the bottom. Harry, as Chief QM, was the eyes of the ship, and he firmly advised the quiet ensign, "When you're OOD, always be sure keen eyes are on deck looking for a landmark, a lighthouse, or a coastal profile you can recognize. Make 'keen eyes' believe that he must keep looking—even if it appears foggy there will be daytime breaks. Worry about visibility, spend as much time as you can outside looking steadily landward, and never leave the deck 'empty.' Plan ahead and look at the coast; the terrain profile makes a big change at Pt. Sur."

Ensign Morrow said, "I'm lucky to have you as a friend. It hasn't been easy for me to get candid advice from seasoned seamen." He thanked the chief and said, "Someday when it's quiet, I'd like to walk you through the procedure to determine the ship's midday latitude and longitude."

The chief nodded, and reminded Morrow, "You will soon stand alone on your first OOD watch."

Morrow's mind jumped. He thought about that responsibility; his first OOD watch, being the lead ship in the squadron column, alone on the bridge, nighttime, moving steadily at 20 knots into the Santa Barbara Channel, overtaking and facing oncoming commercial and recreational traffic. In a lighthearted tone, he continued, "Chief, what do we do if we run over a couple of sailboats?"

"You and the lookouts stay awake," the chief replied. "Stay alert. Keep the ship well lighted, don't change course, double your lookouts, and put someone in the crow's nest. You have a big horn and a searchlight—any sailor will get out of your way if he sees or hears you"

Tuesday, September 4, Afternoon

It was a warm San Francisco day with a max temperature up to 80 degrees and an average wind speed at Pt. Reyes of only 13 knots. Fair weather extended southward to San Luis Obispo, where the max temperature reached 94 degrees.

Lieutenants (jg) Sam Dalkowitz and Max Wellborn, deck officers on the *Kennedy*, met and headed for lunch on the waterfront. They found a fisherman's restaurant where they picked up seafood and took it outside. They ate sourdough bread and crab salad with an extra serving of crab piled on top of the meager original. Dalkowitz said, "This is Fleet-Week weather, the only time that it's clear, warm, and windless here."

Wellborn replied, "It's a good day for motorboats, but lousy for sailing—the average wind on the Bay will be lucky to reach ten miles per hour."

Impressed with the clear visibility, Dalkowitz said, "This would be a great day to steam south—a day when we could identify the different profiles of the headlands along the route."

Wellborn, an avid reader about coastal weather, replied, "It's never clear and warm along the coast for long. By the time we get started it'll be lousy with fog before you can even get a suntan. I've read that the greatest caution should be exercised in thick weather. Depth soundings should be taken frequently." Both officers expected Saturday would be a regular summer day, cooler than the one they were now enjoying, and with some fog. Neither lieutenant foresaw, however, that the day of their departure would find the San Francisco max temperature down to 64 degrees, the sea breeze howling, and the Pt. Reyes average daily wind speed up to 33 mph. As they parted, Dalkowitz said, "I'm keen on September, keen on no storms."

Wellborn replied, "Let me tell you how to recognize the most foolish mariner on the coast: he's the guy who thinks that the lack of summer storms means steaming the coast will be a safe bet."

Wednesday, September 5, Afternoon

The day was the warmest of the week, the max temperature reached 87 degrees, and the average wind speed at exposed Pt. Reyes barely reached 9 knots. South, at San Luis Obispo, the max temperature reached 93 degrees.

Lt R.F. MacNally, navigator of the Division 32 flagship, *Kennedy,* met for a real lunch with OODs Dalkowitz and Wellborn. All three agreed on beer, grilled fish, crab, prawns, shrimp, lobster, oysters, garlic bread, baked potatoes, and salad.

"Let's go to the Cliff House," Wellborn suggested.

Dalkowitz said, "Too far away. I'd rather walk along the waterfront to Alioto's at Fisherman's Wharf." Instead, they stopped at the first okay place they came to and ordered almost everything not obtainable on shipboard. After lunch they relaxed and enjoyed Lt MacNally's kind remark about how each of them was certainly the best OOD in the squadron.

Lt MacNally was not one to visit without a purpose. He was soon talking about the use of the radio compass (RC) on the run to San Diego. Both young officers knew MacNally was an excellent navigator, and valued his opinions about the RC.

"The RC is your best friend when visual piloting is impossible," Lt MacNally said. At MacNally's request, Dalkowitz hauled an old nautical chart out of his backpack and pointed to the RC station they would use: the navy's station at Pt. Arguello, 255 miles south of

San Francisco. MacNally said, "You need a fix on Pt. Sur and on Pt. Arguello—the lighthouse and RC are next to each other." (Refer to maps in Illustrations **3** and **28**.)

MacNally continued, "Following your radio request, the RC station will take a bearing on your ship's radio signal and give you their bearing on that signal—the direction from the station to your ship. If the *Kennedy* is well seaward, say ten miles, the ship's passage of Pt. Arguello will be confirmed by a sequence of RC bearings that back—that is, shift counterclockwise. For example, expect an RC bearing indicating you are to the northwest of the RC, then a west bearing indicating you are abeam of the station, and then a south bearing indicating you've passed the station." (The RC bearings received by the *McDermut* are shown in Illustration **12**).

"Here's your homework. Early next Saturday our destroyer, *Hull,* will be running southward alone. Assume you are Officer of the Deck on the *Hull* as it steams by Pt. Arguello. Will you feel comfortable signing off an entry in the ship's log that confirms these directional bearings and times: (264 deg at 6:45 A.M.), (211 deg at 7:14 A.M.) and (177 deg at 7:31 A.M.)?" Both men said yes. Each was ordered to check the *Hull*'s deck log in San Diego.

Wellborn asked, "What is the range of the RC station?"

"The useable range of the RC is about 140 miles," MacNally answered.

Dalkowitz asked, "What is the chance of a bearing misreading—getting a reversed bearing direction?"

MacNally replied, "The chance for a misreading is about one to two percent. A misreading can occur when you approach the RC station blindly from a distance near the station's limit of reception. It also depends on the strength of your ship's signal source. Far distance and a weak source signal can be a problem whenever you make your first RC request. One way to avoid that is let the station know you've entered their range when you request your first bearing, and get the radioman to confirm your ship's source signal is okay. Our purpose in using RC bearings is to confirm our passage of

Pt. Arguello. Bearings are not precise enough to fix our ship's position, but they're well suited (plus or minus four degrees) for confirming your passage of the RC station." (See Appendix II for the RC bearings.)

MacNally was good at giving advice. "Pay attention to your radioman. Ask him to intercept RC bearing radio messages addressed to other squadron ships. It's not easy, but he can do it." This was old news to Wellborn, and he chimed in with a question: "Assuming we're alone, what should I do to resolve a misreading quandary?"

"Ask them for a repeat," MacNally said. "Then, if it's necessary, make a course change 45 degrees to the right for a fixed distance, and then request and verify a new RC bearing by its conformance to your known course change. That's it, gentlemen, no more questions."

Wednesday, September 5, Evening

Capt Watson was dressed for comfort in a well-fitted, rumpled cloth coat with a choker collar. He looked trim, and he had a pleasant smile as he finished dinner and went over to the *Melville* to visit with RAdm Kittelle. The visit was routine until Watson asked, "What criticisms did you hear after the *Henderson* rammed my *Zeilin* in Seattle?"

After a pause, the admiral replied, "Embarrassing. Your squadron's newest destroyer got bent like a door hinge on the morning of the Presidential Review. Thank the angels that your men were rescued."

Capt Watson knew the admiral was not pleased and that more grief might be coming, so he switched the topic to the recent earthquake in Japan. Kitelle said, "The navy did a good job there. The destroyer *Borie* led the rescue group and made headlines, as they were the first to bring relief supplies to the disaster area."

Thursday, September 6

It was the fourth pleasant day in a row in San Francisco. The max temperature reached 84 degrees, and the average wind speed at Pt. Reyes increased to 16 mph. South, at San Luis Obispo, the max temperature reached 96 degrees. This ended the three days of fair weather from San Francisco to Pt. Arguello (data in Appendix IV). The Weather Bureau predicted, "One more day of pleasant Fleet-Week weather." The sailors enjoyed Thursday and planned to enjoy Friday.

Friday, September 7, Morning

It was a pleasant San Francisco day, but there were signs that the warm weather was ending. The afternoon temperature struggled to reach a pleasant max of 76 degrees—down eight degrees, and the average wind speed at Pt. Reyes moved up to an average 25 knots—up nine knots from the previous day. By Saturday the beautiful coastal fair weather south of San Francisco would end.

RAdm Kittelle summoned the two squadron commanders for a meeting aboard his flagship. The August 31 Order 29-23 m was released: "Depart San Francisco 7 A.M. Saturday, 8 September 1923. Rendezvous off San Francisco Lightship and proceed to San Diego on cruising turbines at standard speed of 20 knots." Capt Watson would lead Squadron 11 at a standard speed of 20 knots, while the commander of Squadron 12 would lead his squadron at a standard speed of 20 knots or less as the sea conditions warranted.

Friday, September 7, Afternoon

Capt Watson assembled his squadron's division commanders for a pre-voyage conference about the endurance run. Watson presented RAdm Kittelle's order and emphasized that he expected Squadron 11 "to make an excellent run."

Squadron Staff Engineer LCdr Donald said, "I expect to see a big red "E" for excellence ... on our smokestack."

Cdr Pye, Div. 31, asked, "What will be our course after we clear Pt. Arguello and Pt. Conception?" (A map and chart of this area are in Illustrations **3** and **28.**)

"I'll get back to you later about the course change," replied Capt Watson.

The engineers expressed concern about engine reliability—until recently, a fuel-economy order had limited the engines to fifteen knots.

The division commanders were known for their different traits. Capt R. Morris, Commander, Division 33, was the ranking division commander and deputy squadron commander. He was known for being differential to Watson. Cdr William S. Pye, Commander Division 31, was forty-three, and known for behaving commendably in difficult situations. Cdr Walter Roper, Commander, Division 32, was forty-eight, and known for candidly expressing his views.

Friday, September 7, Late Afternoon and Evening

It was late afternoon. Capt Watson was in the lobby of the San Francisco Hotel when he met his old friend from Japan, Third Secretary of the U. S. Embassy Eugene Dooman. Watson said, "Why don't you be my guest and come along with me to San Diego?"

Dooman replied, "I'd enjoy that. I have a lot to tell you about their navy, and a day at sea with you sure beats a train ride." Later, Mr. Dooman and his "luggage" were escorted to a "vacant cabin." The next day the two men ate breakfast and reminisced. Mr. Dooman was a diplomat. He never attracted attention, and was identified years later as the "phantom passenger, who arrived with heavy baggage reportedly containing $3,000 in silver."

Late Friday evening, LCdr Donald Hunter, skipper of the *Delphy*, was walking the deck and checking *Delphy*'s readiness. The crew was at ease and ready for an early-morning departure. Hunter was surprised to see a light in the navigation cabin, and to find Ltjg Blodgett inside. Hunter gave no greeting, but sharply queried the lieutenant, "What are you doing here?"

"Getting ready for tomorrow's trip," replied Blodgett.

"Not necessary," Hunter said. "I'm planning to navigate tomorrow."

Blodgett, the ship's assigned navigator, was speechless. Hunter continued, "I will be the navigator tomorrow. You will do routine."

Nonplused, Blodgett asked, "Have I done something wrong? Have I offended you."

"That's all," Hunter closed. "Captain has big plans. See you in the morning."

The relationship between the two men deteriorated as they faced each other in the cramped navigation space, the emergency cabin to the rear of the bridge. The closeness of the little cabin was intimidating. Ens Morrow and Chief Cummings were nearby. Morrow said, "I hope we don't hear one of them say something we'll be sorry to hear."

"Hunter is a very fine officer, and well liked by everyone," Cummings said." I have yet to see him make a major mistake."

Saturday, September 8, Morning

Typical San Francisco high-fog weather prevailed—the max temperature headed for a cool 64 degrees, and the average daily wind speed at Pt. Reyes reached 33 knots.) Corday Counts, the young meteorologist at the U. S. Weather Bureau, San Francisco, completed his analysis of the surface weather map, and issued his regional weather forecast at 7 A.M.: variable coastal fog, low stratus clouds, and northwesterly wind along the Central California Coast. (The U. S. Weather Bureau's surface weather map for the western U. S. and eastern Pacific for 5 A.M., 8 September 1923 is shown on the map in Illustration **7**. The predominant summer airflow pattern along the California coast is shown on the map in Illustration **8**.)

[In WW II, Mr. Counts was senior supervisor in the U. S. Weather Bureau's San Francisco office, and an outstanding professional example for the young Army Air Corps meteorologist, Lieutenant Spencer Duckworth, during the period when he was assigned to the Oceanic Air Traffic Center.]

Navigational Background: Charts, Piloting, and Lighthouses

Charts

Navigating the coastal area starts with nautical charts. A 1923 destroyer traveling southward from Seattle to San Francisco to San Diego would have known about lighthouses, tides, currents, climate, sunrise, and sunset, etc. They would have a set of "navigator's notes that included names, descriptions, and locations of lighthouses and coastal landmarks." The navigator of a 1923 destroyer was an important person. His signature and the captain's were required on the last page of the ship's daily deck log.

Early ship captains found that their sailing charts included inaccurate drawings of the coastlines and an excess of unnecessary names, and lacked geographic references, so they sought out sailors familiar with the route their vessel was planning to sail, and drew terrain profiles of the harbor entrances and coastlines. Savvy captains and navigators made notes on their charts about difficult tideways, daily weather, water resources, harbors of refuge, and safe channels. Captains carried their notes with them from ship to ship, and when planning a voyage on an unfamiliar route, they frequently haunted seaport libraries and scouted the harbor yards for words about coastal landmarks. Any land encounter—clearing a point, entering a seaport at night—could be scary, and the loss of cargo or ship might mean the end of a career. A lighted landmark made the difference, and the demand led to the first lighthouses in the San Francisco Bay in the 1850s.

Piloting

Piloting is the ability to interpret all available information, and keep "ahead of the vessel." Captains know that "piloting is not the same as dead reckoning (DR)." Piloting captains and navigators search for landmarks, talk to nearby navigators, and sound the sea bottom to confirm that their DR estimates are real. Captains of large cargo vessels are met offshore by pilot boats.

Piloting the coast is different: it requires continuous alertness because of hazards from shoal water and underwater reefs, and it requires a periodic fix of the vessel's position. Nearness to land or other vessels, lack of a position fix, and opposing traffic patterns increase the risk of collision or an error that might in the open sea be considered minor, but could be disastrous near the coast. Navigation on the high seas can be a comparatively leisurely process with a midday fix by latitude and longitude.

Most coastal navigators of the day had a talent for recognizing terrain profiles such as the major change in the coastline at the start of the northern Pt. Sur coast. They also liked sailing along a safe depth contour to clear a promontory like Pt. Conception (Illustrations **28** and **12**).

Lighthouses

In 1923, identifying lighthouses and prominent landmarks was key to safe piloting along the California coast. Sharp lookouts aboard ship were valued, and when they reported decreasing visibility, everyone on the bridge took note. Seeing and recognizing landmarks and getting compass bearings and a distance away from a lighthouse was a favored way to get a position fix. Each lighthouse had its own characteristics: a unique shape, tower height, siren or horn, and the land profile on which it sat. At night each was distinguished by a unique light characteristic.

Five lighthouses were important to the southward bound pilot from San Francisco (Illustration **3**). The first was Pigeon Pt. (Illustration **14**), south of San Francisco. Here the navigator got a fix and started his initial DR course. The second light was Pt. Sur (Illustration **15**). The third was Pt. Piedras Blancas, the midpoint of the leg from Pigeon Pt. to Pt. Conception. The fourth was Pt. Arguello (Illustration **9**), and the fifth Pt. Conception (Illustration **10**). Each of the primary lights was established before 1890, and each had a first-order Fresnel lens, a height above the ocean of more than 100 feet, and a penetrating fog siren. These lights (or landmarks) were the places to visually confirm a DR-estimated position. Otherwise, a combination of depth soundings and RC bearings was used (Illustration **12**). Heading for San Diego, and lacking confirmation of a DR-estimated position, a wise choice was to go west of San Miguel Island (Illustrations **3**, **12**, **28**).

The fifty-foot-high Pt. Sur Light was on top of a 200-foot-high escarpment (Illustration **15**). A fix on Pt Sur Light was important to the *Delphy*'s navigator, as a position fix here could show the reliability of his DR-estimated position. Without a fix on Pt. Sur, it became important to get a fix on the next landmark or on the Pt. Piedras Blancas Light. That light's ninety-foot tower sat alone on a grassy knoll at the seaward edge of a flat promontory just north of San Simeon. The tower's height above sea level was 142 feet. Afternoon fog layers were usually above this light, and its fog signal was notoriously earsplitting. Given a fix on Piedras Blancas, and visibility more than six miles, the navigator could prepare for a fix on the Pt. Arguello Light (Illustrations **9** and **28**), and the Pt. Conception Light (Illustrations **10** and **28**), 72 feet above the sea. It was also noted for its fog signal—a powerful compressed-air siren—and the navy's adjacent radio compass tower. Without a fix on Pt. Arguello, or RC bearings confirming a safe position offshore, it was necessary to confirm that the ship was a safe distance offshore by taking depth soundings.

Chapter 3

The U.S. Battle Fleet Heads South to San Diego

I was the OOD on the cool, windy, and foggy night that we departed on our annual full-speed solo run to San Diego. We cleared the lightship, headed south, powered up to 32 knots, and stayed there until 2 P.M.

—Ens T. A. Kelly, USS *Reno*.

Introduction

The route southward from San Francisco to Pt. Conception is shown in Illustration **3**, Pt. Reyes to San Miguel Island. Destroyer Squadrons 11 and 12 typically took a 150-deg true course along the coast until they cleared Pt. Arguello, and then a 130-deg course until they cleared Pt. Conception and turned into the Santa Barbara Channel (Illustration **12**). The critical part of that course was to get a fix before Pt. Arguello, and a fix on Pt. Conception. No fix was obtained, so, as Destroyer Squadron 11 approached Pt. Arguello, they came near the coastline and into the afternoon west-northwesterly airflow blowing onshore over the coastal lowlands.

Illustration **3** illustrates a course line from Pt. Sur to Pt. Arguello of 150 deg. It shows that a ship on this course is vulnerable to serious error if the navigator cannot confirm the ship's DR-estimated position. The *Delphy* never confirmed its DR-estimated position. *Delphy*'s position was wrong due to a compass error and onshore flow pushing the ship into shoal waters.

Ships of the Fleet Make Successful Transits Southward

USS *Seattle,* a powerful armored cruiser and flagship of the U.S. Battle Fleet, steamed past Alcatraz Island at 12:30 A.M. and the San Francisco Light Vessel at 1:30 A.M. on September 8. The ship's captain and the navigator had no interest in hugging the coastline, so they chose a deep-water offshore course.

By 4 A.M., the *Seattle* was steaming on a course 156 deg true, with its magnetic and gyrocompasses operating. Its speed of 12 knots was determined by the hourly count of propeller revolutions, and its total distance traveled by a taffrail log towed from its stern. *Seattle* planned to confirm its passage of Pt. Arguello by radio compass bearings in the evening from the Pt. Arguello RC Station, and they requested bearings. As shown in Appendices II and III, their RC bearings confirmed their passage southward by backing from 282 deg to 200 deg. *Seattle* avoided the Santa Barbara Channel and went west of San Miguel Island (Illustration **3**).

At 8 P.M., *Seattle*'s latitude was "34-10 N, 121-00 W," well to the west of San Miguel Island, and in agreement with the 218-deg radio compass bearing they received at 8:24 P.M. The ship was to the south of San Miguel Island when it turned toward San Diego.

USS *Corry* was a Squadron 12 destroyer making a power run alone at speeds above 30 knots. As it passed offshore from Pt. Arguello, *Corry*'s RC bearings backed from 258 to 168 deg in one hour. (See RC bearings for *Corry* in Appendices II and III.)

USS *Melville*, the 7,200-ton tender and flagship of the destroyer squadrons, was built in 1915 and was well equipped to serve its squadrons. It departed from Berth 2 and headed out of San Francisco Bay just after midnight on September 8. It steamed south on a course of 150 deg true at a speed of 13 knots. By 5 P.M., it was preparing to pass Pt. Arguello and began requesting radio compass bearings. The RC bearings confirmed their passage as they consistently backed (shifted counterclockwise): (310 deg at 5:43 P.M.); (262 deg at 6:20 P.M.); and (168 deg at 7:18 P.M.)

The nautical chart (Illustration **28**) shows the 50-fathom water-depth contour along the coast. At 4 P.M., the crew of the *Melville* started taking depth soundings every fifteen minutes to confirm their distance offshore. After 7 P.M., they found 41 fathoms of water, and 15 minutes later they could find no bottom with 300 fathoms of wire out—evidence they were in the deep-water Santa Barbara Channel.

Shortly afterward, they changed course to eastward. At 8 P.M., *Melville*'s latitude and longitude position was consistent with its last radio compass bearing. The *Melville* procedure exemplified the use of RC bearings to verify that it was clear of Pt. Conception and was safe to turn eastward, and the use of depth soundings to confirm it was in the deep-water Santa Barbara Channel.

USS *McDermut*, 1,200-ton Flush Deck Class destroyer and flagship of squadron 12, departed San Francisco Berth 18 at 7 A.M. and steamed westward into the offshore waters where it conducted gunnery exercises. Near noon it headed south on a course of 160 deg per its gyrocompass (pgc). At 2 P.M., it changed course to 149 deg per gyrocompass at a speed of 18 knots. The captain and his navigator decided to navigate past Pt. Arguello and Pt. Conception by using frequent RC bearings from Pt. Arguello. Accordingly, as shown in Illustration **12**, they requested and used RC bearings. The first seven bearings showed that they were north of Pt. Arguello, and then the bearings shifted counterclockwise: (305 deg at 9:31 P.M.); (204 deg at 10:24 P.M.); (172 deg at 11:07 P.M.). At 10:20 P.M., fog settled in and they slowed to 10 knots. Illustration **12** is the map showing the *McDermut*'s classic use of radio compass bearings to clear Pt. Arguello and Pt. Conception.

USS *Reno* of Division 32

It was foggy, cool, and windy in San Francisco. At Pier 36 the *Reno* was wet and cold—a typical night for the working sailor. The wind at Pt. Reyes, north of the Golden Gate, was northwest at 36 knots.

The *Reno* was ready to depart alone on its annual smoke-prevention and full-speed solo run to San Diego. It was eight bells, the end of the last watch of September 7, and the start of the first four-hour watch of September 8—midnight to 4 A.M. (A bell was struck each half hour, and two bells on the first watch was 1 A.M.) The engineer and crew had been on duty for hours, and the ship's turbines were idling when the genial LCdr "Dick" Barry came on the bridge. The chief quartermaster was on deck forward of the bridge, and an experienced helmsman held the wheel. Young Ens T. A. Kelly was the OOD. The navigator was in the spacious chartroom below the bridge, looking at the nautical chart. He noted the sequence of headings, lights, horns, and buoys he would use to exit

San Francisco Bay, head westward to the San Francisco Lightship, and then southward to a fix on the Pigeon Pt. Light.

The *Reno*'s boilers were ready at 12:30 A.M. The young deck hands cast off the dock lines, the ship backed out of its mooring nest, and its port anchor fouled the *Stoddert*'s stanchion. *Stoddert*'s OOD blew his whistle, and the *Reno*'s OOD graciously apologized. By 2 A.M., the *Reno* was out of the Golden Gate, with the San Francisco Lightship on its port beam at a distance of one mile. As visibility was restricted due to fog, the captain set a standard speed of 15 knots. The OOD made the departure entry in the day's deck log. (Excerpts from the deck logs of the *Seattle* and *Partridge* are in Illustration **13**. Note the entries and the clean, sharp typewriter record on these logs—one from a heavy cruiser, the other from an oceangoing tug.)

The surface weather map (Illustration **7**) shows a typical summer pattern along the coast south to Pt. Conception, with broken low clouds, variable fog, northwest winds over the open ocean, west-northwest wind over the coastal waters, and westerly winds near the coastal lowlands. The predominant summer airflow pattern along the coast is shown in Illustration **8**. Climatological data for summer, and meteorological data for Sept. 1–8, 1923, are given in Appendix IV.

USS *Reno* was at sea and started its full-power run at 8 A.M. It continued powering with an average hourly propeller revolution count of 404 and a speed of 31 knots until about 2 P.M. [Some ship!] The *Reno*'s speeds and revolutions during the power run are given in Appendix V. *Reno* confirmed its passage of Pt. Arguello with three radio compass bearings between 11 A.M. and noon, when the RC bearings backed from 286 deg to 238 deg and 215 deg (Appendix II).

Reno was alone when it moved to pass to the west of San Miguel Island (shown in the map in Illustration **3**). Sighting loaded lifeboats, the crew changed course and decreased speed to investigate. They found the boats held survivors from the wreck of the Pacific Mail steamer SS *Cuba*—loaded with cargo and passengers from Panama—which had run aground early that morning and had been unable to request help because its radio was out of order.

Reno's radio message to Capt Watson told of the wreck and the start of their rescue work. The heroic actions of the *Reno* were reported in plain language in its deck log, and signed by the OOD, Ens T. A. Kelly. "At 1:35 P.M. sighted boats adrift. Changed course, discontinued power runs... At 2 P.M. got whaleboat from SS Cuba alongside with 22 passengers... At 2:20 got another whaleboat alongside with 24 passengers. At 4 P.M. sighted wreck of Cuba and passengers on beach. Stopped engines, lowered boats, reported our actions to Commander Destroyer Squadrons Battle Fleet... Two men got lacerations getting survivors aboard..."

The *Reno* kept busy rescuing the *Cuba*'s passengers until 5 P.M., when it anchored in 12 fathoms of water. Near 7 P.M., a whaleboat arrived with 25 more survivors—a total of 71 survivors were now on board. One of the *Cuba*'s boats was still missing. The destroyer *Selfridge* (Appendix V), unable to make a steady 20-knot run with its sister ships, was nearby and slowly cruising with the *Melville*, RAdm Kittelle's flagship. The master and purser of the *Cuba* were still on the wreck, and were confident that the *Selfridge* would find their remaining lifeboat, so *Reno* got underway at 7:30 P.M. The *Selfridge* was successful, and its log for September 9 shows the names of twelve "destitute seamen from the Cuba..."

USS *Cuyama*, a tanker, carried fuel oil for the destroyers and was affectionately known as the "destroyer's friend." (*Cuyama*'s role is easy to see if you picture it as the large ship in the center of a dozen destroyers, all stacks smoking and all bows pointing forward.) By 6 A.M., *Cuyama* completed filling its bunkers with 4,100 barrels of oil at the Union Oil dock in Port San Luis Obispo and prepared to depart.

Cuyama cast off its dock lines near 10 A.M. and headed southward from Port San Luis Obispo. The captain was conning from the pilothouse, the navigator was on the bridge, and the leadsman was in the chains. The ship's draft was 24 feet forward and 28 feet aft. Although some fog was present, the harbor bell buoy was easy to hear. The ship moved southward, fog signals were occasionally sent, and a sharp lookout was kept to identify the coastal landmarks visible from time to time. The loaded *Cuyama* was moving at 13 knots when the officer of the deck heard the Pt. Arguello fog signal. At 1 P. M., the quartermaster logged the ship's passage of Pt. Arguello; later, he used a hand-held bearing bar to take a 26-degree bearing on Arguello. He sighted Pt. Conception at 2 P. M., as expected. The crew of the *Cuyama* safely piloted the coast by identifying landmarks visible whenever they could see the coastline through the variable high fog.

USS *Partridge* was a seagoing tug under the command of Chief Boatswain J. A. Pierce. It was of particular interest on this voyage because it was the most frequent user of RC bearings as it navigated past Pt. Arguello, and then "countermarched," as ordered by RAdm Kittelle, to the rescue area. At 10 P. M., it radioed the *Melville:* "We are off Pt. Arguello, holding our position, awaiting further orders. We can hear the Pt. Arguello Light's siren." (Extracts from the *Partridge*'s deck log are shown in Illustration **13**.) According to its deck log, its senior staff held the rank of chief boatswain. There was no signature in the space for "U. S.N. Navigator." By convention, this meant that the ship's commander, Chief Boatswain J. A. Pierce, was also the navigator. The log showed that *Partridge* was, at the start of the voyage, in the company of the *Seattle, Melville,* and the destroyers *Farquhar* and *Farenholt.* It logged visibility of two miles in fog for most of the day, except for visibility of 4–5 miles from 1 to 5 P. M.

Destroyer Squadron 11 Steams South to Disaster

USS *Delphy,* flagship of Destroyer Squadron 11, and one the oldest destroyers in the fleet, departed San Francisco in the early morning of 8 September 1923, arrived at the San Francisco Lightship at 8:30 A. M., and conducted gunnery exercises as it moved southward to Pigeon Pt.

Destroyer Squadrons 11 and 12 were under orders from RAdm Kittelle to test their cruising turbines by proceeding to San Diego at a nominal speed of 20 knots; however, the commander of Squadron 11 decided to make the run southward at a steady 20 knots. The commander of Squadron 12 decided to proceed at 20 knots unless sea conditions warranted a slower speed.

The *Delphy*'s ship captain, LCdr Hunter, assumed the navigator's authority on departure. At 2:30 P.M., he decided the ship was abeam the Pt. Sur Light—though the light was never sighted. The squadron commander, Capt Watson, then changed the ship's course to 150 deg true.

Between 6 and 7 P.M. the *Delphy* requested RC bearings from the navy's Pt. Arguello RC Station. In a period of an hour *Delphy* received three 320-deg RC bearings. These bearings signaled that the ship was *to the northwest* of the Pt. Arguello RC station and headed for it. Shortly after 8 P.M., the *Delphy* intercepted two RC bearings that had been sent to the *Stoddert*. Those bearings showed the squadron was still *to the northwest* of Pt. Arguello (Illustration **28**).

About 8:30 P.M., the *Delphy* received another bearing that it had requested. It showed the *Delphy* was still *to the northwest* of Pt. Arguello. LCdr Hunter decided that that RC bearing was in error, and demanded the RC station send him a "reciprocal" of the bearing without first asking the RC to confirm the "doubted bearing." The RC station complied at 8:35 P.M. (That message was "reciprocal—168 deg," an approximate reversal of the actual bearing.) But LCdr Hunter assumed the 8:35 P.M. "reciprocal" message he had demanded from the R C station—was likely a "bearing." Thus he started dead reckoning his final DR-estimated 9 P.M. position (Illustration **28**).Then, at the last minute, without any verifiable techni cal reason, Hunter and Watson conferred and decided to increase *Delphy*'s estimated speed-made-good to 21 knots.

The *Delphy*'s crew had no fix, nor took any depth soundings, to confirm the ship's estimated distance from shore. This was a major error, since the distance offshore was a critical piece of the navigational puzzle as they approached Pt. Arguello (shown in Illustration **28**).

By 8:50 P.M., LCdr Hunter and Capt Watson had reviewed and manipulated the available navigational data. Watson decided, "We'll turn the squadron eastward at 9:00 P.M." Hunter asked, "Should we say anything to the division commanders?" Watson was quiet. The two were convinced that *Delphy* was past Pt. Arguello, could turn eastward, clear Pt. Conception, and safely turn into the Santa Barbara Channel. Tragically, the *Delphy*'s actual position as this time was just three miles north of Pt. Arguello, and one and a half miles west of the rocky coast at Pt. Pedernales (Illustration **28**). Summaries of the activity for ships mentioned are given below for each of the eight shipboard watches.

First shipboard watch (Mid to 4 A.M.*)*—Div 32 *Kennedy,* Div 31 *Farragut,* and Div 33 *Young*. The new helmsman and the new OOD came on the bridge at 4:00 A.M. Cdr Walter Roper, Commander Div 32, Lt MacNally, navigator, and deck officers Ltjg Dalkowitz and Ltjg Wellborn were on the *Kennedy*. Cdr William Pye, Commander Division 31, was on the *Farragut,* and Cdr Calhoun was in command of the *Young,* in Div 33.

Second shipboard watch (4 to 8 A.M.)—*Delphy*. The boiler fires were lighted. Capt Watson came on the bridge at 7 A.M. He decided he didn't want to worry about the detail of the day's navigation, and asked LCdr Hunter, "How is it with your young navigator?" He was relieved when Hunter said: "I will be the navigator today. Ltjg Blodgett will do the routine work."

The rumble of the turbines awakened Eugene Dooman, Capt Watson's civilian guest. Dooman arrived in the captain's spacious cabin as the steward finished setting the table, and was warmly greeted. He visited with the captain, and they discussed their earlier experiences together in Japan. Dooman said, "I sure feel more comfortable here than I did last night in the cigar-laden atmosphere of that damn hotel lobby. I'm enjoying the clean bay air and the coffee aroma."

Watson looked forward to the forthcoming discussion about the Japanese Navy's plans. Dooman was concerned about passing on any sensitive diplomatic material. Watson was quiet. The steward arrived with breakfast: juice, thick and flavorful French toast, ham and eggs, and enough coffee and cool, fresh water for the rest of the morning. By 8 A.M., the OOD finished checking the standard magnetic compasses he would use for steering. Next he logged the starting count of the propeller revolutions that he would use for estimating the ship's hourly speed. In the day's log, he noted: "The ship's gyrocompass is not working."

Third shipboard watch (8 A.M. to noon)—*Delphy,* with Div 31 *Farragut* and Div 32 *Stoddert.* At 8:30 A.M., when the three ships were southeast of Pt. Reyes, Capt Watson formed the squadron's three divisions abreast (Formation 5, Table 1) and conducted maneuvers as the squadron moved slowly southward in light fog. Watson issued special orders: "*Delphy* will navigate for the squadron. All ships will maintain 20 knots."

Cdr Roper was unhappy and spoke accordingly when he found out that his excellent navigator, Lt MacNally, was not a part of the *Delphy* navigation team. The well-navigated *Stoddert,* from Cdr Roper's division, signaled: "Have visual fix on Pigeon Pt. Lighthouse, 11:30 A.M. Light is abeam at a stadimeter distance of 4,250 yards."

Cdr Pye, Commander Division 31, was annoyed to find no mention—as promised—of when he would be told the squadron's intended course after it cleared Pt. Conception. The watch was in its last hour when Cdr Pye noticed his *Farragut*'s course of 160 deg true would be dangerous if continued. He called, "Change course to avoid Pigeon Pt." (That lighthouse, 45 miles south of San Francisco, is shown in Illustration **14**.)

Aboard *Delphy* the word spread—"LCdr Hunter is the navigator, Ltjg Blodgett is doing routine work." But Hunter discouraged any mumbling about why he had taken that action, and Ens Morrow, Chief Cummings, and others obliged. At 11:20 A.M., LCdr Hunter told Blodgett, "Start a dead reckoning course from our fix on Pigeon Pt., use a course of 160 deg and a speed of 20 knots to estimate future DR estimated positions."

Fourth shipboard watch (noon to 4 P.M.)—Div 32 *Kennedy,* DesRon's *Melville,* and Div 32 *Reno.* These three ships were underway when the *Kennedy*'s radioman intercepted a message from Division 32 *Reno* addressed to RAdm Kittelle, on the squadron flagship *Melville:* "We have sighted lifeboats from a shipwreck." Cdr Roper radioed Capt Watson, "Request permission to take my division to the aid of our ship *Reno* in its rescue of a ship in distress." Capt Watson replied, "Good to hear about *Reno*'s rescue—something seaman-like to offset that *Zeilin* disaster—have your request. However, permission to leave squadron formation is denied." Watson's rebuff—over the not-so-private ship-to-ship radio telephone—embarrassed Roper, and he "spoke stiffly" to Capt Watson over the radio telephone, and spoke "salty words" to his bridge crew. The *Kennedy*'s captain remarked, "Capt Watson sounds harsh, after all the *Reno* is one of our ships in need."

[Watson rebuffed Roper because he did not want to dim the *Reno*'s success by making it into a Division-32 rescue. Watson was reluctant to send Division 32 off on its own, because it would have interfered with the full squadron getting credit for a fast—record-breaking—endurance run to San Diego.]

Capt Watson modified his RC order: "*Delphy* is navigating for the squadron. However, the *Reno* is free to request RC bearings to aid the rescue. Other RC traffic will be conducted by *Delphy*." The *Reno,* however, never requested any RC bearings after Capt Watson's order.

At 1 P.M., Capt Watson and Mr. Dooman finished their pleasant lunch, and the captain suggested they organize their discussions to facilitate his visits to the navigation cabin.

By 2 P.M., the *Delphy* was well down the course leg to Pt. Sur. CQM Cummings reported, "Visibility three miles in light fog, winds west-northwest 16-knots, waves 5-feet." He listened for the horns and looked for the Pt. Sur Light, one of the finest on the coast because of its First-Order Fresnel Lens and its 250-foot height above the water (Illustration **15**). Cummings counted on seeing the light, and was disappointed when the variable fog and the *Delphy*'s distance offshore blocked his view of it. He reported, "Sir, Pt. Sur Light not visible, cannot hear its horns. Cannot identify the Sur escarpment"(Illustration **11**). CQM Cummings asked the OOD, "Have we any word about visibility down south?" The OOD replied, "Have no word on that." No one on the bridge knew that the "Pt. Arguello fog signal had been on since early Friday."

Hunter continued navigating by dead reckoning, using only the ship's compass course and the ship's speed by propeller revolutions. Thus Hunter had a series of DR position estimates—but he had no fix, no confirmation of any DR-estimated position.

Around 2:15 P.M., LCdr Hunter called the Pt. Arguello RC station, 140 miles away, and requested two RC bearings. Blodgett cautioned, "We're near the limit of the RC's range, and we are sending them a weak radio signal." The RC bearings came, indicating that the ship was south of Pt. Arguello. The vexed LCdr Hunter radioed the RC station, "I know we are to the northwest, send us another bearing." The RC radioman promptly sent a northwest bearing (that correction appears in Appendix II, the log of the RC Station).

At 2:30 P.M., *Delphy*'s DR indicated Pt. Sur was abeam. Chief Cummings listened carefully, and steadily scanned the coast, but he did not see the Pt. Sur Light or hear its foghorns (the light is shown in Illustration **15**). Capt Watson presumed they were at Pt. Sur, and ordered the course changed to 150 deg, but no sighting of Pt. Sur was made. Since the marked coastal change continued for hours south of Pt. Sur, it was a time for all the ships to begin a serious lookout for the appearance of the Pt. Piedras Blancas Light, the next light to the south. Blodgett suggested moving one of the more eastern ships closer to shore to ensure a fix on Piedras Blancas. Hunter said nothing, and made no plan to get a fix on the Piedras Light.

The DR line of positions was extended.

[The windage on the *Delphy*'s lightly loaded 300-foot-long profile, and the sea waves impacting on its stern quarter, caused it to yaw and become unstable directionally. In yawing conditions, it is difficult to steer the given course and hold a fixed speed over the bottom—the conditions necessary to make reliable DR position estimates. The yawing fostered a slight but continuous movement of the hull toward the coast, a movement not reflected in *Delphy*'s DR-estimated straight-line course.]

Fifth shipboard watch (4 P.M. to 8 P.M.)—*Delphy,* Division 32 *Kennedy,* and *Stoddert*.

The squadron was in "Formation 5" (Table 1). Capt Watson decided to put Squadron 11 into "Formation 18," and the *Delphy* showed yard-arm signal flags for the squadron to form in column. This maneuver was completed before 5:30 P.M. The bow-fantail distance between ships was now 200–300 yards, and the column order as shown in Table 2.

On *Kennedy,* Ltjg Max Wellborn was the new OOD. He saw the helmsman's steering difficulty and noted that the ship was not making 20 knots. Looking at the charted water depths, he saw that a few depth soundings [from Pt. Piedras Blancas south to Pt. Arguello] would give him an estimate of his distance offshore (Illustration **28**), and he chafed at not being allowed to slow down and take a sounding. No one on the bridge suggested that the last ship in column, *Thompson*, could slow, sound, report, and easily return to formation.

At 6 P.M., Lt MacNally and Ltjg's Dalkowitz and Wellborn were in the spacious chartroom of the *Kennedy.* MacNally reported, "The true heading by standard compass has changed. Even though we are in column formation—the heading is now 127 deg—two deg more eastward than the 129 deg we used for the previous two hours. Our actual true course is now 148 degrees—despite the *Delphy*'s statement that the given true course is 150 degrees."

"We've made a two-degree change in our true course," Dalkowitz said.

"Yes," agreed Wellborn.

MacNally continued, "I notice the engine revolution counts for the 5–6 P.M. hour are different than those for the previous hour. Our speed is 19.4 knots, and not the assigned speed of 20 knots. The three vigorously reported to Cdr Roper, "You need to call Capt Watson about this."

"Don't call the *Delphy,*" Roper corrected them. "Squadron 11 knows what it is doing. It has all the navigational information."

[Evidence of a speed less than 20 knots was not just a *Kennedy* affair: the average speed for four Division 31 and Division 32 ships, calculated later from the engine revolution counts in their deck logs, indicated their 4 to 8 P.M. average speed was 19.3 knots, not 21, as the navigator of the *Delphy* assumed.]

On *Delphy.* Between 6 and 7 P.M. *Delphy* requested three RC bearings. A threesome request is a sign of a ship looking for a counterclockwise shift in bearing direction to confirm the start of its passage of Pt. Arguello. *Delphy*, however, received three 320-deg bearings, indicating the ship was *northwest* of Pt. Arguello. Blodgett spoke up, "We are on a dangerous course, heading directly for Pt. Arguello. We need to change course."

"No," replied Hunter. "I'm sure we are well seaward of Pt. Arguello. Hold the current course."

Capt Watson and Eugene Dooman finished their simple dinner before 7 P.M. Mr. Dooman returned to his cabin. LCdr Hunter, Ltjg Blodgett, and Capt Watson gathered elbow to elbow in the small navigation cabin.

Just after 7 P.M., the *Delphy* intercepted an RC bearing to the *Melville*—168 deg—indicating it was *south* of Pt. Arguello. Hunter knew the *Melville* was ahead of him, and was convinced that *Delphy* would soon receive a south RC bearing.

The navigation cabin's size was barely adequate to two people. When Watson and Hunter were present, junior officer Blodgett was always in the cramped position. Nevertheless, Blodgett spoke up, "We need soundings to confirm our DR estimated position." Blodgett's proposal had merit, which was evident to the two senior officers as they looked at the water-depth contours on the chart (Illustration **28**). They saw the 50-fathom water-depth contour wrapped around Pt. Arguello at a distance from shore of about four miles. Now, Hunter and Watson dominated the talk: "Our DR shows we are eight miles distant from the coast, at an indicated depth contour of more than 100 fathoms," Hunter said. "There is no need to slow down for soundings."

Watson shook his head. "Sounding not much use—probably can't even reach bottom," he replied.

"Slowing will spoil our engineering run," added Hunter.

Although Capt Watson stifled the discussion of taking soundings, he sensed his faux pas and continued, "I understand the need for soundings, and I wish we had a sonic depth finder onboard like the new fathometer the British have on their destroyer leaders." Capt Watson's words convinced Hunter that the captain was satisfied with his decision, but Hunter was still uncomfortable, because he knew that Watson's mind was not navigating.

LCdr Hunter had a long-standing and pervasive distrust of the radio compass. He didn't like the RC because it was not on his ship and under his control. He emphasized the general view: "The radio compass is inaccurate for *precise* navigation." Hunter went on with balderdash, however: "RC bearings are frequently not reliable for approximating the ship's position relative to the RC station." Blodgett remained quiet.

At 7:30 P.M., Hunter was concerned about the DR-estimated 8 P.M. ship position he was required to send to RAdm Kittelle. He yearned for a batch of RC bearings or depth soundings showing his DR was okay, but he requested no RC bearings, and failed to exchange his estimated positions with those held by other squadron navigators.

[Later, during the Court of Inquiry, Hunter would say, "We could not request RC bearings at that time, because there was an RC traffic problem, too many ships requesting RC bearings at the same time." This was untrue. The record shows the 7–8 P.M. RC traffic for three commercial and five navy ships was handled promptly.]

Having decided on the *Delphy*'s DR-estimated 8 P.M. position (Illustration **28**), LCdr Hunter consulted Capt Watson. They erred, however, and sent that DR-estimated 8 P.M. position to the admiral without first sending it to the division commanders for comment.

Worse, Hunter *never* sent his position to the division commanders, nor requested a position from them.

RAdm Kittelle assumed all was well with his two destroyer squadrons. His flagship, *Melville,* was moving southward at 12 knots, and its captain was taking depth soundings until he got a depth of 300 fathoms—proof that the ship was in the deep water of the Santa Barbara Channel. The *Melville*'s captain was a steady user of RC bearings, and his ship's passage of Pt. Arguello was marked by a classic counterclockwise set of radio-compass bearings: (310 deg at 5:43 P.M.); (262 deg at 6:20 P.M.); and (168 deg at 7:18 P.M.). The admiral presumed that the *Delphy* was proceeding with care, because *Delphy*'s 8 P.M. report carried no comment about the uncertain nature of that DR-estimated position.

Sixth and last shipboard watch of the day (8 P.M. to midnight)—Division 32 *Kennedy* and *Stoddert*, Division 31 *Farragut* and *Somers,* Division 33 *S. P Lee* and *Young,* plus flagship *Delphy.* As Ltjg Dalkowitz took over as OOD on the *Kennedy,* the departing OOD said, "We're using a course of 148 degrees and speed of 19.7 knots for the DR position estimates." Dalkowitz called out, "Our DR track will put us close abeam the Arguello Lighthouse at 9 P.M., and in dangerous shoal water."

Navigator MacNally called the radioman, "Intercept every radio compass bearing sent from RC Arguello."

Dalkowitz advised Cdr Roper, "*Delphy* and the leading squadron ships will be close to the coast and in danger at 9 P.M."

"Don't worry," Roper assured. "The *Delphy* is on that course to be sure it picks up the Pt. Arguello Light."

LCdr Bratton, commander of *Stoddert,* was concerned about his ship's position, and he requested two RC bearings between 8 and 8:30 P.M. They came as 326 and 330 deg, showing the *Stoddert* to be northwest of Arguello. These bearings, intercepted by the Division 32 *Kennedy,* were found to agree with their ship's DR-estimated position to the northwest of Pt. Arguello, and with their projected track that passed close to Pt. Arguello. Those two commanders were not alarmed, however, because they did not know that the *Delphy* had decided to turn eastward in thirty minutes.

Kennedy and *Stoddert* estimated they would pick up Pt. Arguello close by and at a distance of two miles at 9 P.M. The OOD on the *Kennedy* assumed that *Delphy*'s navigator, with all available navigational information on hand, was confident in his estimated positions—the two the *Kennedy* had intercepted. The *Kennedy*'s OOD questioned his navigator: "Doesn't make sense, the *Delphy*'s DR–estimated 9 P.M. position is twelve miles further south and six miles further from shore than our estimated 9 P.M. position." (Illustration **28**) After serious thought, the *Kennedy*'s OOD said, "We should radio *Delphy* and call attention to the difference between the DR estimated positions of our two ships." Cdr Roper, however, said, "*Delphy* knows what it is doing, it's trying to pick up the Arguello Light." No one on the bridge suspected the *Delphy* had decided to turn the squadron eastward at 9 P.M.

Other Division 32 ships had DR position estimates different from those of the *Delphy*. Division 33's *Young* estimated it was seven miles north of *Delphy* at 8 P.M., and Cdr Pye's Division 31's *Farragut* and *Somers* estimated they would not reach Pt. Arguello till 9 P.M. The thing everyone was looking for, and never saw, was the Pt. Arguello Light, atop a 28-foot tower near the end of a jagged projection of the rocky coast. Also, they listened for, but never heard, the light's powerful compressed-air fog siren, which was sounding full blast. (The Arguello Lighthouse and RC Steel Tower are shown in Illustration **9**.)

On *Delphy*, Ltjg Blodgett suspected the ship was in danger, but he had no evidence to wave around, because LCdr Hunter had declined his request to gather position information from other squadron ships. Hunter now projected the *Delphy*'s aging and unverified DR track (Illustration **28**). That projection indicated they would pass Pt. Arguello Light on the port beam at 8:30 P.M., at a distance of eight miles. The *Delphy*'s DR-estimated position was alarmingly different from the DR of the ships *Young, Kennedy,* and *Stoddert,* but *Delphy*'s bridge did not know about that difference, because they never exchanged estimated positions with the *Delphy*.

Capt Morris' *S.P. Lee* and Cdr Calhoun's *Young* intercepted *Delphy*'s transmission of its 8 P.M. estimated position to RAdm Kittelle, but Capt Morris had little reason to query *Delphy* about the reliability of their estimated position, because he was navigating in a parallel fashion. In addition, there was linkage between the *Lee* and the *Delphy* due to Capt Morris' rank and his ship's #2 position in the column. As division commander, however, Morris was responsible for contacting his ship commanders, asking for their 8 P.M. positions, and passing those positions on to the squadron's commander. This did not happen. Cdr Calhoun, in the #3 column position, had an estimated position seven miles north of *Delphy,* but he took no action, because the bridge of the *Young* assumed Morris and Watson had all available information.

Delphy. LCdr Hunter was fixated on his projected DR track (Illustration **28**). It indicated that San Miguel Island lay directly ahead, a hazard fresh in his mind since the wreck of the *Cuba*. After 8 P.M., there was a flurry of radio compass bearing reports. *Delphy* intercepted two bearings sent to *Stoddert* (330 deg at 8:11) and (326 deg at 8:32). Refusing to believe those bearings, Hunter made his own request to RC Arguello, and received an RC—330 deg—meaning *you are to the northwest of this RC station.* Hunter rejected that 330-deg bearing and sent a demand to the RC Station: "Give us a reciprocal, we are to southward." He received a reply at 8:35 P.M.: "*Reciprocal 168 deg*." LCdr Hunter then used that 168-deg reciprocal and a speed of 21 knots to project a DR position estimate for 9 P.M. This sequence was marked by hurried words between Hunter, Watson, and Blodgett. Hunter became concerned about running into San Miguel Island (shown on the map in Illustrations **3, 12,** and **28**). But LCdr Hunter and Capt Watson decided that the *Delphy*'s final DR-estimated 9 P.M. position was probably a bit ahead of their original DR estimate, and was a safe place to turn eastward. Capt Watson ordered. "Turn the squadron on a course 095 degrees true at 9 P.M." The order to turn eastward was not sent to the squadron's division commanders. Thus, a few minutes later, each ship's commander was startled when the ship ahead suddenly turned eastward at 20 knots.

Delphy made two final requests to RC Arguello for RC bearings, and received (333 deg at 8:39) and (323 deg at 8:58). Both indicated that *Delphy* was to the *northwest* of Pt. Arguello. Hunter ignored them.

On the *Delphy*'s bridge at 8:59 P.M., Ens Morrow was one hour into his first OOD watch. He heard that Capt Watson's estimate of the emergency stopping distance in clear weather for a destroyer at 20 knots was 600 yards. Cummings, outside and looking forward in fog, had no reference point to use for a visibility estimate. Looking down the column in the fog, he reported he could see the lights on the ships three positions to the rear. The 9 P.M. time to turn eastward arrived, and the *Delphy* turned.

Cdr Pye's and Cdr Roper's divisions, in column behind the *Delphy,* were in the dark about Capt Watson's decision to turn the squadron eastward. They were expecting to be advised, inasmuch as Capt Watson had said at the pre-voyage conference, "I will advise you later about the course to be taken after clearing Pt. Arguello." Cdr Roper was expecting to see the Pt. Arguello Light, because his estimated position was only several miles from shore. If Commanders Calhoun, Pye, and Roper had known of each other's situations, and of the order to turn eastward at 9 P.M., they would have radioed a warning to *Delphy* and immediately acted to save their ships.

Two divisions blindly followed the *Delphy*'s turn. Cdr Roper's Division 32 did not turn. The followers were convinced that the *Delphy*'s positions were based on a fix determined by RC bearings and navigational data they did not have. Hence no ship commander considered the *Delphy* might turn eastward without a position fix, without knowing where it was, and without informing them in advance. Cdr Roper was not convinced, and Division 32 did not turn.

Capt Watson's order to turn eastward at 9 P.M. was made at 8:50. Once the turn was started, Capt Morris' ship, #2 in column, received the turn signal, but Morris did not pass the turn command down the column. The deck log of Cdr Pye's *Farragut* states: "At 9:01 guide changed course to 095 degrees without previous signal."

Most amazing, as *Delphy* turned, Capt Watson and LCdr Hunter were insensitive to the nine signposts indicating that they were on a pathway to disaster:

- Fog, darkness, forward visibility and depth of water unknown;
- No grasp of the accumulated error of their DR-estimated position; no sighting of a lighthouse or a recognizable landmark; no sound of a lighthouse horn or siren, and no confirmation of their DR-estimated line of position;
- No sighting of a lighthouse or other known coastal landmarks after Pigeon Pt.;
- No RC bearings to confirm their passage of Pt. Arguello;
- No depth soundings;
- Squadron 11 moving in column, in fog, at an excessive speed;
- Five RC bearings in a row indicating the *Delphy* was northwest of the RC Station;
- No idea of the estimated positions held by Commanders Calhoun, Pye, and Roper;
- No advance notice given to the division commanders that the squadron would turn eastward at 9 P.M.

Aboard *Farragut*, Cdr Pye, Commander Division 31, was nonplused when the ships ahead of him turned. He followed blindly, because he was convinced that the squadron commander aboard *Delphy* must have the navigational facts required to justify changing course. Pye was shocked, because he had expected the *Delphy* to slow and take soundings to verify that they were in deep water. Now, *Delphy* had turned without giving advance notice, and Cdr Pye's ships were in imminent danger.

The bridges on *Kennedy and Stoddert* were alert and thinking for themselves. As the radioman intercepted the *Delphy*'s bearings, *Kennedy*'s OOD, Ltjg Dalkowitz, and the former OOD, Ltjg Wellborn, huddled over the nautical chart. They agreed that the *Kennedy* was on a true 148-deg course, not 150 deg as the *Delphy* compass indicated, and they agreed that the *Kennedy*'s speed was only 19.5 knots. Wellborn said, "Our more landward direction and slower speed was due to the difficult steering." Alarmed, Dalkowitz replied, "It looks like the squadron is headed for the beach." Agreeing with the two OODs, Lt MacNally ordered, "Report this to LCdr 'Baldy' Bell, and to Cdr Roper."

Roper's first reaction surprised them: "Seems like you think you know more than the squadron commander. Watson gave me hell about the *Cuba*, and I don't want to stick my neck out unless we're sure we're right." He paused, "All right, if you are afraid, get over to the right."

Dalkowitz gave the order. The division moved 200 yards to starboard from the line of formation. This opened up a gap of 350 yards between the *Kennedy* and the ship ahead, the *Chauncey*. The rest of the division's ships did likewise. At 8:58 P.M., the *Kennedy*'s radioman intercepted, and called out, "RC bearing addressed to *Delphy*—323 degrees." The *Kennedy*'s bridge was alive. Ships were bunching ahead. The *Kennedy* and its other division ships slowed and stopped. At that time, the *Chauncey* was on the port beam and about 1000 yards ahead. Cdr Roper signaled, "Do not turn eastward. Slow, move your ship seaward, take soundings, keep me advised." Ships soon reported having sounded depths of more than a dozen fathoms. Cdr Roper ordered his ships to move slowly westward, take soundings, and prepare to anchor.

Seven Destroyers are Stranded on the Rocks

The sea below the Pt. Honda Mesa is a dangerous place. When visible on a windy day at low tide, its seascape is a fearsome sight: you can see the rocky escarpments stretching into the sea, and the rocks along the coast (Illustration **2**). At high tide, however, the seascape is misleading, as many of the rocks are underwater or barely awash. (Illustrations **16-A** and **16-B** show the accident scene on a high-tide day in September 1994. The deterioration of the *Nicholas* on the reefs is evident in Illustration **18**.)

The Disaster Sequence

At 9 P.M., the *Delphy* turned left, sharply and blindly, at a speed of 20 knots, and a distance from the shore of about one and a half miles (Illustration **28**). At 9:06, at 20-knot speed, *Delphy* ran onto the mainland of the rocky coast at Pedernales Point. Stranded hard, bow pointed north (the rudder was put "hard left" just before it hit), the stern of the ship started breaking free at once. She sounded her siren and radioed the signal "9 turn [left] ... keep clear to westward."

Two other ships followed. *S.P. Lee,* #2 in column, managed to avoid running into the stern of the stranded *Delphy*, and to reduce its speed to 8 knots before it ran into the mainland and stranded with bow pointed north (Illustration **2**). *Nicholas,* #5 in column, passed the stranded *Lee* and sheered left until its bow was pointed west. It was then impaled, and stranded on the pinnacles of an offshore reef (Illustration **2**).

Young, #3 in column, was heading onshore when it was cut open by an offshore reef. It turned starboard side down and came to rest on its beam end 100 yards offshore, its portside two feet out of the water, bow pointed south (Illustration **5**).

One ship turned right. *Chauncey,* #10, managed to maneuver past the *Young* and got stranded on the mainland with bow pointed south (Illustrations **5** and **20**).

Two ships struck dead ahead on offshore rocks. *Woodbury,* #4, was first, wedging itself between a small island and Pinnacle Rock, bow pointed southeast. *Fuller*, #7 (in the center-right of Illustration **19**), hit rocks astern of the *Woodbury,* and stranded, bow pointed more eastward. The location of the *Woodbury* is shown in Illustration **5**, **19**; the positions of all the wrecked ships are shown on the map in Illustration **17**.

Twenty-three seamen were lost: twenty from the *Young*, and three from the *Delphy*. Despite a major salvage effort, seven new, pride-of-the-navy destroyers were lost.

Three ships from Cdr Pye's Division escaped: *Farragut, Somers,* and *Percival.* A sense of what happened to the *Farragut* and *Somers* is shown in the excerpts from their deck logs.

The following is from the deck log of Cdr Pye's Division 31 *Farragut,* column position #6:

> At 9:01 guide changed course to 095 degrees without previous signal. At 9:05 changed course to follow … had hardly settled down when siren sounded ahead and ships began to break formation. Called Commander … out of chart house and Captain took the deck … 9:09 changed speed to ⅔, then stop, then full speed astern … the ships ahead were on the rocks … all boats were ordered manned to go to rescue of men in water … collision quarters sounded … we were struck on side by *Fuller* … boats damaged … engines backed full … ship stopped, shuddered and then we gathered sternway …

The following is from the deck log of the Division 31 *Somers*, column position #9:

> At 9:08 ships ahead seemed to be crowding up in confusion. Put rudder hard right and stopped. Went ⅓ speed ahead to clear *Percival.* At 9:10 a ship ahead sounded siren and there seemed to be collision

> ahead as oil was burning on the water. At 9:11 sighted breakers dead ahead on port hand ... went astern full speed ... At 9:12 hit rocks ahead and slipped off as gained sternway ... at 9:24 starboard engine astern ⅓, port engine ahead ⅓ to get clear of other vessels and bring ship to westerly heading. At 10:05 steadied ... At 10:20 depth 26 fathoms ... Foggy, visibility during watch 600 yd.

All the ships of Cdr Roper's division were saved. This excerpt is from the deck log of *Kennedy,* Division 32, column position #11, and signed by the OOD, Lt Dalkowitz:

> Intercepted bearings from Pt. Arguello to *Stoddert* 8:12—326 deg, 8: 32—330 deg and following to *Delphy* at 8:35—*reciprocal* 169 deg; 8:39—333 deg; 8:58—323 deg At 9:05 changed to ⅔ speed. 9:06 standard speed, 9:11 (⅔), 9:12 (⅕), 9:13 stopped, 9:19 touched unknown object forward causing jar on bridge. Backed full speed. 9:20 stopped both engines. Took sounding, 7 fathoms. 9:22 sounding, 13 fathoms. 9:29 RC to *Kennedy* 000 ½ deg. At 9:31 steadied on course 270 deg true.

This excerpt is from the deck log of *Stoddert*, Division 32, column position #13:

> At 9:08 went two-thirds speed followed immediately by stop. Changed course westward to keep clear of ships ahead and get to seaward. *Kennedy* was on port bow sounding backing signals. Backed till dead in water, took sounding and obtained 12 fathoms. Heard train ... immediately went to westward with hard right rudder ... At 9:50 formed with division *Kennedy,* #11, *Hamilton,* #12, and *Thompson,* #14.

Division 32 formed offshore and steamed slowly southward and northward during the night. The division's progress is shown in the RC bearings below addressed to ComDesDiv32.

Summary of RC bearings to Squadron 11, 9:16–11:57 P. M.
(*ComDesDiv32 is slowly moving southeastward)

USS *J. F. Burns*	9:16 P. M.	312.5 deg
USS *Kennedy*	9:27 P. M.	0.5 deg
USS *Stoddert*	9:37 P. M.	317 deg
* ComDesDiv32	9:43 P. M.	303 deg
* ComDesDiv32	9:52 P. M.	286.5 deg
USS *Somers*	10:17 P. M.	320 deg
* ComDesDiv32	10:28 P. M.	243.5 deg
* ComDesDiv32	11:04 P. M.	234.5 deg
USS *Farragut*	11:57 P. M.	323 deg

Twenty-six individual ships called for, received, and successfully used RC bearings to navigate past Pt. Arguello. (All the RC bearings are referenced in Appendix II.) None of the other southward-moving ships of the U. S. Battle Fleet Pacific, or the civilian ships in transit southward on September 8, had any RC problems.

Chapter 4

Survival and Loss

The ship turned over fast, starboard side down, and we scrambled to the port rail. The men were in a precarious position, and Chief Boatswain's Mate Arthur Peterson swam below, found the fire axe, returned, and smashed the portholes to make handholds for the men.

—Lt E. C. Herzinger, USS *Young*

Overview

Here are the stories of what happened, ship by ship and sailor team by sailor team. They are the stories of the heroics of LCdr Walter Seed, Machinist Mate 1st Frank Moon, and Chief Boatswain's Mate Arthur Peterson. The official citations given by the Naval Court of Inquiry and by RAdm Kittelle tell how each was earned, and are listed at the end of each ship's story, but it was impossible to identify and commend all of the deserving people. There is scant detail about the lost men, the heroics of the three men lost while adrift in a life raft, the heroics and the agony of the men who struggled up from below decks, and those who drowned in the oily water as they were swept seaward. "Capt Watson obtained the name of the fishing smack, so the heroic work of those fishermen—they saved about 100 men—made the newspapers."

This account is based on statements by the survivors, the rescuers, those testifying at the Court of Inquiry, the court martial, the Court of Inquiry's written report, the available ship's deck logs, pertinent personal records, newspaper accounts, and the writings of the main chroniclers of this event: C. Hice, C. Lockwood and H. C. Adamson; J. and M. Silva, and Elwyn Overshiner. (Elwyn's brother, Gordon, was one of the firemen lost when the *Young* capsized.)

It was 9:10 P.M., 8 September 1923. The ocean at the tragic site was cold, rocky, coated with oil, and hazardous. The tide was turning seaward. On the rocks and reefs of Pt. Honda and just offshore were seven wrecked destroyers and 600 men in peril.

The survival story for each ship is different, but the unpleasant conditions the crews faced were similar. The crews did not know they were on the mainland until 10 P.M., when a train blew its whistle. Since they did not know the lay of the land, the survival effort developed as a series of improvised steps. Many of the men started this phase with injuries they suffered when their ships collided with the rocky coast. No one was properly clothed or prepared for the survival effort. Rescuers found it difficult, in some cases impossible, to grasp and aid the oily, slippery injured. Wind and cool water chilled everyone. The crews wore what they were wearing at the time of the crashes; only a few men had boots or jackets.

The ships soon lost power, and darkness was the rule. The available lanterns and flashlights were not adequate. It was extremely difficult for the below-decks men of the *Young* to escape. Even some of those who got up on deck found it impossible to survive immersion in a layer of fuel oil, a seaward tidal flow, submerged rocks, chunks of floating debris, a blow, an eyeful, a mouthful of oil, a little oil inhaled into the lungs. One raft with three men aboard disappeared into the night. Another raft was rescued through a joint effort of the Navy RC and Lighthouse crews at Pt. Arguello.

Each commander had to make immediate decisions about what to do as each emergency occurred or was discovered, and decide how to survive until daybreak. Each had to decide whether his ship was grounded or stranded. He had to decide if his ship would hold together, capsize, break in two, sink, or do something else. The skill, courage, and perseverance of all the cold, wet, oily men—in various kinds and levels of distress as they strove to survive the night—merit our attention and praise. The disaster tested the ability of men of all ranks to make and carry out lifesaving decisions. They were not found wanting in discipline, stamina, bravery, or leadership. A complete story of this disaster would tell of every man's heroic role.

[According to a statement in Overshiner's *Course 095 to Eternity,* RAdm Kittelle failed to order an immediate and comprehensive search for the *Young*'s three men, adrift on a raft in the open sea, an action that might have saved them.]

The men who were recommended for citations by the Court of Inquiry or by RAdm Kittelle are listed at the end of each ship's section, following the text describing the conditions under which their letters of commendation were earned. These lists include the names of all of those cited.

The men of the *Chauncey* aided the *Young, Lee*'s men aided the *Nicholas, Woodbury*'s men aided the *Fuller,* and the *Roma* aided *Woodbury* and *Fuller.* The men saved themselves, saved each other, and then went on to help the men on the "next ship," an exceptional example of bravery and heroism.

Considering that seven nearly new destroyers were lost, it is remarkable that the loss of life was not much greater. This exceptional outcome was due to the outstanding survival efforts of the men of Destroyer Squadron 11, the men of the Southern Pacific Railroad, the people of the Lompoc community, the fishermen who arrived on the *Neuva Roma* on Sunday morning, and the fortunate location and timing of the disaster: near a mainline railroad track on a summer night, rather than on an isolated seacoast on a stormy winter's night.

On Sunday, the sailors were thrilled by the community's warm-hearted, immediate, and effective help and the railroad's rescue efforts. The days following were marked by memorial services, the court of inquiry, and the court martial. There was no parade to honor these brave men, many of whom would rise to high rank and be the future leaders in the U. S. Navy, because this military mishap was not that kind of military misfortune.

Illustration **17** shows the locations of the wrecked ships in their geographical grouping at the time the last ship stranded. The northern group and their column positions were *Delphy,* 1st; *S. P. Lee,* 2nd; and *Nicholas,* 5th. The central group was *Young,* 3rd, and *Chauncey,* 10th. The offshore group was *Woodbury,* 4th and *Fuller,* 7th. The destroyers in column positions 6, 8, 9, and 11-14 escaped. (See the column formation in Chapter 2.)

USS *Delphy*'s Men Climb to Top of Bridge Rock; Three Men Lost

The lead ship hit Bridge Rock, the mushroom-shaped headland in Illustration **17**, as the helmsman made a frantic last-minute effort to turn left. Everyone not braced continued forward into the nearest fixed object. Lt Blodgett's knee was damaged. The ship ended up on a rocky ledge, rolling and banging against a large protruding rock. The men called this "first rock." It is a lower part of Bridge Rock. The bridge is a narrow connection over the ocean from the rock to the mesa. *Delphy*'s hull shows in the lower right of Illustration **5**.

Three sets of survival activity were necessary. Each was developed on the spot. One hundred men moved, one at a time, from the ship to first rock. Upon reaching that small space, each man moved up to the top of Bridge Rock, then each exited, along what they perceived in the dark as a narrow "path," to the mesa. Few realized that that path over the water was a narrow land bridge, and that a couple of steps sideways meant going into the sea.

The *Delphy,* shown in Illustration **5**, rolled on impact and water entered its hatchway. The waves bashed the hull against first rock, causing a hole on the starboard side. LCdr Don Hunter sensed the ship was beginning to break up and ordered, "Abandon ship." Men jumped to first rock from the stern, but this opportunity vanished as the ship changed position. Men jumped from the bow, fell into the sea, and got caught in the oily water between the ship and the rock. Engineman R. L. Rhodehamel saved four of these men, pulling them in one by one as he clung to the steel sea ladder on the ship's starboard side.

Fireman James Pearson was the last to be pulled in. He was in critical shape, his eyeglasses broken and small pieces of glass jammed into his eyes. Pearson was in severe pain, covered with oil, slippery, and violent. The ship's lights were out and the deck was a mess. Ens Morrow held Pearson and the flashlights. Chief Pharmacist Mate

G. E. Jordan and Lt Blodgett tried but could not render proper aid. Jordan could not see the glass slivers. Blodgett and Morrow tried to hold the patient motionless, but failed. Jordan said, "Stop, I don't have the proper medical instruments."

Lt Blodgett decided to tie Pearson in a raft and move him to shore until his violence could be controlled. Through an outstanding effort by Gunner's Mate H. J. Fontan, a life raft was launched, but before Pearson could be placed aboard, the raft was sucked away from the ship's side. Fontan just had time to make a frantic grab for the steel sea ladder. Later, Blodgett tried again, but Pearson was so slippery, and struggled so violently, that it was unsafe to continue. At this stage, Pearson was a menace to anyone aboard with him. To secure him until he could be safely removed, a strap loop was placed around him to prevent him from being washed overboard, and he was placed in comparative safety on the base frame of the steel searchlight tower.

The crew spotted a knob-like shape on top of first rock, a shape suitable to hold and adjust a ship-to-shore survival line. But it required someone to swim, and climb to first rock, above the water and over twenty feet away. Radioman E. R. Weisendanger, volunteered, and started out through the oily surf carrying the needed line. He lost the line, but survived the swim, and reached first rock. With much effort, Boatswain's Mate H. H. Wilgus rigged a heavier mooring line, but the sea twice washed him off the propeller guard and twice slammed him back. Once the line was rigged from the top of the after deckhouse to the knob on first rock, a few strong men were able to traverse the line to first rock. This traverse-type system would work for the rest of the crew only if the line was alternately tightened and slackened to compensate for the ship's continuous rolling. LCdr Donald (squadron staff engineer), Lt Cruzen (*Delphy*'s engineer), and Seaman W. J. Ekenberg went over to do this job.

Seaman Ekenberg realized they would need to move the men again, from first rock near the water up to the top of Bridge Rock. Ekenberg made the traverse to first rock with a length of boat falls—the line used to lower or raise the whaleboat to its davit heads. He immediately set about finding a route to the top of Bridge Rock, and strung rope along the way. LCdr Donald tested the rope and found that it held. The scene was now set for survival. LCdr Donald was on top of Bridge Rock. Lt Cruzen, with volunteers, was on first rock, and Ens Morrow and Chief Cummings were on top of the after deckhouse. Superb craftsmen, these "volunteers" anticipated each roll of the hull, and slacked or tightened the line between first rock and the hull to compensate for the hull's roll toward or away from the rock face.

One man at a time, the uninjured stepped off the top of the deckhouse, grabbed the line, hung on to it with hands, arms, and legs, and worked their way landward using something akin to a Tyrolean traverse. Several injured men could not make this trip, and were placed in a tied raft. Radioman Weisendanger pulled the raft ashore, but while the injured were being unloaded, the raft broke loose, so only one trip was completed.

The first batch of men on top of Bridge Rock heard the sound of a railway train. Until that time they did not know they were on the mainland. The problem remained of getting up to the railway. They finally found a narrow path in the dark and moved quickly up to it. As shown in Illustration **17**, this path turned out to be the "bridge" connecting Bridge Rock to the mesa. In daylight, they later noted that the "path" was narrow and 30 feet above the water.

Fireman T. C. Farnham lost his grip and fell into the sea while trying to reach first rock. Three men, Ship's Cook A. A. Bayes, Gunner's Mate J. C. Rosboro, and Fireman W. C. Etheridge, dived into the sea between the ship and the rock and saved Fireman Farnham.

When the line from the ship to first rock unexpectedly tightened, Fireman Conway and Cabin Cook Dalida were heaved, lost their grip, and were plunged into the raging mess of oil and salt water between the ship and the rock's face. Gunner's Mate James Ferrell and others went into the water. Farrell managed to grab Fireman Conway, but Conway, too slippery to hold, fell into the sea. The men lost were Fireman 3rd Class James W. H. Conway and Cabin Cook

Sofronia Dalida. At daybreak there was no sign of Fireman 1st Class James Pearson.

Three Men Lost from the *Delphy*

James W. H. Conway, Fireman 3rd Class
James T. Pearson, Fireman 1st Class
Sofronia Dalida, Cabin Cook

Delphy Men Recommended for Citations

By the Court of Inquiry:
—R. L. Rhodehamel, Machinist's Mate 1st Class, for extraordinary heroism in saving the lives of four shipmates at the risk of his own life after the *Delphy* had stranded.
By RAdm Kittelle:
—Lieutenant Commander D. T. Hunter, for coolness and efficiency during the crisis, doing everything possible for his ship, and material assistance to the squadron commander (*Delphy*).
—Lieutenant Commander H. G. Donald, for valuable service in securing boilers and planning lifesaving appliances (*Delphy*).
—Lieutenant (jg) L. F. Blodgett; Lieutenant R. H. Cruzen; D. F. Aivtey, Watertender 1st Class; A. A. Bayes, Ship's Cook 1st Class; G. E. Burke, Yeoman 1st Class; G. F. Connon, Machinist's Mate 1st Class; L. Cook, Chief Signalman; H. C. Cummings, Chief Quartermaster; W. J. Ekenberg, Seaman 2nd Class; J. W. Ferrell, Gunner's Mate 1st Class; H. Fontan, Gunner's Mate 1st Class; J. C. Holdorf, Chief Yeoman; H. A. Isbell, Coxswain; L. V. Lattimore, Chief Radioman; J. F. O'Hara, Quartermaster 1st Class; E. B. Palmer, Coxswain; J. B. Rob, Engineman 2nd Class; J. C. Rosboro, Gunner's Mate 3rd Class; J. C. Wittaker, Chief Carpenter's Mate; H. H. Wilgus, Boatswain's Mate 2nd Class; and H. B. Wilson, Chief Torpedoman, were cited for displaying coolness, courage, and efficiency in the abandoning of the *Delphy*.

Men of the USS *S. P. Lee* Climb To the Mesa; Aid the USS *Nicholas*

Cdr William Toaz commanded the *S. P. Lee*, #2 in column. The *Lee* had completed an awkward left turn, and Cdr Toaz was sighting on the *Delphy* when he noticed that *Delphy* had crashed into a rocky cliff and stopped dead, and that *Lee* was closing rapidly. He put the *Lee* full astern, maneuvered hard left, and missed the *Delphy*'s stern. Now the *Lee* crashed into a rock wall at a speed of 8 knots, stranded, and rolled slightly. Water entered the aft fire room at a rapid rate. (The location of the *Lee* is shown in Illustration **17**.)

Cdr Toaz and his E. O., Lt Tarbutton, looked for a way to abandon the ship, but the cliff was high at this point, and the only immediate place to go was a two-foot-wide ledge at its base. Using a small doughnut raft, Coxswain C. M. Carlson and Seaman C. G. Stahl took a coil of signal halyard and made for the ledge 50 feet away. The men on the raft were able to take the sea by spinning and tilting. Bounced into the cliff, they secured their line on a projecting rock, reached the ledge where they got footing, and clung spread-eagled. They finally found a rocky bollard strong enough to hold the heavy line they had hauled over from the *Lee*. They fastened the line to the rock, and went hand over hand back to the destroyer. The trip took 30 minutes. At this stage they saw problems: the ledge would hold only a fraction of the crew, and there seemed to be no exit upward from it. Nonetheless, they started to "ferry" men from the *Lee*, eight men per trip in a large raft, the passengers tugging on the "ferry lines" that stretched overhead. (A photograph of the stranded *Lee* is shown in Illustration **2**.)

The first men to reach the ledge, Coxswain Carlson and Seaman Stahl, struggled to find a way up the cliff. It was hard work, but they reached the top and located a shorter, more negotiable route for the following crew. Ens W. D. Wright rigged a rope along the rocky path—the trail left by Carlson, Stahl, and Wright. All the sailors were on the top in an hour. Most were cut and bleeding. Pharmacist's Mate M. C. Watts rendered aid at the mesa's edge, bandaging the cut feet and hands with cotton fabric cut from the life preservers.

The *Lee*'s signalman contacted the *Nicholas* and found out that they were hard and fast on the reef below, and LCdr Roesch was prepared to wait until daybreak before abandoning ship. A signal watch was established on the mesa to keep in touch, and Capt Morris settled down to watch, walk, and plan till daybreak. The *Delphy*'s crew was in dire need; Cdr Toaz, two officers, and a dozen seamen headed south along the mesa's edge to aid them. Other heroes are listed below.

S. P. Lee Men Recommended for Citations

By RAdm Kittelle:
—Captain Robert Morris, indefatigable in the rescue of men from the *S. P. Lee* and *Nicholas*.
—J. F. Ryall, Radio Rigger from Mare Island, rendered meritorious service in saving crew of *S. P. Lee*.
—W. Short, Chief Quartermaster; N. C. Brown, Chief Gunner's Mate; Haynes, Torpedoman 2nd Class; Cushner, Radioman 2nd Class; Stillwaugh, Radioman 2nd Class; and Carlson, Coxswain, for particularly meritorious service and commendable conduct aboard the *S. P. Lee.*

Men of the USS *Nicholas* Survive Overnight; "Ferry" to the Beach

LCdr Herbert Roesch commanded *Nicholas*, #5 in column. His ship turned left, following the ship ahead. After a few minutes LCdr Roesch noticed confusion ahead—ships sheering left, and he immediately sheered *Nicholas* to the left., barely clearing the *S.P. Lee*. *Nicholas* completed a "U-turn," got her bow pointed seaward, then swung broadsides and violently ran into a reef of pointed rocks

(Illustration **2**). LCdr Roesch tried to get the *Nicholas* off the reef and escape seaward, but without success. Pinnacles had penetrated both fire rooms, the tide was ebbing, and the ship listing 30 degrees to starboard. Depth soundings found a 5-foot depth on the starboard and a 10-foot depth on the port. (The location of *Nicholas* is shown in Illustration **17**.)

Nicholas was on the weather side of Pedernales Pt. (locally called "Honda"), and the seas were striking its bow and carrying off to the *Lee,* which was at right angles. The searchlight showed an increasing number of rocks as the tide ebbed. It did not look as though they could even lower a boat without capsizing or dashing it to pieces on the hull or reef. LCdr Roesch decided to wait till daylight before abandoning his ship. Word was passed about the ship—"stay with her."

At this time LCdr Roesch thought it possible the ship might turn over on its starboard side, so everyone was advised to keep to the port rail spread lines and to make lines fast fore and aft. As the tide ebbed, however, the ship rested easier, and it seemed she was safe till dawn. At first light it would be easier to get ashore and get help, so that intent was signaled to the *Lee*'s signalman. By now, everyone wore life preservers, and gathered for the long wait until daybreak in the more protected spots on deck and in the few enclosed places not filled with water—spaces easy to get out of.

At daylight, with Capt Morris on duty, volunteers from the *S. P. Lee* assembled: Engineering Officer Lt. Paul Steinhagen, Coxswain C. H. Carlson, Chief Gunner's Mate E. G. Brown, Chief Quartermaster W. Short, Chief Torpedoman I. Yukovic, Quartermaster H. A. Bixler, Torpedoman P. C. Haynes, Machinist's Mate L. M. Goddard, Water Tender L. M. Woodson, and Radioman P. M. Kushner. They worked their way down from the mesa and ferried themselves back to the abandoned *Lee* aboard one of the rafts used the night before. (A photograph of *Lee* and *Nicholas* is in Illustration **2**; their locations are shown in the Illustration **17** map.)

The *Lee*'s bow was now pointing toward a narrow strip of beach just north of Pt. Honda, and oriented 90 degrees to the *Nicholas*.

Considering this geometry and the onshore wind, Lt Steinhagen set up the line-throwing gun, and the gunner aimed at the *Nicholas*'s bow. The lightweight cotton line made it a tricky shot, and the first shots either missed, or hit where the receiving crew could not reach them. Finally, the *Nicholas* crew grabbed the line, and one end of a cable was pulled from the *Lee* to the deck of the *Nicholas*. Another line was now shot from the *Lee* to the men on the "beach." Those men used that line to pull the other end of the cable from the *Lee* down to the beach, where it was secured to a boulder. A two-way line from the beach to the *Nicholas* was now rigged along this cable, and a ferry operation began, eight men per trip. The ship had been stranded twelve hours, had settled considerably, and the seas were breaking over the deckhouse. A few men embarked as the raft was being readied. Fireman Knox was swept overboard and slammed on a rock. Fortunately, the unconscious Knox was saved by the quick action of Seaman A. E. Dominick. (A photograph of the *Nicholas* a day after it stranded is in Illustration **2**; a later photograph of the *Nicholas* deteriorating on the rocks is shown in Illustration **18**.)

The procedure the crew of the *Nicholas* followed was to jump in the raft, work their way to the beach, then wade through hip-deep water into the arms of the men waiting to help. The ferry line gradually worked northward over the rocks, increasing the distance to shore, so on the last trip the ferry raft containing all the officers capsized and they were all thrown into the sea. Everyone swam, then waded and walked ashore. One seaman was washed overboard with his life preserver on. He made a game fight, and two men on the beach went out and grabbed him.

Men Climb to the USS *Young*'s Portside; Twenty Men Lost

The *Young* was #3 in column. Feeling a slight trembling, her skipper, Cdr William Calhoun, headed for the bridge. A terrific shock knocked him to the floor, and he thought the ship had been rammed. He could feel her slowing, but everything happened so fast that he did not sense that one of the turbines was still running and its propeller still turning. The ship had slowed, but was still moving, and the helmsman was steering slightly to the right. A quick decision was made to let the ship go for a sandy-looking inlet several hundred yards ahead, but hidden rocks ripped through the hull plating almost the full length of her starboard side. The ship stranded, and now started filling with water and listing to starboard. Concerned that the men might start leaving the ship, Cdr Calhoun ordered, "Don't leave her; she is on the rocks. Stick with the ship." The location of the *Young* is shown in Illustration **17**; the capsized *Young* is shown in Illustrations **5** and **19**.)

The *Young* listed. Unconscious from the fumes, Engineering Officer Lt Frederick C. Sasche was dragged up to the deck. There was imminent danger from the oil burners still pouring heat into the boilers: the increasing steam pressure might cause the boilers to explode. One of the brave men aboard ship was Fireman F. T. Scott. The E. O., Lt Herzinger, called for an engineer to go below. Fireman Scott shouted, "I know where the master valves are," and disappeared down the fire room airlock, but the water had risen so high that he could not complete the job. [The master valves were below the floor plates in the flooded fire room.]

The *Young* turned over fast, starboard side down. The men scrambled to make the port rail, and reached the portside of the ship, now two feet out of the water. The turnover time was 90 seconds. To the men on the hull, safety looked far away, and the tidal flow was seaward. The men were in a precarious situation—they went flat on the hull, looking for a handhold. Chief Boatswain's Mate Arthur Peterson decided to make handholds for them. He swam below, found the fire ax, and returned. He then created handholds by breaking out the exposed portholes.

By now the *Chauncey* had managed to pass the *Young*, get stranded upright in a shallow inlet, and set its anchor. Chief Peterson had a tough time swimming a line to *Chauncey,* but was spotted by Chief Mike Frye's searchlight and pulled to safety. A two-way set of lines was rigged to the ship's raft. All eighty men on the hull were saved by ferrying, alternately towing the raft to shore and pulling it back to the *Young*.

LCdr Booth of the *Chauncey* got his men safely on the mesa and then helped the *Young*'s survivors. Booth and his executive officer, Lt C. V. Lee, gave medical aid to the disabled Lt Sasche. Cdr Calhoun climbed on the hull and tapped for survivors, but heard nothing. Where were the twenty missing men? (The capsized *Young* can be seen in Illustrations **5** and **19**, and its location in **17**.)

Engineman C. E. Juri was below on the forward throttle. He said the crash sounded like the rattling of knives and forks in a big dishpan. Water came into the engine room immediately. He and most of the others below deck struggled to reach the escape hatches—the water reached the top of the escape hatch just as they did. Men were in the oily sea, mostly firemen and enginemen, plus crew who never made it to the port rail. They were exhausted, injured, and unable to swim through the thick oily layer now covering the sea around the ship. Swimming away from the ship—seaward with the tidal flow—seemed possible.

A glimmer of hope came when the *Farragut* arrived, lights blazing and dead in the water. Out swung the boats ready to help, but from the ship's deck the officers saw only a dismal scene of destruction. Suddenly, *Farragut* backed away.

Eight men escaped from the *Young* on two rafts: three on one raft and five on the other. They got the two rafts tied together, but the wave action soon broke the ties. The five-man raft ran into Pt.

Arguello, where the lighthouse keepers and nearby radiomen from the radio compass station rescued all aboard. The three-man raft carrying Radioman Reddock, Seaman Martin, and Coxswain Salzer was never seen again.

(The upper middle of the navy's aerial photograph, Illustration **5**, shows the capsized *Young*).

Twenty Men Lost from the *Young*

Thirteen had fireman or engineman designations. Seventeen bodies were reported as recovered from the sea, and two from the hull of the *Young*.

Everett Grady	Fireman 2nd Class
Earnest Harrison	Fireman 1st Class
Edward Kirby	Fireman 3rd Class
Henry Kirk	Fireman 3rd Class
Wade Morris	Fireman 3rd Class
Gordon Overshiner	Fireman 3rd Class
Leo Rogers	Fireman 3rd Class
Hugh Skipper	Fireman 3rd Class
Joseph Slimak	Fireman 3rd Class
Max Taylor	Engineman 2nd Class
Vern Van Schaack	Fireman 3rd Class
John Young	Fireman 1st Class
August Zakrewski	Fireman 2nd Class
Earl Duncan	Seaman 2nd Class
James Martin	Seaman 1st Class
Ralph Buchan	Chief Pharmacist
Ernest Jones	Cabin Cook
Clitus Reddock	Radioman 1st Class
Charles Salzer	Coxswain
Enrique Torres	Cabin Steward

List of *Young*'s Men Recommended for Citations

By the Court of Inquiry:
—Commander William L. Calhoun, for the coolness, intelligence, and seaman-like ability he showed after the vessel under his command (*Young*) stranded, which action on his part was greatly responsible for the much-reduced loss of life on that occasion.
—Lieutenant E. C. Herzinger, for especially meritorious conduct in connection with saving the crew of the *Young* after that ship had capsized.
—Chief Boatswain's Mate Arthur Peterson, for extraordinary heroism in swimming with a line from the *Young* to the *Chauncey* in heavy and turbulent sea.
By RAdm Kittelle:
—Commander W. L. Calhoun, who displayed leadership and personality that saved three-quarters of the crew of the *Young*.
—Arthur Peterson, Chief Boatswain's Mate, who bravely and at great personal risk swam to the *Chauncey* with a line by which the crew of the *Young* were landed.
—Lieutenant E. G. Herzinger, for coolness and great assistance in the face of grave danger; for personal courage and the excellent manner in which he made arrangements for landing the crew of *Young*.
—Lieutenant (jg) C. V. Lee and M. Frye, Chief's Mate, who greatly aided in landing the *Young*'s crew.
—Lieutenant (jg) A. H. Donaldson, who, as officer of the deck, was cool, calm, and most officer-like, and conducted himself in a commendable manner in a grave crisis (*Young*).
—Lieutenant Commander R. H. Booth, who rendered invaluable service in rescuing the crew of the *Young*
—J. Scott, Fireman 1st Class, for attempting to close the master burner valve of the *Young*.

Men of the USS *Chauncey* Reach the Mesa, Aid the USS *Young*

The *Chauncey* was #10 in column and commanded by LCdr Richard Booth. At 9 P.M. he was in the emergency cabin, with all its portholes open so he could hear what was happening on the bridge. He heard that there was confusion ahead, something about the squadron flagship suddenly turning left. (The *Chauncey*'s terminal location is shown in the map in Illustration **17**; photographs are in Illustrations **19** and **20**.)

Chauncey was closing on the two ships ahead, the *Somers* and the *Percival*. Thinking there was a collision ahead, LCdr Booth slowed, as did the ships ahead, but he still kept closing as those two started to back. The squadron order came, "Nine turn (left)." Booth could not turn left because there was another ship—probably *Percival*—in that space, so the skipper eased *Chauncey*'s throttle and executed a right and left rudder to slow down and miss the ship in his way.

As the ship's searchlight swung across the bow, Booth saw his real problem: the overturned *Young*, men clinging to her portside, shouting, "Don't hit us." The *Chauncey* maneuvered—to the left, full back, stop, and ahead port engine only—and "cantered" past *Young*'s stern. The *Young*'s still-rotating propeller cut *Chauncey*'s hull, and she stranded at 9:08 P.M. in a small cove below and south of the bluff of rock on which *Delphy* had crashed. (Illustration **19** shows the *Chauncey,* DD 296, stranded on the "beach," with the *Woodbury* on the rocks in the background; illustration **20** shows *Chauncey* stranded in the rocky cove, and a model of this class.)

The lights went out, and *Chauncey*'s crew dropped anchors and found the ship stable and out of danger. While preparing to send a line to the *Young,* they saw Peterson, *Young*'s Chief Boatswain's Mate, struggling in the water, the needed line in his hands. The survival of the men on the hull of the *Young* was now assured. Only 25 yards away, Bridge Rock rose above the *Chauncey,* but the surge of sea between the ship and the rock was rough. Two lines were rigged under the direction of Lt Lee. Two Carley rafts were used as ferries. The backbreaking job was getting the men of the *Chauncey* and *Young* over to the base of Bridge Rock and then up to its top. The men from *Young* were soon exhausted and lacerated. Everyone, including a few from the *Delphy* who had some energy left, lent a hand.

The lead men were Watertender George Bleam, Ens William E. Stock, and Boatswain's Mate J. M. Reynolds. The pharmacist's mates of the two destroyers tended the injured. One man was found floating in the water. Six men "got him up the rock wall" without cutting him on the jagged rock outcrops. Among those who proved indefatigable was Seaman Patrick Connell, who carried messages on foot to the Pt. Arguello RC, three miles distant. Connell also carried injured men over the three-foot-wide "bridge" from Bridge Rock to the mesa.

LCdr Booth located Capt Watson and the group of sailors on the mesa. Soon, *Chauncey*'s sailors moved quickly to get most of the ship's food, blankets, lanterns, and other needed items up to the mesa.

Chauncey's Men Recommended for Citations

By the Court of Inquiry:
—G. C. Ostergard, Machinist Mate 1st Class, for remaining at his post in the engine room of the *Chauncey* until the water was above his waist.

Men of the USS *Woodbury* Reach "Woodbury Rock," Link with USS *Fuller* and SS *Neuva Roma*

The fate of the *Woodbury*, #4 in column, became intertwined with that of the *Fuller* when *Woodbury*'s bow ended up on Woodbury Rock, and *Fuller*'s bow on the reef about 100 yards farther west. The fishing smack *Nueva Roma* arrived at daybreak, and its Capt Noceti saw a handful of survivors on an exposed reef. He and his three-man crew carried those survivors to shore and then returned for the crew of the ship. Later, they shared the rescue with whaleboat crews from the destroyers anchored nearby. The "Woodbury Rock" of 1923 is now called "Destroyer Rock" on the nautical chart. (*Woodbury* and *Fuller* are shown in Illustration **19**, and their locations in Illustration **17**.)

Cdr Louis P. Davis, commander of the *Woodbury*, came on the bridge, and the OOD reported that the *Young*, #3, just ahead, had stopped, and the *Lee*, #2, had sheered out of column. Davis was reaching for the telegraph to signal "stop" just as the ship struck heavily amidships and he slid forward. The lights went out. To warn the ship astern, the whistle and siren were blown. Ens H. Ridout and about fifteen men—firemen, enginemen, and machinist's mates—went below, restored power, and remained in the steaming boiler room until the power was lost. The generators came on for a short time, and the searchlights were turned on to help the *Young*. The engineer reported that three compartments had been bilged. Three firemen and Watertender E. J. Cook went into the No. 2 boiler room to make a final attempt to restore power again, but failed.

Cdr Davis made a heroic effort to back his ship off the rock. Engines were put full speed astern, and attempts were made to back. As the water rose in the engine room, Cdr Davis realized they would not be able to hold steam much longer, despite the immense effort by the men below decks. (The *Woodbury* and its "rock" can be seen in

Illustration **19**.) The ship was close to the rock it hit. Several men were put on a part of that main rock, and they rigged lines to control the listing of the ship. The quartermaster took soundings and prepared the whaleboats and motor dory for use. At 10:15 P.M., it became obvious that the ship was stranded, rolling somewhat, and in danger of sinking. The waves had now pushed the bow 40 feet from the rock, and the pounding of the ship had carried away one of the lines.

The crew put a towing hawser around the rock, and, little by little, the bow was hove in to a distance of 25 feet. Three 5-inch lines were also secured to the one good place on the rock. The crew prepared to abandon ship. A weak cry was heard from the water: it was Braden, a sailor from the *Young*, who had been washed overboard. Seaman H. F. Williams tied a rope around his waist, jumped in, got his hands on the nearly drowned Braden, and both were pulled to safety. Ninety men went to Woodbury Rock using the secured lines. As soon as most of them were on the rock, food, water, ponchos, blankets, and other supplies were passed over. By 2:15 A.M., everyone except the captain and boatswain's mate had been landed on the rock. LCdr Davis realized that he would get no help from shore. The wind changed at daylight, and they heard the siren at Pt. Arguello.

(*Woodbury* is shown in the center right of Illustration **19** and the upper center of Illustration **5**. Its bow is near Woodbury Rock, and *Fuller*'s bow is about 100 yards farther west. The ship lying on its side between the mesa and Woodbury Rock is the *Young*. High-tide views of the coastline are in Illustrations **16-A** and **16-B**. At low tide, you can see the dangerous underwater rocks and reefs.)

Men of the *Woodbury* Recommended for Citations

RAdm Kittelle cited the following men, who went below and remained in the steaming boiler room until all power was lost aboard the *Woodbury:* Ensign H. Ridout; M. E. Tilley, Chief Machinist's Mate; V. L. Griswold, Machinist's Mate 1st Class; J. L. White; Engineman

1st Class; C. Thomas, Engineman 2nd Class; G. Herbert, Engineman 2nd Class; S.V. Sage, Ship's Fitter 3rd Class; E. Bangaban, Fireman 1st Class; W.W. Pullen, Fireman 3rd Class; F. Sylvia, Watertender 2nd Class; C.E. Van Buskerk, Fireman 1st Class; E.N. Castleberry, Fireman 2nd Class; B. Caolgosz, Fireman 2nd Class; E.J. Lowman, Fireman 2nd Class; and D.P. O'Brien, Fireman 3rd Class.

—E.J. Cook, Watertender 1st Class; C.N. Sordyl, Fireman 2nd Class; H.C. Wilson, Fireman 2nd Class; and G.W. Groen, Fireman 3rd Class, also of the *Woodbury,* were cited as men who went into No. 2 boiler room and attempted to get up steam, though without result.

—N.F. Owens, Quartermaster 1st, and H.W. Williams, Seaman 2nd (of *Woodbury)*, were cited for being instrumental in saving the life of Braden, Boatswain's Mate 2nd of the *Young.*

Men of the USS *Fuller* Struggle to Reach Woodbury Rock

LCdr Walter Seed, commander of the *Fuller*, #7 in column, was on the bridge and noted his ship was closing rapidly on the ship ahead, *Farragut,* which was backing. LCdr Seed put engines full astern, and felt a tremor as the *Fuller* continued to drift forward, scrape the *Farragut*'s side, and quickly clear. Now, *Fuller*'s crew tried to back and maneuver, but without success. Firemen Lord and Moore, and Watertender Vasvinder remained at their posts in the engine room until driven out by the rising water. *Fuller* was stranded. (Location of the *Fuller* is shown in the map of Illustration **17** and a photograph in Illustration **19**.) Five men attempted to leave ship and get to Woodbury Rock by jumping onto a reef projecting barely out of the water. The ship moved away from the men and left them stranded on that reef. The five could not reach the ship or the large rock, and clung to the wet reef all night. At daybreak, they fell limp into the arms of their rescuers, the crew of the fishing boat *Neuva Roma.*

A whaleboat was launched, and its crew made an unsuccessful attempt to get a line from the *Woodbury* to the rock (Woodbury Rock). Concerned that his listing ship might capsize, LCdr Seed decided that he must get a line from the ship to the rock in order to move his men off the ship. As daylight came, the crew tried to get a raft to Woodbury Rock, but failed. The whaleboat crew, which had been rowing for hours, tried to get a hawser to the rock, but the end of the line was carried away, frustrating their second strenuous attempt. The crew manned the whaleboat throughout the night, in the face of constant danger.

One of the young men in that whaleboat, Seaman 2nd Class Casey Bass, was cited. His letter from the assistant secretary of the navy awarding him a silver Lifesaving Medal, and a commendation from Secretary of the Navy Edwin Denby, are pictured in Joe Silva's book, *Honda Left Turn 095.*

LCdr Seed, the *Fuller*'s captain, talked to Frank M. Moon, Machinist's Mate 1st Class. They agreed that LCdr Seed would swim for Woodbury Rock, and if he made it, Moon would swim after him with a heavy coil of line. (If he didn't make it, Moon would be on his own.) Walter Seed dove in and swam to the rock. He was spent on arrival, and *Woodbury*'s men tossed him a line and hauled him up. Then, Frank Moon, carrying a heaving line, swam over, and was helped up onto the rock. Several lines were finally strung between the *Fuller* and Woodbury Rock (Illustration **16-B**).

The *Fuller*'s crew started to abandon ship, and found they were about 2 feet below the rock ledge when they arrived. *Woodbury*'s rescue team would wait till a wave lifted each man, then grab his lifejacket and pull him "aboard." One hundred men fought their way over along that line without injury—LCdr Seed called it a "remarkable rescue."

Men of the *Fuller* Recommended for Citations

By The Court of Inquiry:
—Lieutenant Commander Walter D. Seed, for great bravery in swimming a distance of about 75 yards through a turbulent sea in order to test the feasibility of and make arrangements for the salvage of his crew (*Fuller*).
—Ensign B. S. Jones and the men who, with him, comprised the crew of the *Fuller*'s whaleboat: Lucian Barger, Shipfitter 3rd Class; Frank Sparta, Seaman 2nd Class; George E. Trenn, Fireman 1st Class; Glen M. Melvin, Fireman 2nd Class; Casey M. Bass, Seaman 2nd; Lloyd A. Campbell, Seaman 2nd; Alfred M. Titus, Seaman 2nd; Sumpter L. Gillespie, Fireman 3rd Class; and James R. Collins, Fireman 2nd Class, for displaying courage in volunteering and manning a whaleboat, which they pulled throughout the night in the face of constant danger.
—Frank M. Moon, Machinist's Mate 1st Class, for extraordinary heroism in swimming with a line from the *Fuller* to a rock in a turbulent sea in order to salvage the crew of that vessel.
—Valierus Vasvinder, Watertender 1st Class, Frank C. Colpits, Fireman 1st Class; George C. Lord, Fireman 3rd Class; and James Moore, Fireman 3rd Class, for meritorious conduct in remaining at their post in the fire room of the *Fuller* until driven out by the inrush of rising water.
—Lieutenant Commander W. D. Seed, by personal effort and leadership saving his entire crew.

Citations Recommended for Men Who Were Not on the Wrecked Ships

By The Court of Inquiry:
—Commander W. G. Roper (*Kennedy*), for the seaman-like ability and judgment he showed in handling the division under his command (DesDiv 32) on the night of the stranding of Squadron 11.

By RAdm Kittelle:
—Commander W.S. Pye, for saving certain vessels of his division (DesDiv 31) by prompt action (*Farragut*).
—Lieutenant Commander J.F. McClain, for extricating the *Farragut* from a serious position.

Fishermen of the SS *Neuva Roma,* and the USS *Fuller*'s Whaleboat Crew, Save Lives

At dawn, LCdr Seed and Cdr Davis could see land ahead, and fog to seaward. There was no help in sight. They decided to load men aboard the *Fuller's* whaleboat and try for a landing near the *Chauncey*. This turned out to be an arduous task; the men had been rowing for hours. But two boatloads of men were rowed ashore.

Capt Giovanni Noceti of the fishing boat *Neuva Roma*, and his crew, Nicolo Ghio, Giacomo Stagnaro, and Federico Ghio, left Santa Barbara at 1:00 A.M. Sunday morning. At daybreak, they suddenly found themselves trolling past a long, narrow shipwreck, the destroyer *Fuller*. Putting in closer, Capt Noceti could see the five men who had clung all night to a reef projecting from Woodbury Rock, unable to reach the main rock because of the running seas. The captain launched his skiff, tended the distressed sailors back to his boat, and delivered them to shore near the *Chauncey*. The *Roma* returned to the rock, saw the destroyers *Somers* and *Percival* some 800 yards away, and started delivering the distressed men to the nearest one. *Roma* continued its lifesaving work, later joined by whaleboats from *Percival* and *Somers* that had been standing by.

There are varying estimates of how many men were rescued by the four fishermen on the *Neuva Roma*. The chronicler Silva (*Honda Left Turn 095*) gives the number as "one hundred and fifty." According to him, "The *Roma* was damaged on the rocks when she landed one party of shipwrecked men, and leaked badly on the balance of the fishing trip." One of the public records shows the financial reimbursement from the navy to Capt Noceti as $20. There is no record of navy funds given to cover the cost of repairing the *Nova,* or of any financial award to the *Nova* crew for their lifesaving efforts. Although no commendations were given to the fishermen of the *Neuva Roma*, there is a letter, dated Oct. 18, 1923 (reproduced in Silva's book), from Acting Secretary of the Navy T. Roosevelt, addressed to Mr. Giacomo Noceti, Master of the Vessel *Neuva Roma*. It reads, "The Navy Department desires to thank you for the excellent work done by you on the morning of September 9th, in taking survivors off the destroyers on the occasion of the grounding of destroyers at Honda, California."

A story by James Schermerhorn appeared in the *Santa Barbara News-Press* in September 1923:

> "Mama" Ghio remembers it was Fred Ghio who saw the Navy ships and men from the top of the fishing boat's mast. The crew of the *Roma* then worked for hours in the heavy fog and pulled in and out of the dangerous surf—when they could only see a few feet ahead of the boat—taking men off the rocks and sinking ships. The U.S. Navy credited them with saving 150 men. They worked until the seas became too rough, taking men back to the destroyers that had avoided the collision, Mama Ghio said.
>
> [*Roma* took two boatloads to shore, and a third to ships standing out to sea.]

Capt Watson got the name of the *Roma* and praised the fishermen. The five men on the rock said, "It was a most cheery sight to see the *Roma* crawling towards us through the fog." Capt Watson said, "Captain Noceti and his men should be recognized for their courage and perseverance."

By midday Sunday, the mesa was alive with railway men, people preparing food, medical help, tents, rescue workers with clothing and blankets, horses, wagons and observers. (Illustration **22** is a photograph of the scene on Monday afternoon, and Illustration **21** is a photograph of the observers at the rescue site.)

Men of the Wreck and Death Watch Patrol Do Their Duty

Sixteen men were assigned to the Wreck Patrol under the command of the *Chauncey*'s Executive Officer, Ltjg Clarence Lee, assisted by Ens William Wright of the *S. P. Lee*. As the special rescue train departed, the patrol was left—without a supply of food or shelter—to recover bodies and prevent looting of the battered ships. (The photograph in Illustration **23** shows sailors moving a recovered body up to the mesa.) The seas prevented the boats from offshore vessels bringing essential things ashore. On September 11 the *Santa Barbara Daily News* printed a story, *Castaways at Honda*:

> Apparently there is a loose cog in the U. S. Navy's machinery. Nearly three days have elapsed since the disaster and yet those men on the Wreck Patrol are still camped like refugees on the wind swept bluff without shelter or adequate supplies. A car load of supplies was sent by the Santa Barbara Red Cross. The men are on the main rail line and within miles of supplies they need, yet to all intents they are still in the condition of castaways.
>
> These men are on official duty and have the sad task of guarding government property and caring for the bodies of their dead comrades. The railway building at the scene has been converted into a morgue. The living sleep in the open. Kindly disposed people have brought the sailors cakes, cookies, and doughnuts. Leftovers from the tourists lunches—who have come to see the millions of dollars worth of junk warships—"gladden the hearts of the men engaged in doing the nation's work." It is difficult to understand why conditions are as they are. It surely takes Uncle Sam a long time to unwind the

red tape in which the Navy is bound. During the days of their grim watch for dead bodies, the patrol was dubbed the 'Death Watch' by the newspapers.

By October 17, after the patrol was withdrawn, five more bodies were recovered. This brought the total to 17. "At long last, the Devil's Jaw … settled down to wait … for the jinns to provide another feast."

The newspaper's complaint was called premature. As the seas subsided, boatloads of supplies were brought in alongside the *Chauncey*. A member of the patrol, Frederick Fish, Radioman 1st, wrote a lengthy, picturesque, and timely comment:

> This patrol with shattered nerves and bodies weak from loss of sleep and insufficient food, performed the hardest of tasks for a period of many days. With but sixteen men they guarded the wrecks night and day to keep off looters, patrolled the beach from dawn to dark for bodies, worked like giants to salvage material from the wrecked ships, and served as pack horses to lug bodies and materials from the wrecks to the Railway Station and Section House at Honda. These duties were performed under the hardest of conditions, irregular and scanty diet, sleeping quarters on the ground where the blankets were soaked by the continued fog and drizzle. Most of the patrol obtained but 2 or 3 hours' sleep a night, and many became so exhausted they could not sleep even when opportunity offered.

Too much credit cannot be given to the good folk of the surrounding town for their generous response to the patrol's needs.

The destroyer men's character was revealed in the stories of survival and loss, and the recommendations for citation. The character of the Wreck Patrol's leader, Ltjg Clarence Lee, and of his friend, the railroad's Section Foreman, John Giorvas, are evident in part of a handwritten letter from Ltjg Clarence V. Lee to Section Foreman, John Giorvas:

My dear John,

It is just a week since I left Honda Section House, and I have been busy every minute or I would surely have written to you sooner to thank you again for the hundreds of things you did for me and all the Navy men at Honda.

I am sure that a number of our sailors owe their thanks to you for saving their lives, and a great many, for keeping them from sickness, cold and exposure. It is a wonderful thing how much you did on the night of the wreck, and I don't believe anyone will ever forget it. Believe me, John, I appreciate what you did.

Your men at the Section House were good to us too, and I want you to remember me to them and thank them again for me. None of us will travel along the coast division without asking to have the train flagged so we can stop to say hello, at least. And if I ever can get away, I'm coming up to Honda sometime to see you all once again.

Joe Silva's book contains stories about Squadron 11 survivors George Wallace, Watertender 2nd Class, *S. P. Lee;* Joseph Gianni, Seaman 1st Class, *Delphy;* Gene Bruce, Seaman 2nd Class, *Chauncey;* Harry C. Crawford, Fireman 3rd Class, *Farragut;* Melvin Schrock, Quartermaster 1st Class, *Woodbury;* Walter Watts, Pharmacist's Mate 1st Class, *S. P. Lee;* Robert Greenwald, LCdr *Chauncey;* Harold Hooker, Fireman 2nd Class, *S. P. Lee;* Ivan Vukovic, Chief Torpedoman, *S. P. Lee;* Jack Kramer, Signalman 2nd Class, *S. P. Lee;* John Becker, Seaman 1st Class, *Young*; John Kolster, Seaman 2nd Class, *Delphy;* and Harold Harris, Seaman 2nd Class, *Kennedy*.

Chapter 5

The Lompoc Community Responds to the Disaster

The sea at Saddle Rock was rough as it always is, but it was calm in comparison with what it is in a stormy sea. Had the sea been that angry on Saturday night the loss of life would have been appalling.

—Ronald Adam

Articles Written in 1923 by Ronald Adam, Editor of the *Lompoc Record*

Ronald Adam, editor of the *Lompoc Record,* wrote more than forty-five short newspaper articles and started printing them in the *Record* on 14 September 1923. Each article is unique, and reading them provides insight into the "way things were seen in 1923," when Adam was on the scene.

Adam's articles were republished in the 1998 Lompoc Valley Historical Society quarterly, *Lompoc Legacy* #79 and #80, edited by Vance A. Newcomb. The *Legacy* article also includes Newcomb's pertinent comments about the disaster, photographs taken by Vance in 1963 and 1974, and photographs taken by his father, Leighton C. Newcomb, in 1923. I am indebted to Vance for permission to use a few of his photographs, to the Lompoc Historical Society's *Legacy,* and to the *Lompoc Record* for the Adam stories it originally published.

Adam wrote his short news articles just days after the wrecks, and they occasionally differ in technical detail from other reports. I have made no changes to Adam's articles, because they have the priceless flavor of the person who was at the scene, a nuance not found elsewhere. Forty of Adam's articles and titles are given below. A list of the Lompoc rescuers is in Appendix VII.

The Call for Help. When the call came in from Honda on Saturday night that help was needed at that point, no one realized that one of the greatest naval disasters in history—one that would make the famed battle of Manila Bay look like a ten-cent side show—was happening at that moment at our door. The message come to City Marshal W. S. Bland that a ship was reported ashore near Honda station and the officer quickly summoned Glenn Baker, motor traffic officer, Clifford J. Smith and the editor of the Record to go with him to investigate the report. The message was received in Lompoc about 10:30 P.M., and in a very few minutes this party has loaded a coil of rope into

Bland's car and was rolling toward Surf at a high rate of speed. At Surf a motor track car was waiting to take us to Honda and the perilous dash was made over the Southern Pacific rails. G. T. Gunderson and Harry Seerey joined our party at Surf. Railroad man at Surf operated the track car—or attempted to. Something was wrong with the timer on this particular car—anyway the timer got all the blame—for the vehicle balked about every mile. Once during a stop for repairs the train which we were expecting came rushing upon us and the track car was removed barely in time to prevent a smash-up.

Night Extremely Dark. The night was pitch dark and a heavy fog made it impossible to see but a few feet even with the aid of a lantern. The track car rushing... through the black, chilly night together with the dread of meeting a train head-on was one of the thrilling incidents that the rescue party experienced. [The *Somer*'s deck log reports the visibility on the water at 9:12 P.M. was 600 yards.]

Distress Signals. As we arrive at Honda station we discovered that a vessel was sending up distress signals from off Saddle Rock and the party was hastened to this point. Although the fog was extremely thick, the rockets that were sent up made it possible for us to distinguish the outline of a vessel close in shore. The vessel that we could see was the *S. P. Lee*, ship No. 310, and we did not learn until later that another vessel further out than the *Lee* was the one sending up the distress signals. [Perhaps the *Nicholas*.]

Meet Captain. A consultation was held by the party and it was decided that the best aid we could render would be the building of a big bonfire on shore and to have our coil of cable on hand if it was needed. No wood was to be had in this bleak region and some of the party started back to Honda section house to procure wood and kerosene for building the fire. On the way to the section house the party encountered Captain R. Morris who was wandering in a bewildered state on the sandy mesa that separates Honda from the ocean. It was from Captain Morris that we learned that there were several vessels in distress and that all of his men had been landed from his ship, the *S. P. Lee*. He did not know where his men had disappeared to and inquired and was given direction to the station.

Uproar is Heard. Going to the south side of the Saddle Rock the shouts and screams of hundreds of distressed men reached our ears and on arriving at this point we found three more vessels pounding on the rocks. The men from these vessels were coming ashore and their shouts and cries could be heard above the booming of the surf. There were no lights to aid them as the generators on the vessels went out of commission as soon as they struck, and rendered the large spotlights useless.

Build Fire on Cliff. Some of the Lompoc men took it upon themselves to go back to Honda section house, secure wood and kerosene and enlist the aid of the sailors from the Lee in helping them carry the fuel to the beach. A fire was soon built that was real effective in furnishing light for the rescue work from the three vessels—the *Chauncey*, the *Delphy* and the *Young*—which came ashore at this point. The fire also furnished light for the doctors to work by, and warmth for the wet and half-clad boys that came ashore. In addition to this bonfire on the bluff, an immense fire was built near the section house and here the sailors gathered by the hundreds soon after they got on shore.

Local Doctors There. Dr. M. S. Kelliher and Dr. L. E. Heiges were the first and only doctors on the scene. They had arrived about midnight and had their hands full for the next few hours. About a dozen men were seriously injured and after they were given first aid treatment by the doctors they were placed aboard train No. 102 at about 4:00 A.M. and taken to a Santa Barbara hospital. The majority of these casualties were men from the boiler rooms who had been gassed by the smoke following the crash. One sailor had a broken arm and another a broken collarbone the doctors reported.

Hospital at Section House. The section house at Honda was made into a hospital for the time being as it was the largest building in the locality. About one hundred were treated there by the doctors, the majority of these cases being cuts and gashes that were sustained by men who jumped bare footed on the rocky reefs and clambered up the slippery rocks.

After getting the big bonfire going at the top of the bluff where three of the ships were ashore the writer returned to the section house. Hundreds of the men were huddled around the bonfire that had been built there. This was a pitiful sight indeed. Half of the men were without shoes and some were clad only in their under clothing. Nearly all the men had been drenched in the sea. A cold wind was blowing from off the ocean and the heat from the bonfire was most welcome to the men.

Men Were Cheerful. But with all they were the most cheerful lot of men one could hope to find anywhere. They had saved practically nothing of their personal belongings but as they stood around the fire turning around to warm first one side and then another, they laughed and joshed with one another much the same as a crowd of young fellows will carry on after a football game.

Mexicans Help. The Mexicans of the railroad section gang had already begun to hold "open house" for the sailors. Every one of the huts built of railroad ties where the Mexicans laborers live had a fire going and cans of coffee stewing. All were full of sailors who sat on bunks and stools and sipped the red hot coffee.

Coffee is Made. In the kitchen at the section house there were as many sailors in the room as could possibly crowd inside. A roaring fire was going in the range and two big cans of coffee were boiling. A sailor who had lost all but a thin suit of underwear was dispensing the coffee as fast as he could but as there were only three cups on the premises and the beverage was steaming hot the service was rather slow. The kitchen was stifling from the heat of the range and the steam from the garments of the sailors. Several of the boys who had been hurt were curled up on the floor and the others who crowded within the room were driven there by the cold without.

Injured Cared For. The living room was almost as crowded as the kitchen. Doctors Kelliher and Heiges were working over the injured. The men who were in a bad way were lying along the walls. They were the first to receive attention from the doctors. Others with minor injuries were waiting their turns. The two telephones—one of the railroad company and one of the Santa Barbara Telephone Company—were in this room that was serving the purpose of a receiving hospital. Several of the officers from the ships were here sending out messages when we arrived. Messages were sent out over the Southern Pacific wires and over the telephone company's lines by way of Lompoc. Other messages were dispatched by railroad motor cars to the Arlight Radio Station three miles south.

Install Special Wire. By 2:00 A.M. Sunday morning the railroad company had run a wire into a hand-car shed across the track from the section house and a dispatcher was installed therein and was busy with the telegraph instruments.

Supplies Arrive. Train No. 102 arrived at Honda at about 4:00 A.M. with blankets and comforters from Lompoc, dozens of them, and these were distributed among the sailors. It is needless to say that they were a welcome gift to this mass of shivering humanity. On this same train the dozen badly injured men were loaded and sent to a Santa Barbara hospital. Twenty-five or more people had arrived from Lompoc by 4:00 A.M. but there was nothing that they could do for the comfort of the men. Some of the people came on the early morning train while others made the trip in automobiles by way of the Sudden grade.

Life Raft Heard From. The doctors had just finished with the last of the injured at the section house when a call came that they were needed at Pt. Arguello where five men had come ashore on a raft. Don Sudden was there with his automobile and took the doctors to Arguello.

More Wrecks Discovered. It was not until daylight on Sunday morning that we knew that more than four destroyers were ashore. The ships that were accounted for on Saturday night were the *Chauncey*, Ship No. 296, the *S. P. Lee*, No. 310, the *Young,* No. 312, and the *Delphy*, No. 261. These four ships had landed all of their officers and most of their crews, but it was not until after daylight on Sunday morning and after the fog had lifted somewhat that the full proportions of this maritime tragedy was revealed. [Ships shown in Illustration **5**.]

Find the *Nicholas*. The first ship that was sighted on Sunday morning was the Nicholas, No. 311. This vessel was just a little ways out from the *S. P. Lee* and was the vessel whose distress signals we had seen the night before. There was not a sign of life on the *Nicholas* when the ship was first discovered at daylight and it was thought for a time that all aboard had been lost. After repeated signals from shore an answering signal came from the vessel and we were soon able to distinguish human forms aboard. [Ships shown in Illustrations **2**.]

Morale Still High. On the cliff above the little beach a bonfire had been built and here the men gathered to warm themselves. Around the campfire their spirits were high as boys who had been having a big time in a swimming hole. The officers in their bedraggled gold braid were the only ones who for a moment grasped each other's hands and in low tones congratulated each other on their deliverance. In view of the fact that the sailors had spent the entire night in the upper part of the boat (the hatches having been battened down soon after they struck) and had kept each other warm by huddling close to each other, together with a prospect of almost certain death, their care-free attitude when they reached shore was quite remarkable.

Some Are Overcome. A few of the men were overcome and needed assistance in getting up the cliff but soon recovered. One man was washed from the *Nicholas* while this rescue work was going on and the waves carried him out beyond the big rocks that are out in the little bay. Another wave cast him upon a reef where he held for a moment but he was finally able to swim to shore where he arrived in an exhausted condition. Dr. Kelliher attended the man and expressed the opinion later that he was not in a bad way.

Two More Destroyers. In the meantime the fog had lifted and revealed two more vessels on the rocks between Saddle Rock and Pt. Arguello. These ships, the *Woodbury,* No. 309 and the *Fuller,* No. 297, were against some big rocks about half a mile from land and were lying close to each other. The crews of both vessels had sought safety on these barren rocks soon after the ships struck. The majority were high and dry but a few had sought safety on some very low reefs over which the waves had dashed all night. But even those on the big rocks had suffered severe hardships during the long dark night. From the amount of gear that each brought ashore it was evident that the men from these ships saved more of their personal belongings than any of the others. [These ships are shown in Illustration **19**.]

Other Destroyers Near. That other destroyers were standing by was known on shore early in the morning, as their hoarse sirens could be plainly heard. When the fog lifted in the forenoon four destroyers were seen at anchor but they made no attempt to render aid. A launch came in near shore from one of the vessels and signaled a message once during the forenoon. [The map showing the locations of the wrecked ships is in Illustration **17**.]

A Marine Graveyard. The scene of this terrible marine disaster is the graveyard of many ships that have foundered there in the past... In 1849 the SS *Edith* was deliberately beached so her crew could get to the gold fields sooner. The SS *Julius Ray* went ashore at Pt. Conception in 1881. The SS *King James* was an English collier whose cargo caught fire and the ship abandoned 100 miles at sea in 1891.

No Lights or Wireless. As soon as the vessels struck the fires were banked to prevent an explosion. This made it impossible to use the generators for the big spotlights and the wireless apparatus with the result that the seamen could neither signal for help or furnish light by which the men could land.

Bound Over Rocks. The ships were going at such a terrific speed when they hit that they bounded on top of the low reefs and tore great holes in their bottoms. Oil poured from the tanks and added another problem to the situation as it blinded and choked the sailors whenever the waves dashed over them. The *Chauncey* and the *S. P. Lee* had the least difficulty of any in landing their men. Men from the *Lee* first rowed ashore on a life raft, securing a line on the point of Saddle Rock, and ferried the others ashore on the raft. The *Chauncey* got a line ashore without any difficulty and with a sort of breeches buoy took their men ashore one at a time. Neither the *Lee* nor the *Chauncey* lost any men. [Impact speeds ranged from 8 to 20 knots.]

Landing in Dark. The *Delphy* had great difficulty in landing the men and lost several. They had to jump to a rock. Others that got upon the rock had to wait until the waves would recede when they would run and climb up the slippery cliff. [The *Delphy* hit hard and by mid-Sunday the rear portion of the vessel had broken off from the main hull.]

Young Rolls Over. The *Young*, the second destroyer to strike, lost more men than all the others combined. The terrific speed of this boat carried it up on some submerged rocks further out than the *Delphy* and it immediately began to roll over towards the sea. The men on board claimed that the vessel rolled over in a minute and thirty-seven seconds after it hit on the rocks.

Men Jump into Sea. Some of the men jumped over board when the *Young* rolled over and attempted to swim to the rocky cliffs ashore. Some jumped on life rafts and two of these were heard of hours afterwards when the men were rescued at Pt. Arguello and another raft was seen being carried out to sea. [One raft was lost at sea.]

Cling to Vessel. The majority of the men climbed to the upper side of the boat when it rolled over where they held on for two hours with the sea dashing over them before they were rescued. We heard several of the men say next day that they would have followed the example of those who jumped overboard and attempted to swim ashore if it had not been for the appeals of their captain to hold to the ship. [The *Young*.]

Hero on the Young. The captain called for a volunteer to carry a line to the *Chauncey* and a sailor quickly responded. He was successful but risked his life in the mad whirl of waves. When the line was secured between the *Young* and the *Chauncey* the survivors that were hanging to the side of the overturned destroyer were safely taken to the *Chauncey* and thus to the rocky island where the men from the *Chauncey* and *Delphy* had already been landed.

Many Are Lost. Sailors from the *Young* estimated Sunday that two-thirds of their crew of ninety-six men had been lost but the official list given out that afternoon was that twenty-three men were missing. Our estimate was that about forty men were lost, one hundred injured, and twelve seriously injured. [The official number of dead was twenty-three.]

Undertow Terrific. The men who jumped overboard from the *Young* and those who missed their footing when they jumped on the slippery reef from the *Delphy* had little chance for their lives as the undertow is extremely treacherous at this point. Accounts of other disasters and tragedies that have occurred there show that hardly any who have gone down in ship wrecks and accidents have ever made shore and few of the bodies have ever been recovered. The sea at Saddle Rock was rough Saturday night as it always is, but it was calm in comparison with what it is at some seasons. Had the sea been as angry at this time, as it often is, the loss of life would have been appalling. [Three men were lost from the *Delphy*.]

Hundreds On Rocks. When the party from Lompoc headed by Marshal W. S. Bland and Traffic Officer Glenn Baker, arrived at the place where the *Delphy*, *Chauncey* and *Young* grounded, nearly all the men from the three vessels were crowded upon a barren rock or island that was separated from the mainland by a chasm twenty feet wide. The hundreds of men on the rock could faintly be seen by aid of the local officers' pocket flashlight. Bland and Baker crawled down the slippery cliff where they talked to the captains of the ships. At that time Captain Watson had given orders for the men to remain on the island with the idea of salvaging the ships the next morning. [These ships were "stranded." The "grounded" ships broke free.]

Captains Were [Lost]. The captains [apparently had no idea of where they were wrecked] and were given this information by Mr. Bland. It was also on the advice of Bland that the men were taken off the island immediately. The flashlights of Bland and Baker aided the men in getting across the chasm that separated them from the mainland. Several were wounded and it was risky work to get them over. Husky seamen carried their injured buddies to the mainland on their shoulders and the more seriously injured were strapped upon stretchers and brought across from the island in this manner.

Send Dispatches. As soon as the ships' officers got to the Honda section house they commenced sending out dispatches and were assisted in making their telephone connections by Mr. Bland. No attempt was made that night to get into connection with the other ships that had foundered.

A Real Heroine. The heroine of the great disaster was Mrs. Charles L. Atkins, wife of the "third trick" operator at Surf. Mrs. Atkins left her two babies at home with her husband, boarding the morning train at Surf and arrived at Honda about 2:00 A.M. Sunday. She took charge of the kitchen at the section house as soon as she got there and worked until 12:30 P.M. that day, serving as best she could the hundreds of hungry men. Mrs. Atkins was the only woman on the job and hundreds of sandwiches and gallons of coffee were prepared by her and the "gobs" that helped.

The Lompoc Doctors. Doctors Heiges and Kelliher were at Honda soon after Chief of Police Bland's party got there and they worked for hours under the most trying conditions. One hundred or more injured were relieved by their ministrations. Dr. Kelliher remained at Honda until noon Sunday and his services were often in demand during the forenoon. Surgeons from Santa Barbara arrived there at a little after noon Sunday after all had been cared for and got the credit in the newspapers for doing a great work that the two local doctors had performed. The news of the disaster did not get into any of the newspapers until Monday morning. The writer phoned the news to the Morning Press early Sunday morning and gave them a "scoop" 24 hours ahead of the other papers.

Send Messages Home. The first question of many of the sailors was "where can we find a telegraph office?" as they wanted to send the news home that they were safe. The government had a monopoly on the wires at Honda and G. T. Gunderson and others brought their messages to Lompoc to be transmitted from here.

These messages undoubtedly reached their destinations before the loved ones to whom they were directed had learned of the disaster through the newspapers.

Young Officers. The officers of the ships, with the exception of Captain Watson, were all young men. Captain Watson, the commander of the squadron, appeared to be a kindly gentleman and highly respected by his subordinate officers and men. The writer was by the side of the commander when the daylight came Sunday morning and he could see the wrecks. The scene almost overcame him and he stated that it was the most appalling and dismal sight he had ever looked upon. Nearly all the sailors from the ships were young men and many were mere boys. We came upon four of them at midnight going across the mesa with a canvas in which they had thrown two or three dozen pairs of shoes and they were looking for their buddies who had come ashore barefooted. The supply of extra shoes did not hold out very long as many were barefooted next morning and some had wrapped their feet up in strips from their life jackets to keep them warm. When blankets and comforters came on the early morning train they wrapped these about them and wore them as if they were bathrobes. The Moore Mercantile Company in this city sent every blanket and comforter they had on hand. The boys were served coffee soon after they arrived at Honda section house but their real food came at about 4:00 A.M. by train and they had all they wanted to eat. Mrs. Atkins of Surf, the lady who came and took command of the kitchen, states positively that no one went hungry. Soon after daylight some of the men went aboard a destroyer and salvaged fifteen turkeys, twenty hams, bacon and other foodstuff, and this was cooked at the section house and on the campfire. The men from the *Nicholas, Fuller* and *Woodbury* were fed soon after they were brought ashore. Men from the *Delphy*, *Chauncey*, *Young* and *S.P. Lee* had a breakfast early in the morning and lunch about 10:00 A.M.

Checking Up. The work of checking up the crews started soon after midnight when the officers would call the men together and endeavor to find out who was missing. As the men were scattered it was impossible to get an accurate check. The first passenger train that came through Honda after the men landed there stopped and it seemed like a mighty temptation to some of the sailors to board it. Officers called to them to stand by, and we did not see anyone jump aboard.

Pride of the Navy. The seven destroyers will be a total loss for it is out of the question to float any of them. Some of the equipment may be saved if the sea remains calm for a time. These vessels were built in 1918 and were the best equipped destroyers in the world... The cost of the vessels and their equipment was $1,500,000 each and the total loss is over ten million dollars. Each destroyer carried four (groups) of 21-inch triple torpedo tubes. At 5 P.M. on Sunday afternoon a special train arrived and the officers and sailors of the wrecked destroyers, numbering several hundred men, were taken to San Diego. By this time hundreds of people had arrived from all parts of the country to view the catastrophe and wave good bye. A detail was left at Honda to guard the wrecks and search for bodies of men drowned.

Chapter 6

Rescue by the Men of the Southern Pacific Railroad

Southern Pacific train crews, aided by ranch hands, worked through the night with rope and tackle to bring sailors ashore, at times plunging into the high surf to reach them. The railroad's section foreman, John Giorvas, spent four hours in the water pulling men to safety.

—Ltjg C.V. Lee, USS *Chauncey*

Southern Pacific to the Rescue: the Honda Naval Disaster of 8 September 1923

by Larry Mullaly, Central Point, Oregon

Within a few minutes, on the evening of 8 September 1923, ships of Destroyer Squadron 11 traveling in single file at a speed of 20 knots went aground and stranded at Point Honda, a rocky promontory sixty-three miles north of Santa Barbara. The desolate area in which the disaster occurred would have been one of the most inaccessible stretches of the California coast were it not for the proximity of the Southern Pacific railroad line connecting San Francisco and Los Angeles. During the twenty-four-hour period following this incident—the worst peacetime disaster experienced by the United States Navy to that time—the Southern Pacific played a significant if unheralded role in the rescue effort.

In 1923, the primary connector between San Francisco and Los Angeles was the Coast Route, a single-track rail link that skirted the Pacific Ocean for approximately one-fourth of its 471-mile length. On any given day, in addition to regular freight traffic, seven westbound and seven eastbound passenger trains passed along the high bluffs within 1,500 feet of Point Honda's jagged rocks. Nearby, a 540-foot-wide canyon bridged by a steel railroad trestle cut through the coastal cliffs to the sea. To the north of this trestle was "Honda Station," consisting of a long passing track and a small, seldom-used freight platform. To the south were the Honda section quarters, with housing for a foreman and a crew of thirteen Mexican track workers needed for roadway maintenance.

Since the completion of the rail line through Honda in 1901, section crews stationed at this bleak, windswept bluff had seen more than their share of tragedy. On May 11, 1907, a special train carrying Shriners from San Francisco to Los Angeles was derailed at Honda by what may have been a sand-blocked switch, killing thirty-six passengers and crewmen. Four years later, on July 11, 1911, the *Santa Rosa*, a coastal steamer carrying several hundred passengers, ran aground and sank near the Honda trestle. In both instances, track workers from the section quarters provided emergency aid to survivors.

On Saturday, September 8, from 9 P.M. to midnight, the night was marked by cold wind and fog. Section foreman John Giorvas, who had emigrated from Greece at the age of fourteen and was now in his early thirties, was sitting at his desk in his second-floor bedroom, completing reports of the week's work. Shortly after 9 P.M., he was interrupted by what sounded like a large explosion at the base of the cliffs. This was soon followed by a second blast accompanied by flashes of light in the fog. With the aid of oil lanterns, he and his section crew made their way down to the top of the top cliff face, where they were met, the foreman later recalled, by a din of voices "in every direction calling for help ... 'God, mother, father, help me.'" Looming in the fog, so thick in places that you "could not see your forefinger in front of your nose," the crew saw what appeared to be a destroyer aground on the rocks.

Rushing back to the section house, Giorvas telephoned word of the grounded ship to his general section foreman, W. J. Maes, at Surf, five miles up the line. Maes asked him to repeat his story several times before being convinced that an event of some magnitude was unfolding along the fog-bound coast.

For the next two hours, Giorvas was the sole source of information on the disaster, communicating by phone to the SP telegraph office at Surf, which relayed his messages by telegraph to subdivision train master T. J. Foley at San Luis Obispo and to Night Chief Dispatcher A. Keller at the 3rd Street and Townsend division terminal in San Francisco. Keller, in turn, alerted navy officials and the press.

The first news flashing across the nation's wire service that night was that an unidentified vessel, believed to be a United States destroyer, had gone aground and was without power. The name of the destroyer, USS *S. P. Lee*, was provided shortly thereafter, as well as information that a second vessel, the USS *Delphy,* was also stranded.

At Honda, sailors shivering in the cold and often dressed in underclothes began to emerge from the darkness. Many were boys, some as young as sixteen. To warm the survivors and act as a beacon for those struggling in the breakers and rocks below, the section crew built a large bonfire of railroad ties at the edge of the cliff. Soon afterward they opened their rustic quarters to as many seamen as could fit inside.

As the hours passed and reports continued to arrive, Southern Pacific dispatchers in San Francisco informed the press that a third, and then a fourth and fifth destroyer were on the rocks at Honda. In time, these were identified as destroyers *Nicholas, Woodbury,* and *Young,* part of a fourteen-ship squadron that had left San Francisco that morning on a high-speed test run to their base at San Diego. Word was transmitted on the Southern Pacific Coast Division telegraph lines that all trains passing Honda were to stop and offer assistance if needed.

Meanwhile, regular Coast Route train traffic continued to move. At 10:24 P.M., the *Seashore Express*, coming from Los Angeles, approached the Honda section house and emitted a long whistle blast. Many of the sailors and officers clinging to the rocks had assumed they had struck one of the Santa Barbara Channel islands twenty miles off the California coast. The whistle of the *Seashore Express* dispelled this notion.

Sometime after 10:30 P.M., Surf general section foreman W. J. Maes set out on a motorized track car with a section hand, a reporter from the *Lompoc Record,* and two law enforcement officers from nearby Lompoc. Maes had calculated that there was sufficient time to reach Honda up a one-percent grade before they would be met by a late-night freight coming northward, but in the first two miles the gas-powered, direct-drive motor stopped several times. During one unplanned stop, an SP crewman, feeling vibrations in the rails, shouted to clear the tracks. The group barely had time to drag their motor cars free and fall prone along the embankment before the locomotive steamed past them through the fog.

When the track car with its five additional rescuers reached Honda, section hands had built a second large bonfire near the tracks. Many seamen were covered with heavy fuel oil released into the water by the damaged vessels. Others were barefoot and bleeding from lava cuts. Not everyone had survived. In the heavy surf, the USS *Young* had turned completely over, trapping sleeping crewmen inside, but rescue operations were also going forward. Giorvas' crew had managed to get a light rope to the *Delphy.* A heavy line was then attached and pulled back to land, and more and more men were stumbling ashore.

By midnight Saturday, Mr. Maes had completed a second trip to Surf, bringing with him two badly needed doctors who converted the Honda section master's house into an emergency aid station, though not without some difficulty.

As Sunday September 9 got underway, the commanding naval officer at Honda, Captain E. H. Watson, made contact with train master T. J. Foley, who was in San Luis Obispo, and requested that hospitals in that area be prepared to receive one hundred injured men. No less than five Los Angeles-to-San Francisco trains were available to assist in such a movement: the *Padre* would reach Honda at 12:35 A. M., followed by the *Lark* at 12:56 A. M. Starting at 1:30 A. M., three sections of the scheduled San Francisco-bound *Sunset Limited,* spaced at approximately fifteen-minute intervals, would be passing through. For reasons not entirely clear, however, Captain Watson later decided to send fourteen of the most seriously injured seamen, most of them boiler-room crewmen suffering from smoke inhalation, to Santa Barbara's Cottage Hospital on the next southbound passenger train, which was not scheduled to arrive until nearly 2:30 A. M.

The train that eventually arrived to take off the injured was the *Sunset Limited,* connecting San Francisco to New Orleans in two nights, and one of Southern Pacific's premier luxury trains of this era. The contrast in misery and opulence could not have been greater. The cut and battered seamen were carefully placed aboard, and a naval officer assigned to accompany them later recalled "... how the train crew pitched in to arrange for the comfort of those hurt, oil-soaked bodies of men in the plush fittings and furniture of the club car. Fuel oil oozed everywhere, but it made no difference." About this same time, L. C. Maxwell, a railroad lineman from Surf, succeeded in establishing direct telegraphic communication, in a jury-rigged system set up in the handcar shed located across the tracks from the section house. Later, he was also able to patch two additional telegraph keys into the Western Union Lines.

Meanwhile at Coast Line Subdivision headquarters in San Luis Obispo, train master Foley had assembled a force of repair and steam-shovel crews, both groups familiar with the rope-and-tackle work needed to bring men ashore from grounded ships. From Maintenance of Way cars, Foley also scavenged coffeepots, blankets, quilts, and stretchers. He contacted San Luis Obispo Mayor L. F. Sinsheimer, and soon, taxicabs were rushing food supplies from Sinsheimer's Market to the depot. These items, along with rescue crews, were loaded onto the baggage car of the Los Angeles-bound *Lark* when it steamed into San Luis Obispo at 2:50 A. M. Having done all he could from there, Foley climbed aboard and set out to the scene of the disaster.

It was now approaching 4:00 A. M. on the rescue scene. Following the departure of the scheduled San Francisco-bound *Sunset Limited* from Honda, more Los Angeles-bound trains brought additional help. Soon after 3:50 A. M., the *Sunset Manifest* No. 244 arrived with food, blankets, and medical supplies that had been collected at Lompoc, including a supply of blue coveralls, which many sailors quickly donned. It also brought Mrs. C. L. Atkins, wife of Surf's third-trick SP telegrapher, who alighted from the caboose with an armload of food and coffee. Then, at 4:30 A. M., the Los Angeles-bound *Lark* arrived, bringing Foley, his work crews, and much-needed supplies. Eventually, forty-three Southern Pacific personnel were engaged at the rescue site.

As Foley's railroad men stepped onto the gravel roadbed, they met an unimaginably desolate scene. Along the foggy tracks, illuminated by burning railroad ties, were hundreds of cold and miserable naval personnel. Many exhausted men lay sleeping on the bare ground. In the distance the cries of those seeking help offshore could still be heard.

While his men began moving cables and stretchers to the cliff face, train master Foley met with Commander Watson to arrange for the removal of the sailors from Honda. Working with Coast Division headquarters in San Francisco, it was decided that a special relief train would be put together as soon as possible and be scheduled to leave shortly after *Daylight Limited*'s 7:45 A.M. departure from the City.

As these plans went forward, SP crews, aided by ranch hands from the area, worked through the night with rope and tackle to bring more men to shore, at times plunging into the high surf to reach them. Honda section foreman Giorvas spent four hours standing in the cold water pulling men to safety. His heroics would earn him the title "Honda John," a name that would stick with him for the next thirty-three years of railroading.

In Los Angeles, other efforts were underway to provide assistance. Word of the naval disaster reached the pressrooms of the Los Angeles papers about 2:00 A.M., when two photographers from the *Los Angeles Examiner* sped northward by automobile. Unknown to them, the SP had begun to assemble a short relief train of its own, with commissary supplies. Sometime around 7:00 A.M., Southern Pacific engineer Henry B. Brewer, accompanied by his eleven-year-old son, Darrell, came by the dispatcher's office at the Los Angeles Division's Alhambra roundhouse to check his posting for the day. He was ordered to bring the train to Surf, and was promised the right of way over all Los Angeles-bound traffic. Asking what to do with his son, Brewer was told to put the boy in the coach-baggage car and take him along.

Seen through the heavy mist, sunrise on Sunday was an eerie, long-delayed event that brought no cessation to rescue efforts. Shortly after dawn, the body of a drowned sailor was pulled from the surf—the first of the twenty-three seamen who died in the disaster. By mid-morning the fog had lifted sufficiently to show the full extent of the damage. To the dismay of those on shore, the wrecks of yet another two destroyers, the *Farragut* and the *Fuller*, could be seen on outlying rocks some 400 yards offshore. Sailors were clinging to the vessels or huddled on offshore rock formations. Fortunately, a fishing boat at the scene began the difficult work of extracting sailors. As the day cleared, rescue crews from other destroyers of the flotilla, which had avoided running aground and had spent the night in deeper water waiting for the fog to lift, also moved in and eventually rescued an additional 200 seamen.

Sunday also brought relief to an unfortunate U. S. Foreign Service officer (Mr. Dooman) who had been aboard one of the destroyers and had accompanied the group of injured men sent to the Santa Barbara hospital during the night. At 8 A. M., he found himself standing at the Santa Barbara station platform, still covered with oil and with neither ticket nor money, hoping to board the 8 A. M. *Sunset Express* for Los Angeles. "Come aboard. You're our guest," the conductor said, and led him into the club car. He recounted how the conductor "covered a seat with newspapers ... then disappeared and after a while appeared with ... a sumptuous breakfast of ham and eggs, toast and coffee."

For the sailors on shore, the sunlight brought relief in other ways. From the early hours of morning, coffee was served by a tireless Mrs. Atkins, later to be described in press releases as the Honda "angel of mercy." Western Union telegraphers arrived and set up a transmitting office on the second floor of the section house, making it possible for hundreds of messages to be sent out by sailors to their anxious relatives. Meanwhile, cots, food, and blankets had arrived on a special train from Los Angeles, together with five doctors and several reporters who had been taken aboard at Santa Barbara. The train was unloaded at the Honda section house, and then turned on the wye at Surf.

Throughout the early hours of the day, curious onlookers from Lompoc had made their way to the scene of the disasters, coming through the hills by automobile or wagon or following the sandy construction road paralleling the tracks. By noon, several hundred spectators were on hand. Among them was Ed Negus, a seventeen-year-old young man, who, with a friend named Harold, had walked over the hills and down Honda Canyon. He recalled how many sailors were gathered around the section house, but others stood clustered in small groups in the cold, bracing winds along the ocean cliff, talking quietly among themselves and looking at the rescue efforts still underway. He remembered how young the sailors were, many of them with their feet wrapped in strips they had torn from blankets or lifejackets. "We left them alone," he recounts, "we did not wish to bother them."

Vance Newcomb, Editor of the Lompoc Valley Historical Society's publication, *Legacy*, adds this observation:

> By an interesting coincidence, another source of onlookers was gathering on the California coast that weekend. A total eclipse of the sun was to take place soon after noon on Monday, September 10, 1923. Many people from near and far were gathering at Point Conception to view the event as it came onto the coast of California. Some of the amateur astronomers made their way to Honda when word of the shipwrecks spread to where they were camped to view the eclipse. Years later, a Lompoc resident—a teenager in 1923—reported how eerie the scene became as the midday turned to "night" that Monday when her family was at Honda to view the ships.

As afternoon drew on, the sailors were called back from the beach overlook, and at 4:45 P.M. the Special Relief Train from San Francisco finally arrived. Five hundred and seventeen enlisted men and thirty-eight officers were drawn up at attention along the tracks while the body of the drowned seaman was hoisted into the baggage car. The cars of the train had been preheated, and when the sailors were allowed to board, many of them, exhausted by the past sixteen hours, quickly fell asleep, some in the coach chairs, others on the floors. In Santa Barbara, local citizens stood along the train platforms and passed food and clothing to the men.

"As the special whirled past station after station," wire services reported, "crowds from the surrounding farming country cheered." The outpourings of support slowed the progress of the train, and it was not until 11 P.M. that it reached Los Angeles. There, it paused first at River Station, then switched back to Santa Fe tracks, and was brought down to La Grande Station where a Santa Fe road engine was attached. The ten-car special of Harriman coaches finally pulled into the San Diego station at 3:40 A.M. on Monday, September 10.

[A railroad lounge car and a locomotive similar to the ones used on the *Sunset Limited* rescue train, are shown in Illustrations **24** and **25**].

For the majority of young seamen, the arrival at San Diego meant the worst was over, but the U.S. Navy's honor would require much more time to heal. Due to navigational error, twenty-three sailors were dead, seven destroyers valued at over $10 million and considered among the most modern in the world were declared a total loss, and three others were damaged.

Typical Consist of the* Sunset Limited *in 1923
(San Luis Obispo to Los Angeles)

SP 2433	4-6-2 Pacific
SP 6460	Baggage Express
SP 3228	Baggage Club
SP10105	Dining Car
PC Pickert	Std. Pullman
PC Catlin	Std. Pullman
PC Curwood	Std. Pullman
PC Sunset Beach	Std. Pull-Obs.

A few weeks later, Southern Pacific President William Sproul received a brief letter from the U.S. Secretary of Navy, thanking the railroad for "an invaluable and timely service well done." A similar note of appreciation was also received by several of the railroad men who had assisted with rescue, including section foreman John Giorvas. In the excitement of the event and the ensuing court martial of seven naval officers, these tributes received little notice in the popular press. It was taken for granted that, tragedies or not, trains would run on time, and that the network of technology and skilled personnel that comprised the Southern Pacific system of this era would come through. This it did with flying colors.

John Giorvas retired from the Southern Pacific in 1956, three months short of fifty years' service within the Maintenance of Way Department of the Coast Division. Giorvas, who died in 1957, was posthumously recognized for his services by an act of the U. S. Congress on October 6, 1986.

Chapter 7

The Memorials on 23 September 1923

On September 23, the destroyers of Division 32 were steaming off-shore from San Diego. At 12:30 the Kennedy turned slowly, and the destroyers formed into a circle. The survivors cast flowers over the stern. On signal, engines stopped, all colors were lowered to half mast, and taps was sounded from the bridge…

—Ltjg Max Wellborn, USS *Kennedy*

Overview

It was before noon in San Diego when an eager newspaper reporter headed for the docks to find Commander Roper, whom he had seen earlier, but did not see his face in the crowd gathered for the official memorial ceremony. [This commentary was deduced from various news accounts.]

The reporter reached the harbor and found the *Kennedy* and other ships of Destroyer Squadron 11, but he saw only a few people, a couple of parked vans, and a few gangway guards. A couple of taxicabs pulled up. A batch of sailors and a young ensign got out, opened the vans, unloaded flowers, and headed for the ships. Soon, the fantails of the ships were covered with flowers and wreaths. The turbines of the *Kennedy*, *Thompson*, *Stoddert*, and *Paul Hamilton* rumbled as they prepared to depart. The reporter went up the gangway, but stopped when Commander Roper appeared. Roper's first words were not welcoming, and the reporter quickly made it clear that he was not asking for interviews, he just wanted to know what was going on.

"Sir, it won't hurt to let him stay," Lt Wellborn said. "I'll take care of him."

"All right," Cdr Roper replied, "but I don't want him burdening anybody else."

Wellborn said, "Newsman, I will be your nursemaid. Stay close."

Roper added: "If I see you again, you'd better be close enough to shake Wellborn's hand." The *Kennedy*'s mooring lines were slipped, and she headed for the harbor channel. It was noon.

Lt Max Wellborn was a steady, no-nonsense type, but he was thrilled with the scene unfolding, the destroyers forming in column behind the flagship *Kennedy* and preparing for the memorial ceremony at sea. The reporter wondered about the heaps of flowers covering the fantail of each ship, and the gathering of navy people. Max said, "The flowers are in memory of the men lost in the disaster, and the navy men here are survivors from the *Delphy* and *Young*."

The ships cleared the entrance buoys off Pt. Loma, and headed for the Coronado Islands, which break the sea horizon to the south. Nearing the North Islands towers at 12:35 P.M., with all ships steaming at 15 knots, the *Kennedy* turned slowly to circle. The others followed and the column swept the sea in a 400-yard circle.

On signal from the *Kennedy*, the survivors cast flowers over the stern, and a wreath of color formed on the gently tossing sea. Speed was constant, and the colorful flowers were tossed into the foaming wakes. On signal, all engines stopped, all colors lowered to half-mast, and all hands stood silent. Taps sounded from the *Kennedy*'s bridge. "May God rest their gallant souls" was the prayer as the plaintive bugle notes floated over the sea.

After noon, a crowd of thousands gathered, and another memorial ceremony started in the huge quad of the North Island Naval Air Station. Navy planes flew overhead. Admiral Robert E. Coontz, Commander-in-Chief of the United States Fleet, spoke:

> In keeping with he highest ideals the Naval Services ... our destroyers at Honda upheld the best traditions of the Navy. Trained to be ready for the great moment, those who took our destroyers to sea, and who died ... were true in every way to the trust we had in them ... At Annapolis, the young men ... find on the walls ... the pictures, busts, and records of enlisted men who have made the navy proud. These examples help fill the young officers with the true spirit which breathes in every naval man. It moves them to duty in the face of fear and sustains them in times of woe. In our distress for our dead, we are sad; in our admiration for their conduct, we are exalted.

In 1975, an Anchor Monument and Plaque in memory of the brave men lost was placed on the mesa at the Pt. Pedernales (Honda) disaster site (monument and plaque are shown in Illustration **26**). The stories of this monument, the 1975 memorial services, and the later monuments are in Chapter 13. The Propeller Shaft and Plaque monument carrying the names of the ships lost is shown in Illustration **27**. The Memorial Plaque, carrying the names of all the men lost is shown in Illustration **29.** The Anchor Monument was recently placed in the hands of the Lompoc Valley Historical Society, and is now displayed in their museum.

The failure of Capt Watson's attempt to set a destroyer endurance-run record weighed heavily on the squadron's commanders as they attended memorial services for the twenty-three men lost. No words were adequate to describe the sadness that followed when the court martial found Capt Watson and LCdr Hunter "Guilty of culpable inefficiency and negligence," and only a few people would know of the immense grief carried by RAdm J. C. Watson until he died on December 14, 1923.

Sophoclean

First he was shivering on the shore in skins
Or hunkering behind shell-middens in a cave.
Then he took up oars, put tackle on a mast,
And steered himself by the stars through gales.

Once upon a time from the womb of the earth
The gods were born and he bowed down
To worship them. Then he walked tall
From temple to agora, talking against himself.

The wind is no more swift or mysterious
Than his mind and words: he has mastered thinking,
Roofed his house against hail and rain,
And worked out laws for living together.

Homemaker, thought-taker, measure of all things,
He survives every danger except death
And will lead to nothing else, Nothing
Else, good or evil, is beyond him.

When the truth is in the treadle of his loom
And justice the shuttle, all due honor
Will come his way. But let him once
Overbear or overstep

What the city allows, treat law
As something he can decide for himself,
Then let this marvel of the world remember:
When he comes begging we will turn our backs.

—*Seamus Heaney*

This poem is reproduced with appreciation to, and the kind permission of, the noted poet Seamus Heaney of Dublin, Ireland.

ILLUSTRATIONS

ANGELES Times

Liberty Under Law—Equal Rights—True Industrial Freedom.

SEVEN DESTROYERS ON ROCKS

Navy Ships Pile Up on Rocks

TWENTY-TWO DEAD, THREE MISSING, MANY INJURED

Air Clogged With Messages, Vessels Crash Off La Honda; Deeds of Heroism Feature Tragedy

[EXCLUSIVE DISPATCH]

SANTA BARBARA, Sept. 9.—Confusion in the air caused by the multitude of radio messages growing out of the wreck of the liner Cuba, on the rocks of San Miguel Island, four hours after the big liner went aground, sent seven United States destroyers on the jagged rocks of La Honda, 75 miles north of this city, on one of the most barren stretches of the Pacific coast.

Wedged in between the jagged rocks, which are upheaved from deep water, the seven destroyers went to what is known as "grave of ships" with probably nineteen men of the destroyer Young, while from the

Illustration 1.

Headline and copy from *The Los Angeles Times,* 10 September 1923. (Source: Newspaper Document File, UC Davis.)

Illustration 2.

USN photo looking north on Sept. 9. USS *S. P. Lee* is stranded on the rocky shore, bow pointed north. USS *Nicholas,* DD 311, is stranded on rocky reef, bow pointed west. (Source: Mare Island Naval Shipyard.)

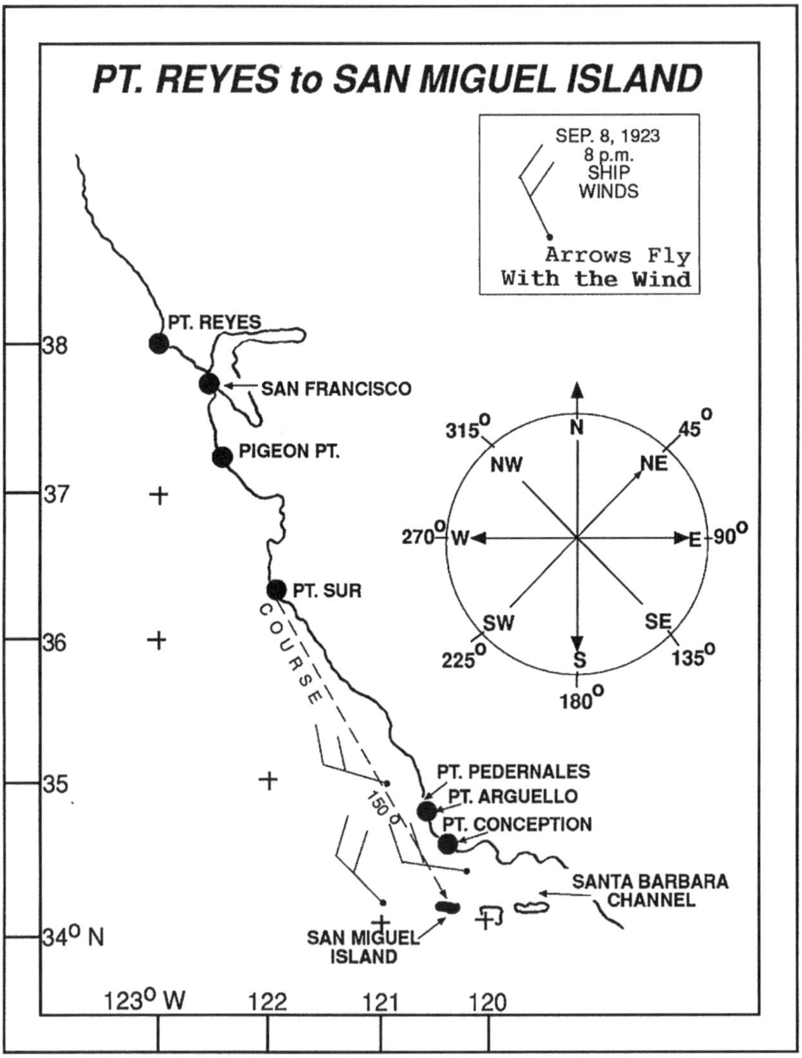

Illustration 3.

"Pt. Reyes to San Miguel Island"
(Original drawing by the author.)

Illustration 4.

USN photo of destroyer USS *Trever,* DD339, under final construction at Mare Island Naval Shipyard on January 2, 1922. (Source: Mare Island Naval Shipyard.)

Illustration 5.

Five of the wrecked destroyers. USN photo taken from a spot on the mesa to the north of Bridge Rock while looking generally westward. The forward part of the *Delphy*'s hull is on its side with bow pointed into the lower right-hand corner of the photo frame. *Delphy*'s stern is in the center of the frame. Just above it is the capsized hull of the *Young,* a slash across the middle of the frame. Woodbury Rock is in the upper center, and the *Woodbury,* partly rolled on its side, is just to the right (north side of the rock). The *Fuller* is partly hidden behind *Woodbury* and partly rolled the other way. At center left is the *Chauncey,* with her flag flying. (Source: Mare Island Naval Shipyard.)

Illustration 6.

USN photo of the destroyer USS *Litchfield,* DD336. Excellent profile of a ship steaming slowly in the Mare Island Channel. (Source: Mare Island Naval Shipyard.)

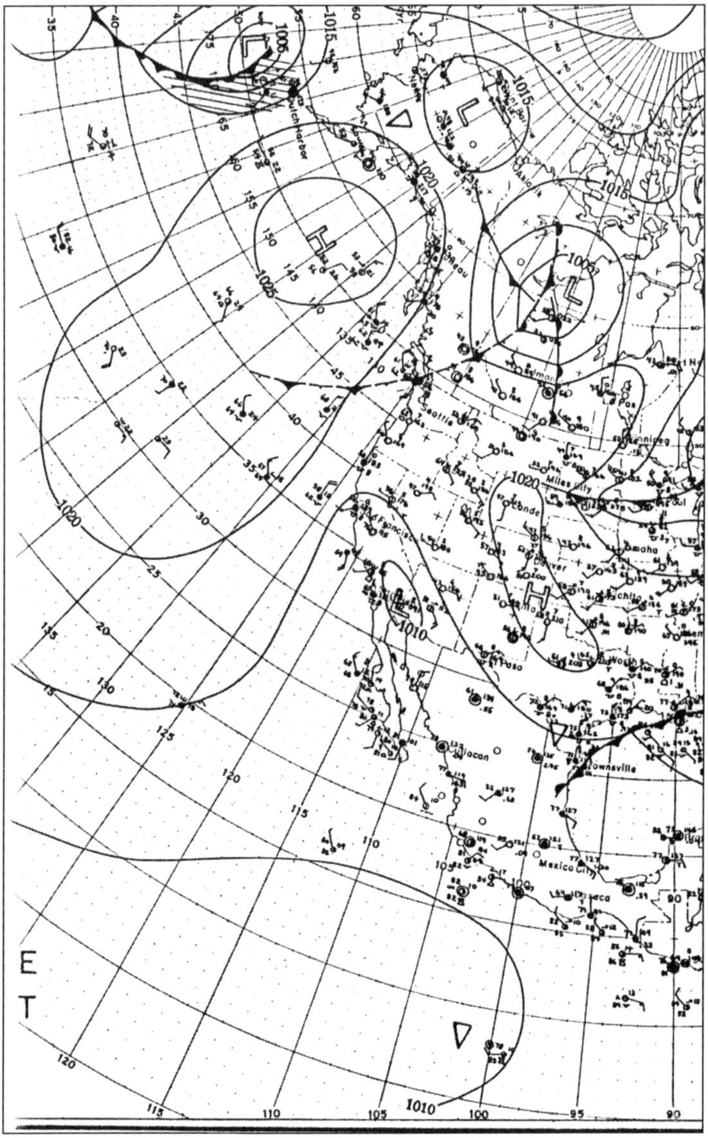

Illustration 7.

Surface Weather Map for Sept. 8th, 1923, U. S. Weather Bureau. (Source: California State Library, Documents Branch.)

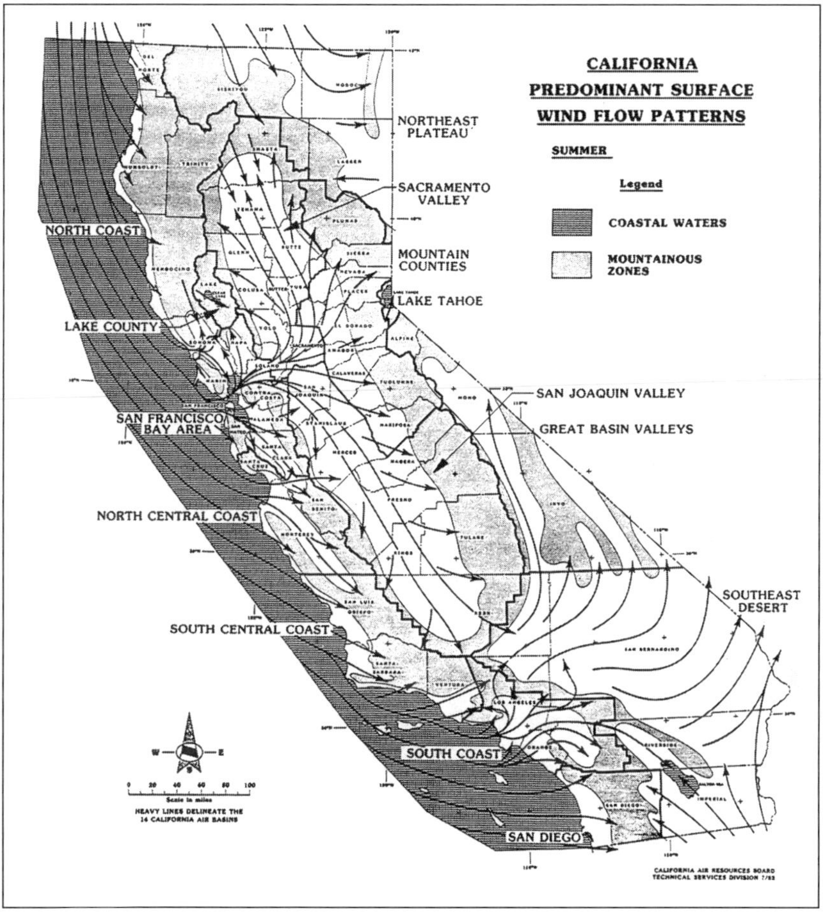

Illustration 8.

"Predominant Summer Wind Flow Pattern Over California Coastal Waters." The Squadron 11 destroyers steamed south in this kind of summer airflow pattern. (Source: California Air Resources Board Library.)

Illustration 9.

Pt. Arguello Lighthouse and Radio Compass Tower, circa 1923, about three miles south of the destroyer disaster site.
(Source: U. S. Lighthouse Society.)

Illustration 10.

Because of the Point Conception's nightmarish reputation—the ocean floor littered with the remains of vessels from American, Spanish, and other nation's ports—Pt. Conception Lighthouse was one of the West Coast's first lighthouses. Construction of the present lighthouse was completed in 1882; the 52-foot tower still stands and guides. (Photo courtesy of Vance Newcomb, Lompoc, CA.)

Illustration 11.

This photo shows the rugged nature of the coastline just south of Pt. Sur. Even the road along this coast is dangerous. Driving southward, the view down to the sea is spectacular, but I favor driving the landward side of the road.
(Photograph courtesy of Jim Neill, Cambria, CA).

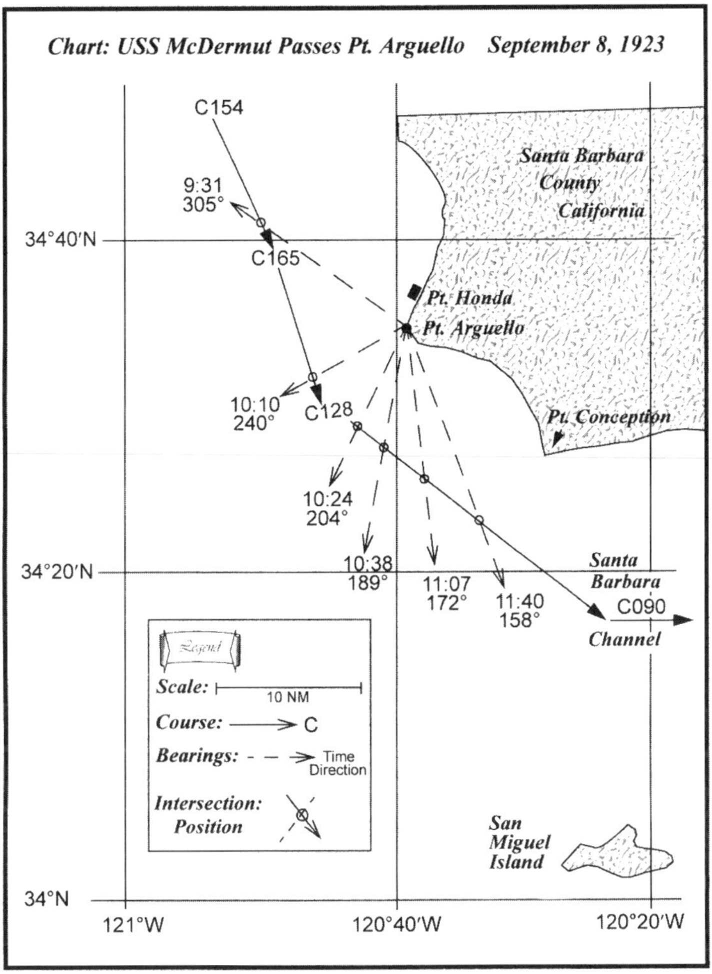

Illustration 12.

Chart: USS *McDermut* passes Pt. Arguello on 8 September 1923. The solid line labeled C154 indicates that the ship was heading on a course of 154 degrees. The dashed line labeled 9:31 and 305 deg indicates that the ship received a 305-degree radio compass bearing at 9:31 P.M. Intersections between the dashed and solid lines show the ship's positions until it was abeam Pt. Conception and preparing to turn eastward into the Santa Barbara channel. (Original drawing by the author; data from the USN Pt. Arguello RC Station and the USS *McDermut*'s deck log.)

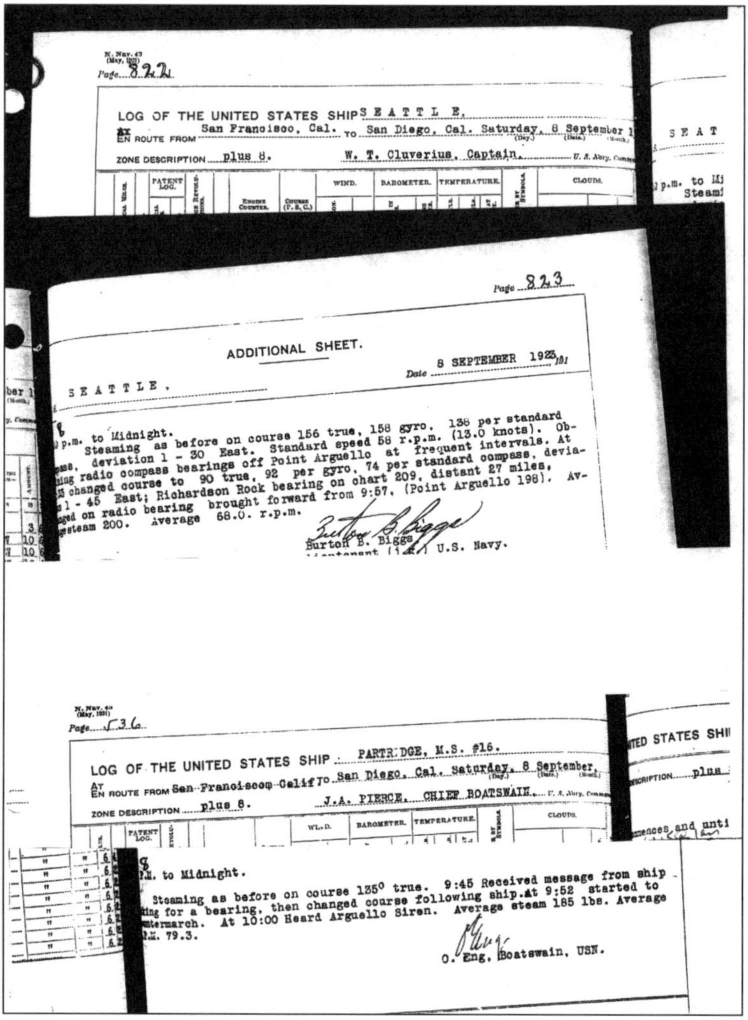

Page 822

LOG OF THE UNITED STATES SHIP S E A T T L E.

EN ROUTE FROM San Francisco, Cal. TO San Diego, Cal. Saturday, 8 September

ZONE DESCRIPTION plus 8. W. T. Cluverius, Captain.

Page 823

ADDITIONAL SHEET.

S E A T T L E. Date 8 SEPTEMBER 1923

p.m. to Midnight.
Steaming as before on course 156 true, 158 gyro, 138 per standard compass, deviation 1 - 30 East. Standard speed 58 r.p.m. (13.0 knots). Obtaining radio compass bearings off Point Arguello at frequent intervals. At changed course to 90 true, 92 per gyro, 74 per standard compass, deviation 1 - 45 East; Richardson Rock bearing on chart 209, distant 27 miles, (Point Arguello 198). Averaged on radio bearing brought forward from 9:57. Average 68.0. r.p.m. Average steam 200.

Burton B. Biggs
Lieutenant (j.g.) U.S. Navy.

Page 536

LOG OF THE UNITED STATES SHIP PARTRIDGE, M.S. #16.

AT EN ROUTE FROM San Francisco Calif TO San Diego, Cal. Saturday, 8 September,

ZONE DESCRIPTION plus 8. J.A. PIERCE, CHIEF BOATSWAIN.

P.M. to Midnight.
Steaming as before on course 135° true. 9:45 Received message from ship asking for a bearing, then changed course following ship. At 9:52 started to countermarch. At 10:00 Heard Arguello Siren. Average steam 185 lbs. Average R.P.M. 79.3.

O. Eng, Boatswain, USN.

Illustration 13.

Excerpts from 8 September 1923 deck logs from USS *Seattle,* Flagship US Battle Fleet Pacific, and from USS *Partridge,* a seagoing tug of the battle fleet. Both logs are for the 8 P.M. to midnight watch. *Seattle* says: "Obtaining radio compass bearings off Pt. Arguello at frequent intervals." *Partridge* says "At 9:52 started to countermarch. At 10:00 heard Arguello Sirens." (Source: National Archives, Washington D.C.)

Illustration 14.

Pigeon Pt. Light was established 50 miles south of San Francisco in 1872. The ground is about 40 feet above sea level and the original tower was 115 feet above the ground, one of the tallest on the coast. The light, which got its name from the Yankee clipper *Carrier Pigeon*, wrecked here in 1853, is still a well-used landmark. (Source: U.S. Lighthouse Society.)

Illustration 15.

Pt. Sur Light. This light was established 30 miles south of Monterey in 1889. The light stands at the summit of a steep-sided sandstone island connected to the mainland by a sandy causeway. The elevation of the tower's base is 200 feet; the light is 250 feet above the sea. (Source: U. S. Lighthouse Society.)

Illustration 16-A.

View looking northward from the mesa above the disaster site. Note the deep gullies made by the wave action eroding the mesa, and the reefs jutting into the sea. (Photo by the author, 1994.)

Illustration 16-B.

View looking southward of a reef extending into the sea. The tide is high, and the most dangerous part of the reef is the underwater area marked by a patch of white water; at low tide the entire reef comes into view. (Photo by the author, 1994.)

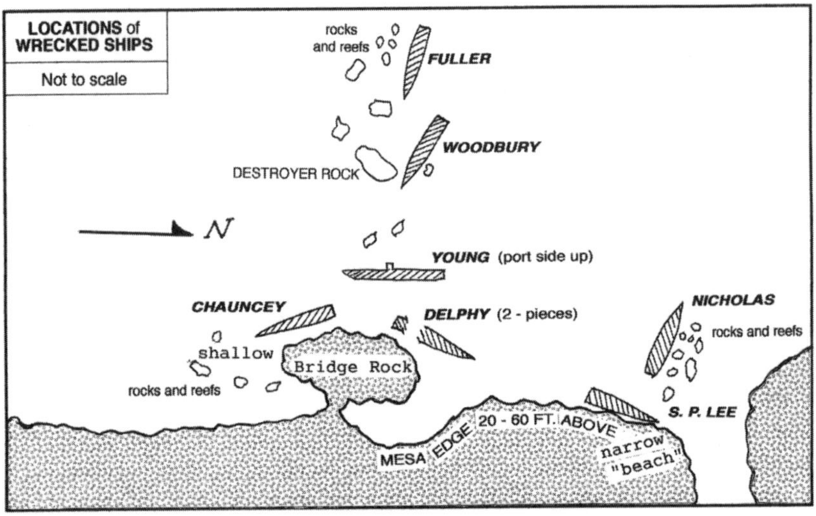

Illustration 17.

A drawing by the author, based on USN aerial photographs, local reports, and a sketch by the USN salvage officer.

Illustration 18.

USN photo of USS *Nicholas* shows its deteriorated condition days after it was stranded. (Source: Print purchased from Maury Hoag, Los Angeles.)

Illustration 19.

USN photo of USS *Woodbury,* USS *Fuller* in background. Vessel to left is USS *Chauncey;* right center is USS *Young.* (Source: Print purchased from Maury Hoag, Los Angeles.)

Illustration 20.

Top: USN photo of USS *Chauncey,* DD296, stranded on a rocky cove, bow pointed southward. Woodbury Rock and *Woodbury* can be seen in the background; dark profiles in right foreground are observers. (Prints courtesy of Myra Manfrina, Lompoc Valley Historical Society.)

Bottom: Model of the destroyer USS *Pillsbury,* DD227. *Pillsbury* fought in the Pacific in World War II; Capt Schofield describes the heroic history of her desperate attempt to reach Australia in his book, *Destroyers-60 Years.* (Source: Model on public display in the Monterey Maritime Museum, photographed by the author.)

Illustration 21.

USN photo of observers on the rocks above USS *Chauncey*. Note the hat on the youngster at the left. (Print courtesy of Myra Manfrina, Lompoc Valley Historical Society.)

Illustration 22.

Photo attributed to the *Lompoc Record* shows afternoon at the rescue site. Most of the people are workers. Note the horses and wagon. Many sightseers were near the ocean, where they could see the wrecks. (Photo courtesy of Myra Manfrina, Lompoc Valley Historical Society.)

Illustration 23.

USN photo of the Navy Wreck Patrol in the process of moving a recovered body from the water's edge up to the temporary morgue on the mesa. (Photo courtesy of Myra Manfrina, Lompoc Valley Historical Society.)

Illustration 24.

This locomotive from the Southern Pacific's famous 1920s transcontinental train was similar to the one used on the 1923 *Sunset Limited,* which traveled the route from San Francisco to Los Angeles, San Diego, Tucson, El Paso, and New Orleans. Connection at New Orleans was made for SP ocean service to New York. The sturdy 4-8-2 mountain-type locomotive—a shining giant with 3,250 horsepower—was built especially for the *Sunset Limited.* Its tender carried 12,000 gallons of water and 4,000 gallons of fuel oil. The total weight was 305 tons for engine and tender; 123 tons of weight was on the drivers. (Photo courtesy of the California Railway Museum, Sacramento, CA.)

Illustration 25.

This railroad lounge car was similar to the one used on the 1923 *Sunset Limited.* It was longer than today's cars, built to last, comfortable, and equipped with huge, six-wheel trucks at each end. Train crews heated the cars on their way to the rescue site, and made every effort to comfort rescued sailors as they boarded. (Photo courtesy of the California Railway Museum, Sacramento, CA.)

Illustration 26.

Top: This is a photograph of the Anchor Monument, in memory of the men lost in the 1923 disaster. The photo was taken on a September day in 1994 when the monument was on the mesa at Vandenberg Air Force Base. In 1923, the rock in the background was named Woodbury Rock for the destroyer *Woodbury* that was stranded there; on today's nautical chart its name is "Destroyer Rock." (Photo by the author, Sept. 1994.)

Bottom: This plaque mounted on the monument says: "Anchor from USS *Chauncey* raised by Vandenberg Aquallier Dive Club, 28 July 1973." (Photo by the author, Sept. 1994.)

Illustration 27.

Propeller and Shaft "In Memory of the Tragedy at Pt. Pedernales / Honda Point" was raised from the sea by father-and-son divers Earnest and Carson Porter, who donated it to the American Legion William Proud Post 211. The monument was placed in the legion's courtyard on Sept. 8, 1983. (Photo by the author, Sept. 1994.)

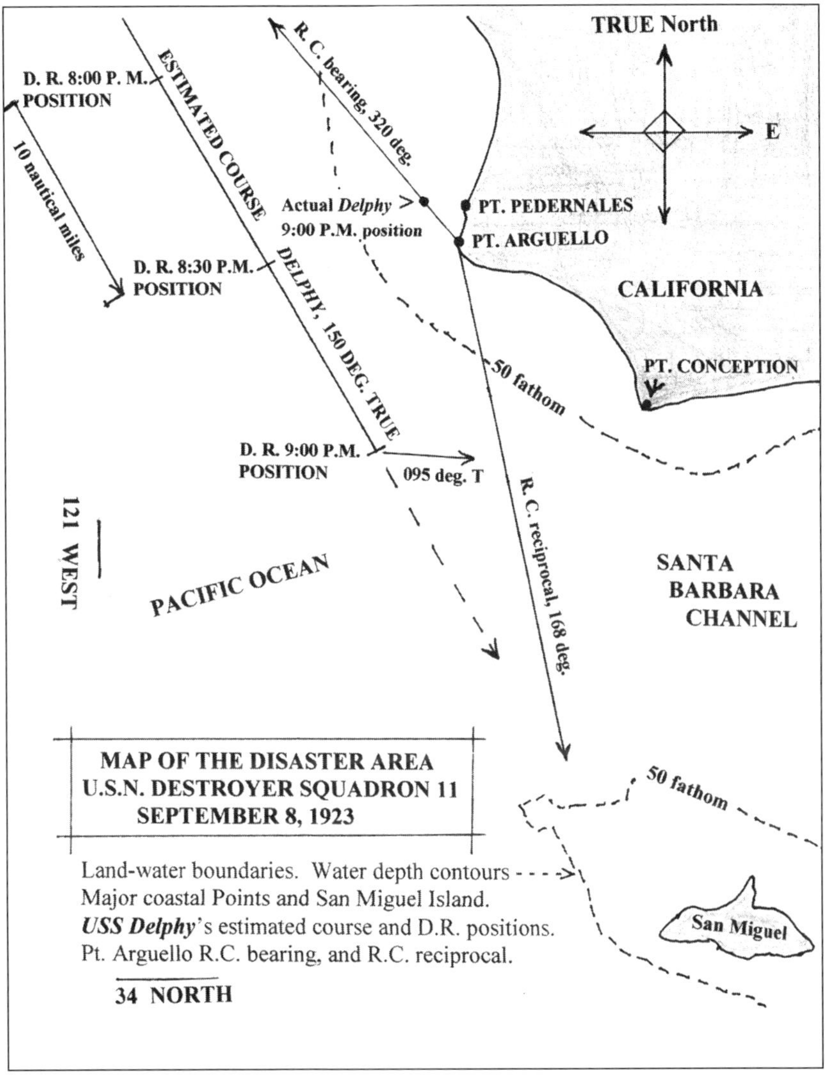

Illustration 28.

Map of the disaster area, USN Destroyer Squadron 11, 8 September 1923. (Original drawing by the author.)

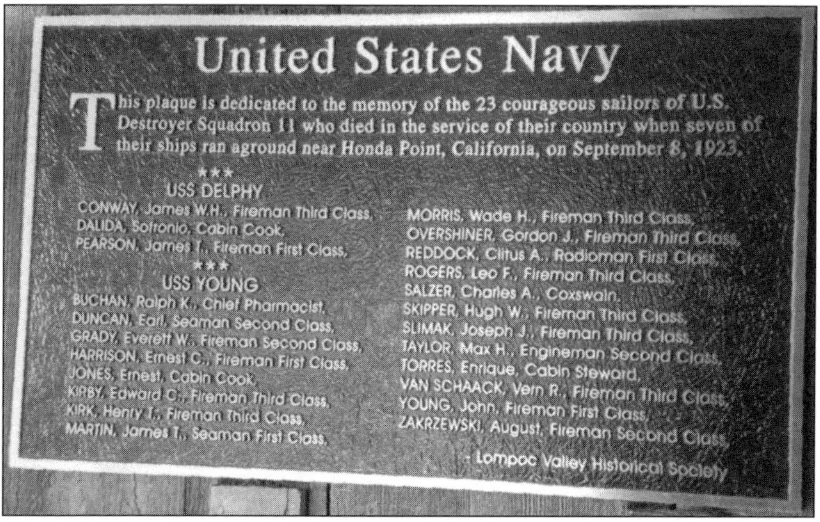

Illustration 29.

Memorial Plaque with the names of the 23 men lost in the 1923 disaster. The Plaque was presented by the Lompoc Valley Historical Society at a service of worship and remembrance conducted in September 1998 by staff from the U. S. Navy, U. S. Air Force, and local dignitaries at the Honda Site, on Vandenberg AFB. (Photo courtesy of Vance Newcomb, Lompoc, CA.)

Illustration 30.

Recent photograph of St. Peter's Chapel, taken during a tour given by Kenneth Zadwick, president of the Mare Island Historic Park Foundation. In 1923 this chapel was on the grounds of the U. S. Navy's Mare Island Shipyard, Vallejo, CA. (Photo courtesy of Janet D. Wilson, Sacramento, CA.)

Illustration 31.

USN photo of the destroyer USS *Sumner,* DD 333, which was one of the destroyers in the Flush Deck Class (Source: Historical records of USN ships recommended by Terry Miller, Executive Director, Tin Can Sailors, Inc.)

PART TWO

Piloting

Chapter 8

Nature of the Disaster, the *Delphy* Men, and Virtual History

I was on the bridge when it happened. The wreck was the result of a blunder in navigation by one man, Lieutenant Commander D. T. Hunter. We had a number of radio compass bearings from Pt. Arguello, which showed us to be 8 or 9 miles inside our laid-down course, but he would not believe them. He was a very fine officer and was well liked by everyone.

—CQM H. D. Cummings, USS *Delphy*

Seriousness of the Disaster

In his 1967 book, *The Last Hours of Seven Four-Stackers,* Charles Hice made the following statement, shown below exactly as it was printed:

> Today, almost a half a century later, the eternal erosion of the sea has erased almost all evidence of the disaster. *There is not even a simple stone marker to tell students and scholars of tomorrow that this is "Honda—scene of the Navy's greatest peace-time disaster."*
>
> **Maybe the Navy had just as soon forget.**
>
> —*Lompoc Record,* Sept. 30, 1966

The loss of seven destroyers justifies the word "disaster." Yet, with the exception of Ronald Adam, editor of the *Lompoc Record,* the magnitude of the tragedy received little attention. He was the man on the scene in 1923, and he stated it clearly in the *Lompoc Record.*

The sea at Saddle Rock was rough on Saturday night, as it always is, but it was calm in comparison with what it is in a stormy sea. Had the sea been as angry at this time the loss of life would have been *appalling.*

An engineering estimate of the human losses if the destroyers had been in a stormy sea would require an extensive technical study of a 1923 destroyer squadron's behavior in a historical storm in this area, such as in the "superstorm" described in the *Marine Weather Handbook, Northern and Central California,* by Kenneth E. Lilly, Jr. Commander, NOAA.

To make a rough estimate of the potential loss that might have occurred in a severe storm, I have projected it happening during a major California coastal storm such as the one described in my article, *Storm in the Gulf of the Farallones: A 1982 Sailing Disaster.* That storm packed ocean waves up to 14 feet and wind gusts up to 70 knots on land. Seven sailboats were lost.

The following is my estimate of the disaster that might have occurred in a storm as severe as that of 1982, had a group of destroyers like those in the 1923 Squadron 11 hit the rocky coast at Pt. Pedernales in a similar stranding pattern of speed and impact:

Ten ships and 700 lives could have been lost.

The initial rescue by the Southern Pacific section men and the Lompoc community would have been delayed and hampered by the storm. Rescue operations would have been exceptionally difficult and subject to periodic curtailment as the storm waxed and waned. Many rescuers would have been injured. Many of the courageous men—railroad workers, civilians, and sailors—who went onto the mesa's seacoast and rocky islands to rescue sailors might themselves have been lost or required rescue.

Delphy would have broken in two before all her crew escaped.

Nicholas would have deteriorated on the reef quickly; there would have been little chance to wait for a daylight rescue, and it would have been impossible to rescue everyone.

Only a fraction of the crews from *Woodbury* and *Fuller* would have escaped to Woodbury Rock. The men on the rocks would not have escaped on Sunday, because the fishing smack *Roma* would have remained in port.

The *S. P. Lee* would have hit the stern of the *Delphy* at a speed between 10 and 18 knots before careening into the rock face at a speed greater than 8 knots. Thus the casualties on the *Lee* would have increased markedly. The escape route to a safe land location would have been extremely difficult; many would have been unable to get onto the mesa and over the narrow land bridge to safety.

One or two of the damaged ships that maneuvered to safety would have collided with each other, the submerged reefs, or the stranded ships. One or two might have become partially submerged, resulting in catastrophic loss of life. The standby destroyers at anchor on Sunday morning would have been unable to mount a successful whaleboat rescue effort that day.

The *Chauncey* would have hit the *Young* and rammed the shoreline.

The ability of the *Chauncey*'s crew to rescue the men of the *Young* and assist them up to the mesa would have been minimal, and most of the men on the hull of the *Young* would have been lost.

There would have been desperate calls for help from the stranded ships. Destroyers not at risk would have responded, and losses from the decks of those rescue ships would have been serious. A rescue ship might have tangled with a rocky reef, and a ship without adequate ballast might have rolled beyond recovery.

During the storm, corollary problems beyond casual estimate might have occurred: there might have been a train accident; a boiler explosion; a large ocean wave, or exposure to two tidal flows. Had the tide been low, instead of high, at 9 P.M., all the ships that grounded, backed off, and maneuvered to safety, and the rescue ships, would have had major exposure to the offshore reefs and rocky pinnacles.

Adverse conditions on the ground would have increased the severity of injuries, overwhelming the two doctors, who were without medical support and facilities. The overpowering forces of the storm winds and raging seas would have overcome the rescuers, the courageous, the skillful, and many of the bravest sailors.

Exhaustion alone is a big factor in a California coastal storm with strong, gusty winds, chill waves, a shoal site, a rocky shore, offshore reefs, and rocky pinnacles.

WWII history shows that destroyers were vulnerable in a storm. They were impossible to maneuver in heavy seas and high winds, especially when their fuel load was light, as during 1944's *Typhoon Cobra* in the East Philippine Sea. In this case, three 1,400-ton Farragut-Class destroyers, built in 1934, were lost. In his book, *Storm*, A. B. Whipple tells how those destroyers rolled to 90 degrees, killing 850 sailors when all three ships went down. One captain said, "The ship is unmaneuverable, I am stepping into the sea." Detail of this disaster is given in S. E. Morison's *History of United States Naval Operations in World War II*. In that stormy situation, the loss of life on the three destroyers accounted for most of the fleet's losses that day.

The following words from the *San Diego Union* give us a feeling for what happened onboard in the 1923 disaster, when there was no storm and the land-based rescue efforts were near.

> There was no time of suspense and preparation, no clearing of the decks, no calls to battle stations, no open and tangible menace of enemy ships and threatening guns. The destroyermen of Squadron 11 had none of the incentive and inspiration that comes in the stern call to naval action in war. Their only ally was their own innate and well-disciplined manhood. That was all—and enough. They met the hour with every ounce of courage that the hour demanded.

Perspectives of Mr. Dooman, Capt Watson, LCdr Hunter, and Ltjg Blodgett

Introduction

The "what-happened view" of the disaster developed in Part I; the "why-it-happened view" begins here, with the perspectives—backgrounds, personalities, and relationships—of the four men who played significant roles.

Capt Edward Watson made major mistakes—he established himself, Hunter, and Blodgett as the *Delphy* command, the squadron's decision maker. He then issued special orders that isolated the *Delphy* command from the division and ship commanders. Worst of all, Eugene Dooman distracted Watson from his command, occupying time that Watson would otherwise have spent observing, listening on the bridge, and supervising LCdr Hunter. This was in marked contrast to the extensive time spent on the bridge by Cdr Pye and by Cdr Roper.

Edward Watson invited Dooman because he was a friend who had interesting news about Japanese war plans, news of value to the U. S. Navy. Dooman accepted the invitation because he was personally burdened with transporting a heavy load to San Diego—3,000 silver dollars.

Inviting Dooman was gracious, but placing him on the *Delphy* was ill advised. Watson had options: he could have placed Eugene on the *S. P. Lee* with Capt Morris, the squadron's deputy commander; he could have delayed his conference with Dooman until they reached San Diego; or he could have planned for a conference at a San Diego hotel on Monday. Any of those alternatives would have left him free to dutifully attend to squadron business on the Saturday voyage. (Also, a San Diego conference would have allowed Watson to invite RAdm Kittelle.) A better choice would have been to defer meeting with Dooman until he came to visit at the Watson's home in San Diego.

Each of these men was an experienced decision maker in his own domain, yet, on this particular Saturday, Hunter moved out of his domain; he took an unnecessary and risky course change without due regard for the squadron's uncertain navigational situation.

Mr. Eugene H. Dooman

In 1921, Eugene Dooman was a secretary in the U. S. embassy in Tokyo, Japan, and Capt Watson was the U. S. Navy attaché. The two became friends during their joint duty. Dooman was a charming man, trained to assess people around him and conduct himself accordingly. On the evening of September 7, he was pleased to run into his old friend, Capt Watson, in the lobby of the St. Francis Hotel. When Watson learned that Dooman was headed for San Diego, he told Dooman he was taking his destroyer squadron there the next morning, and invited him to come along as his guest.

Early on Saturday morning, Dooman was welcomed aboard and guided to a small, newly emptied cabin. He soon became known as Captain Watson's civilian guest, and owner of all the extra baggage that was carried on board. On the voyage, Mr. Dooman was an unusual passenger, but not a mysterious one. The officers knew he was aboard, as did the sailors who carried and dragged his luggage up the gangplank. Shortly after Mr. Dooman's cabin was assigned, the captain's steward made him comfortable, and it soon became obvious to everyone that a big civilian was aboard—an important visitor, a big shot with a private cabin.

The steward guided Mr. Dooman to Capt Watson's spacious cabin. Enthusiastic, Eugene voiced his reaction: "I'm impressed, the view is grand, the cabin is huge, the decor is excellent, and the furnishings most pleasant and comfortable."

"This was the original chartroom under the bridge," the steward replied, "It was completely redone with the captain's personal direction." (See external view in Illustration 4.) Eugene was relieved to learn that he would spend only a few daytime hours in his cramped cabin. The captain arrived, and an ample breakfast was promptly served—nothing fancy, but more than Eugene expected.

After breakfast, Eugene and Edward settled into comfortable chairs and began their morning visit. When the ship had departed, Capt Watson visited the navigation cabin, and Eugene relaxed. He felt uneasy, however, when the ship exited the harbor and started to roll. Then he noticed the vibrations from the turbines, and became diplomatically quiet.

The conversational pattern for the day developed: Eugene talked briefly, then Capt Watson spoke while Eugene listened carefully. Capt Watson had spent a restless night onboard, and soon found the constant interaction with Eugene to be an energy drain. Eugene found it an easy time, listening, snacking, and drinking whatever the steward served, so their conversations continued until lunch was served. Gradually, the talk became less interactive, Watson dominating.

The courteous Eugene repeatedly said, "I hope I am not interfering with your regular duty schedule."

"Don't worry Gene," Edward said. I have competent officers carrying out my orders on each ship, and I have complete confidence in my flagship commander and navigator, LCdr Donald Hunter." Eugene nodded, but wondered about Watson's unconditional confidence in Don Hunter. Occasionally, Watson would leave and go up to the navigation cabin. Dooman wondered what could be accomplished in such short visits. He was correct: Watson's ability to guide Hunter depended on his spending part of each hour on the bridge, observing and listening to the bridge crew, and part in the navigation cabin overseeing the navigators. Instead, Watson seldom interrupted his friend's conversation that afternoon; Watson spent little time on the bridge and only an occasional twenty minutes with the navigators. Thus Watson failed to detect that LCdr Hunter's navigation was awry, and that his navigators, LCdr Hunter and Ltjg Blodgett, were at odds.

Insight into Eugene Dooman's view of his friend Capt Watson is seen in Dooman's 1960s letter to Charles Hice:

> As an individual, he was a most attractive person, witty and a most congenial companion... He did not smoke... you must realize that the assuming of responsibility is what distinguishes a profession from other vocations. Officers of the armed services, diplomats, lawyers, doctors and ministers of religion, are obliged to make decisions which involve the lives and well-being of others, whereas the decisions of a company executive, for example, normally concern only the financial welfare of his corporation...
>
> I am not competent to pass on Watson's decision which led to the disaster... I cannot weigh the extenuating circumstances, but a disaster did occur and the man who made the decision had to assume the responsibility.

When questioned after the crash, the crew remembered that Dooman was agile on the ropes and escaped up to the mesa without special help. The conductor on the rescue train said, "We gave the sad looking, oil-soaked civilian special treatment." Mr. Dooman's whereabouts were evident for a week after his escape. After that, however, there were no stories about his special status or the details of how he lost his valise containing $3,000 in silver. At the trials, members of the audience mentioned Mr. Dooman's role, but we could find no evidence that Dooman was ever officially mentioned during the proceedings of the court of inquiry or the court martial. A member of the naval salvage team told Dooman, "Your valise of silver has been found, but it will harm Capt Watson's case if you go and claim it."

Author Charles Lockwood devoted his 1978 Appendix XI to Mr. Dooman, titling it "*Delphy*'s Phantom Passenger." That this belated discovery of Dooman, an important witness to the disaster, came long after the retired officers of Squadron 11 had talked about "the Captain's civilian guest" is astounding, but Lockwood's third and fourth sentences—in a four-and-a-quarter-page appendix—are equally so: "But, like a phantom, he remained faceless, formless, and nameless. No one knew his name and it showed in no records."

In contrast, we found a section about Dooman titled, "Only Civilian in Wreck" in Charles Hice's 1967 book, *The Last Hours of Seven Four-Stackers.* Quotes from two of Dooman's letters follow.

> September 26, 1966. A couple of days after the disaster, I visited Capt Watson at his home in San Diego. He told me that his wife and daughter had been with him in San Francisco, and his wife had wanted him to take the daughter, then about seven years old, on his ship to San Diego, as the wife wanted to go on a motor trip with a couple of other women and did not want the little girl with them. After he saw me at the hotel, he said to his wife that there was only one empty cabin on his ship and that the daughter could not go. You ask about the money I lost in the disaster.... I decided to take the money, $3,000 in silver... in a leather valise.... When I arrived the banks had closed.... I had to take the bag with me... you can imagine how heavy it was, and as I had to swim ashore I had to leave the money in my cabin.

> October 8, 1966. I am glad you found my previous letter interesting, and it is not surprising when you tell me that you have been researching the Honda disaster for ten years. In my previous letter I wrote you the circumstances of my being on the *Delphy*. I heard later that my money had been found by the salvagers, but I could not claim it without the probability of being called as a witness in the court martial. Watson and his defense were afraid that my testimony might prove harmful to Watson, as I was with him when the ship struck.

Dooman replied to letters from both Hice and Lockwood. Each asked him different questions, and the diplomatic Mr. Dooman slanted his answers accordingly. Neither author asked all the key questions. Hence Dooman's skill in diplomacy is revealed in the differences between the letters he wrote to Hice and those he wrote to Lockwood. For example, the following statements were in one letter, but not in the other:

- I brought 3,000 dollars in silver aboard.
- How lucky it was that I was on board and not Capt Watson's daughter, how providential, as that little girl could never have got ashore!
- Capt Watson, on the mesa after the disaster, stopped at the body of Fireman Conway, silently unbuckled the sword he was wearing and laid it beside the body.

Capt Edward H. Watson was a patrician from Kentucky's well-known Watson, Howe, and Crittenden families. Watson's father, the famous RAdm John Crittenden Watson, had an impressive career. He gained early fame when, as Admiral Farragut's flag lieutenant in battle, he ordered the quartermaster to tie Farragut to the rigging to prevent the admiral from being lost overboard if he was shot. RAdm J. C. Watson was born in the house of his grandfather, John J. Crittenden, who served in the Kentucky legislature, the U. S. Senate, and as governor of Kentucky, and attorney general under

President Fillmore. RAdm Watson knew his son, Edward, would be a naval success.

Capt E. H. Watson was a well-educated man with a huge reserve of self-belief. In the navy he was a much-liked squadron commander with a superior service history and a high place on the promotion list. He had three excellent division leaders: Capt Morris was the passive deputy squadron commander, and a diligent division commander; Cdr Roper was known for his superior squadron staff and his frank honest speech. Roper "found Watson hard to admire"; Cdr Pye was a keen division commander. He asked the critical question at the pre-voyage conference—the one Capt Watson never answered: "What course we will take after we clear Pt. Conception?"

Capt Watson had a solitary operational view of the Saturday voyage. He found it difficult to envision the organized group effort required for its success, and he did not sense the critical need to organize his staff so that all the skills he required would be at the ready.

Watson and Hunter's political priority was ship speed, to the neglect of command and navigation coordination. Many successful teams in history have operated differently: the priority of the Wright brothers was technical; lift and control were critical, and concern for speed came later.

Capt Watson's career was impressive. He moved from assignment to assignment at important stations, commanded ships in difficult seas, and handled diplomatic responsibilities with care and insight. He had a wide range of duty during the Spanish-American War and the Philippine Insurrection. Later, he took training at the Naval Torpedo Station, served in the Bureau of Navigation, and was U. S. Navy representative to the coronation of King Edward VII. He attended the long course at the Naval War College, and served as executive officer of the battleship *Utah*.

Cdr Watson was commander of the battleship *Alabama* in March 1918, and his personality merged with the battleship culture. He was fond of the formal service in the officer's wardroom. In 1919, when diplomacy in the Pacific was stressful, he was moved to the

Office of Naval Intelligence and then to Japan. In April 1920, Watson attained the rank of captain. Nearing age fifty, he was tanned, medium-tall, and sturdy, and carried himself with an air of distinction and authority.

Capt Watson read naval history. He knew that the emergence of Japan as the navy's "bête noire" had led to the secretary of the navy's decision to attach half of the navy's battleships to the Pacific Fleet in 1919. Watson knew that Secretary of the Navy Denby had reorganized the navy in December 1922 so that the bulk of the battle fleet was stationed in the Pacific. Capt Watson was aware that the navy's real striking power—its best battleships and the carriers *Lexington* and *Saratoga*—now lay at harbor in San Pedro, CA.

Capt Watson returned from Japan in 1922 and became Commander, Destroyer Squadron 11. He looked forward to the breadth of his new command—nineteen destroyers—and to being under the command of RAdm S. E. W. Kittelle. On his initial arrival at the destroyer dock, he climbed aboard and paced through the squadron flagship *Delphy.* Taken aback when he entered the destroyer's "small captain's cabin," he promptly declared it "unsatisfactory." Instead, he chose the ship's spacious chartroom for his cabin and had it redecorated with proper fabrics and furniture. When furnished to please him, it was a first-class place. "The chartroom was moved to the captain's emergency cabin—a place with minimal navigation space for two adult men."

Capt Watson was sensitive to his status and his flagship's location at the docks in San Francisco. Hence he arrived at the docks and arranged to have the *Delphy* moored next to RAdm Kitelle's large flagship *Melville.* This made it easy to confer with the admiral, and feasible for him to use the *Melville*'s large wardroom for his squadron meetings.

Aboard his flagship in San Francisco, Capt Watson was a consistent commander. His actions and attitudes were compatible. He gave orders to the division commanders, warmly received the deferential compliance of Capt Morris, disliked the technical questions of Cdr

Pye, and was not pleased with Cdr Roper's frank speech. Watson's general view of his commanders played a major roll in the outcome of the September 8 voyage. Capt Watson believed that orders flowed downward, and he discouraged suggestions or questions that flowed upward. Thus on Saturday he was disinclined to ask for or accept help from Capt Morris, Cdr Calhoun, Cdr Pye, or Cdr Roper.

[Cdr Roper had an admirable command style. His behavior was somewhat brusque, but his staff coped easily with him because he respected their opinions. Roper's navigator, Lt MacNally, was described as "excellent" by VAdm Lockwood. The squadron's officers perceived that Roper's attitude was the reason why he was not promoted to the squadron's recently vacant captain's position, while the deferential Cdr Morris was.]

Capt Watson considered LCdr Hunter ready for promotion, liked Hunter's receptive manner, and thought he was a fine ship's captain. When Watson gave an order, Hunter avoided undue speech, and went to work.

Watson kept his shipboard duties to a minimum on the voyage to San Diego. Nonetheless, he was a shrewd observer, noticed the friction between *Delphy*'s two navigators, and thought it a gentle contest, a match between two professionals. By evening, however, he noted Hunter was outmatching Blodgett by a substantial margin, and it was time for him to play referee and call out, "That's enough." But Watson did not call out, not sensing the serious consequences of that contest.

On this voyage, Capt Watson spent little time on the bridge, and thus was not exposed to the crew's "bridge talk." The importance of such talk is shown by the historian, Capt Schofield, in his book *Destroyers 60 Years:*

> The bridge is the most action-packed place on a destroyer, a place where a squadron commander has a chance to detect the essence of what's happening on a destroyer, as opposed to the limited view available to him when he repeatedly talks to a single subordinate.

> On the bridge a half dozen operations may go on at the same time as vital parts of a tightly coordinated program. Destroyermen—signalman, navigator, messenger, talker, skipper, officer of the deck, helmsman, and quartermaster—may all be seen and heard as they work together, regardless of rank or rating.

Following the disaster Capt Watson was forthright: "The responsibility for the course of the destroyer squadron was mine, a responsibility which I fully realize..." But shortly afterwards, his statement became: "The disaster was due to circumstances beyond our control."

One key question circulated among the squadron's staff at the start of the court of inquiry: "Why did Capt Watson convert a routine endurance run into an attempt to make a record-breaking endurance run?"

On Friday, 27 July 1923, Battle Fleet Pacific was gathered near Seattle for a naval review by President Harding. Capt Watson's Destroyer Squadron 11 was ready, and the squadron's newest destroyer, the *Zeilin*, was scheduled to escort the presidential transport *Henderson.* Everyone was there: flagships, battleship divisions, destroyer squadrons, the tug *Partridge*, and others.

"At 0721 the *Henderson,* accompanied by its Squadron 12 escorts, *Corry* and *Hull,* was steaming on a course 133 deg." Sighted the *Zeilin* close aboard on the starboard bow and crossing the bow. Port rudder hard left and reversed all engines full speed astern. Sounded three blasts on whistle." "At 0752 collided with the *Zeilin* striking her a glancing blow on port side abreast her #2 fire room...."

Capt Watson heard this news with disbelief and embarrassment. He turned to Hunter: "Why did this happen?" The reply was, "The *Zeilin* is sinking and the crew is going overboard."

By September 8, Capt Watson had decided that needed improvement in the squadron's reputation could be earned by making a record-breaking endurance run to San Diego.

In attempting to explain why, when the navigation was clearly confused, Capt Watson gambled, turning eastward when a safe course past San Miguel Island was beckoning, we find that Capt Watson's gamble-to-win decision compares with that made by General John Burgoyne and described in *Patriots, the Men who Started the American Revolution,* by A. J. Langguth.

Capt Watson and Gen Burgoyne were similar in a number of ways. Each leader:

- held a commanding rank in a military hierarchy;
- had a preconceived vision of how their campaign would proceed;
- listened to selected subordinates, but failed to benefit from their opinions;
- had a clear view of future success, and saw his campaign as a challenge that had to be won;
- viewed his activity without seeing reality—piloting difficulties for one, thick mud on the wagon route for the other;
- chose an able and willing officer to assume a specific critical responsibility.

One chose the captain of a squadron flagship. (Thinking he was turning the squadron column eastward into a deep-water channel, he ran into a rocky coast.) The other chose Lieutenant Colonel Baum, the outstanding leader of the Hessian troops. (Trying for a quick and easy capture of the Arsenal at Bennington, VT, he turned his troops eastward—and ran into a wall of revolutionaries.)

When asked what battle action General Burgoyne might take, the American General Gates replied, "Burgoyne is an old gambler. Despair may drive him to risk it all upon one throw." Burgoyne gambled, attacked the Americans at Saratoga, and lost.

Faced with the critical decision to turn east or go west of San Miguel Island, Captain Watson risked it, gambled, turned eastward, and led his squadron directly into the rocky coast at Pt. Pedernales.

LCdr Donald T. Hunter was a high performer as captain of the squadron flagship, and one who looked forward to being a division commander. Capt Watson was confident when he gave Hunter special squadron responsibilities on the trip to San Diego, and Hunter was determined to fulfill those responsibilities.

Ltjg Lawrence Blodgett and Chief Quartermaster Harry D. Cummings talked about Hunter as they departed San Francisco for San Diego. Blodgett began, "I navigated from San Diego to Seattle, inside Puget Sound for the review, and back to San Francisco. Yet I never got one good word from Commander Hunter. Now he tells me, 'I am going to navigate south to San Diego.' Then he reminds me, 'I have a reputation as a destroyer navigator in the North Atlantic during WW I, and 'I was a skilled instructor in navigation at Annapolis.' I already knew that Hunter was a confident, decisive navigator when he worked out of Queenstown, Ireland in WW I, but he surely could have paused a minute and said, 'Good job Larry.' Instead, this morning, Hunter tells me, 'Lieutenant I'm navigating today—you will do the routine.'"

"I'm sorry that happened, Larry," Cummings said. Hunter is one of the best officers I've ever known. He must have a reason for replacing you. Relax. Keep in mind that Hunter spent time hunting subs and returning to port—strenuous, demanding work—in all kinds of weather in the Atlantic, the English Channel, and the North Sea. His business was taking risks and coming home. The word in Queenstown was, Hunter has a homing instinct when headed toward home port."

Blodgett replied, "It's not much of a navigation problem to approach a big port's entrance channel when you know which side of the channel you're approaching. At San Francisco, we came in from the north, and we kept close watch till we saw the traffic pattern and the channel markers. I doubt that getting into Queenstown was much of a group problem. They surely knew which side of the channel was at hand."

Later, Ens Morrow joined the conversation: "On the bridge, Hunter is confident and alert. On deck, he's quick to note every activity, but he tends to be arrogant and avoids simple situations, like chewing the fat with the crew. On the bridge, he's strictly business. His nickname is 'Dolly,' because he can handle heavy assignments and he reminds us of a railroad dolly—a small locomotive. Off the job, Hunter exudes confidence and shows an occasional lighthearted mood and a touch of geniality that suits his slightly round, plump form." Blodgett and Cummings smiled.

On the voyage to Seattle and back to San Francisco, LCdr Hunter was continually cordial toward Chief Cummings. Ltjg Blodgett navigated well on that voyage, and Hunter kept a steady supervisor's attitude. The roles were clear: Hunter was ship commander, Blodgett was executive officer and navigator, and Cummings was chief quartermaster. Navigator Blodgett's performance enhanced Hunter's role as flagship commander. Chief Cummings thought highly of Blodgett, and enjoyed hearing Hunter praise Blodgett's work as executive officer. Nonetheless, the chief sensed that Ltjg Blodgett's role as navigator might have been easier had he graduated from the U. S. Naval Academy.

This was a real plus during and after the embarrassing loss of the squadron's *Zeilin*—the squadron's newest destroyer—just before the presidential review. Hunter, Blodgett, and Cummings worked closely, and that rapport continued during the return voyage southward to San Francisco. Once on the dock at San Francisco, Hunter, Blodgett, and Cummings enjoyed a pleasant, warm week of liberty, but they did little to prepare for the voyage to San Diego, a routine run downwind, through familiar waters to their home port. On Friday, however, the mood changed. Cummings overheard Hunter criticize Blodgett's work as executive officer.

That day, Capt Watson cornered Hunter in the navigation cabin and said: "I'm planning to set a record-breaking time to San Diego, and I'm counting on the two of us to make it happen. That's all for now." Hunter saw a chance to demonstrate his ability, and decided it would be best if he navigated. Accordingly, near the departure time from San Francisco, Hunter took over as the ship's navigator. This produced an unexpected decrease in junior lieutenant Blodgett's navigator status. That change distressed Blodgett and attracted the crew's attention. They wondered why Hunter had made this abrupt demotion, and what he hoped to gain. Blodgett was embarrassed by his loss of status and dignity, and upset when he realized that he had also lost the respect of Chief Cummings.

Hunter's navigational weak spot was his bias against the radio compass. This became a squadron problem when Capt Watson later issued his order prohibiting all ships but the *Delphy* from requesting RC bearings. As the voyage started, Hunter was aware of Watson's impending record-breaking effort, but Hunter was not ready for Watson's special orders, or the quick complications when *Delphy*'s command decided there was no need to share her RC bearings with the other commanders. Hunter's failure to adapt became the trouble as the navigational crisis unfolded.

The ambitious Hunter was determined to make an exceptional showing on this voyage. Yet, all during the afternoon he routinely estimated the ship's DR position each half-hour. By evening he was obsessed with a DR track based only on the estimated line of positions that had started with a morning fix at Pigeon Pt. (Illustration **14**). Hunter lacked vigilance and concern for safety, and failed to see the need for exchanging position estimates with other squadron ships. He was a navigator who was used to working with other navigators, but on this voyage he decided to work alone and rely on capable help from Watson. This did not happen. Thus Hunter found himself in a difficult spot, isolated from the other squadron navigators, and alone with Watson. Now they scrambled to answer the wrong question: when would it be safe to turn the squadron eastward?

After the ship hit the rocks, the injured Blodgett moved to aid a seriously wounded sailor. Hunter moved quickly with Chief Cummings to determine the ship's critical situation, and direct the effort to escape to land.

Hunter describes the heroic roles of twenty-seven crew members in an 8 October 1923 memorandum that he sent to RAdm Kittelle, Commander, Destroyer Squadrons. This remarkable document names the most outstanding crew members, lists and praises their achievements during the rescue, and recommends many for special commendations. The memo shows that Hunter was in charge, was all over the ship, knew what was happening, and was aware of the actions needed to rescue his crew. Cummings was the last sailor, and Hunter the last officer, to leave the ship.

Ltjg Lawrence Blodgett, the youngest in this group, had worked his way up from the enlisted ranks. As executive officer and navigator of the *Delphy* he was competent in his assigned duties, but very much the "junior officer" in the presence of Watson or Hunter. A photograph of Lieutenant Blodgett shows him in a dress-white uniform with striped shoulder boards and chest ribbons, and the firm look of man who has just been promoted.

Blodgett was born in New England, where the tradition of the sea is strong, and he enlisted in the naval reserve in December 1917. He was young, energetic, strong, an avid reader, and a keen observer. Despite having no Naval Academy background, Lawrence adapted quickly to destroyer work, and his wartime service was exemplary. Early on, he showed a talent for mathematics and navigation, steadily worked his way up the ranks, and won a commission in 1918.

Subsequently, he served as an able deck officer and assistant navigator aboard the destroyers *Belknap* and *Chase,* where he earned a reputation as one who learned quickly and kept a keen OOD watch on the bridge. The *Chase*'s executive officer admired the meticulous way Lawrence inspected the magazines and smokeless powder samples. *Belknap*'s navigator was impressed with Lawrence's eye for nautical charts and his enthusiasm for working them.

In February 1920 he qualified as a navigator and was promoted to Lieutenant, junior grade. Ltjg Blodgett joined the *Delphy* in 1920 as navigator, and was soon given the title, and additional duties, of executive officer. His personality fitted his duties, and he easily adapted to the ship's life. He got along well with the crew, who readily accepted assignments from him. Prior to this voyage, the comments about Ltjg Blodgett's navigation ability were complimentary, and it was well known that Ltjg Blodgett and LCdr Donald Hunter enjoyed talking about mathematics.

Blodgett's personality favored clean decisions. He was an effective officer in extracting the ship from a tight mooring array alongside an oiler transport. His exits out of a broadside array were done smoothly, fostered cooperation, and avoided hurt feelings. There was little yelling, horn blowing, bumping, or scraping. On the other hand, the crew noticed Blodgett had little skill in the art of personal nudging and making convincing lawyer-talk. If you had crossed paths with an officer and were looking for another officer to smooth things over, you would have been wise to choose an advocate other than Ltjg Blodgett.

Blodgett successfully navigated the *Delphy* on the trip north from San Diego to Seattle, during the presidential review, and on the return to San Francisco. Chief QM Cummings was Blodgett's friend, and thought he was a good navigator because of his facile understanding of nautical charts and his savvy of the new navigational aid, the radio compass. On the morning of September 8, Blodgett was ready to navigate and win LCdr Hunter's praise, and was shocked when Hunter told him, "I will be the navigator today and you will do the routine duties." Blodgett was dismayed and angry. He felt overwhelmed by the hierarchy. As the day progressed, he chafed under this unfair treatment, and the crew of *Delphy* viewed Blodgett's loss of status and embarrassment with sympathy. "How come?" they asked.

During each watch, Blodgett made pertinent piloting suggestions, which LCdr Hunter rejected. After the *Delphy* missed the fix on Pt. Sur, Blodgett cited the uncertainty of the DR-estimated positions, and suggested they make a special effort to get a fix on the next lighthouse, Piedras Blancas. Hunter said, "Not now. It's too far abeam." Hour by hour, Blodgett became more concerned about the uncertainty of the ship's DR course. He pointed to the water-depth contours on the chart (Illustration **28**), and repeated the advantages of taking depth soundings to confirm the ship was a safe distance offshore. Hunter said, "We're not going to slow down." Capt Watson arrived, and said, "I don't want to slow down, won't do any good, water is too deep." Blodgett was unable to work past these rejections. He thought about arguing the common rule: "Sail the bottom in coastal waters whenever there is doubt about the ship's position." If I say those words, he thought, I'll get a hot rejection.

Ltjg Blodgett's mettle was tested to the extreme that evening. Hunter and Watson talked about changing course, and Blodgett's career crisis developed. He tried to change Hunter's decision or influence Capt Watson about the decision to change course eastward without confirming the ship's position. But Blodgett found out that he could not prevail in a three-way conversation in the confinement of the small navigation cabin, squeezed between two senior officers. Despite his reduced status, Blodgett made a steady, diligent effort to convince Hunter that each RC bearing, intercepted or directed to them, was correct, but Hunter replied unwaveringly: "The bearing is wrong; the bearing is a misreading." So, Blodgett requested they take depth soundings to confirm their distance offshore, but Hunter and Watson denied that soundings were needed or would be meaningful.

Virtual History

Introduction

The changing conditions, the ups and downs that impinged on Squadron 11, started before September 8 and continued long afterward. They warped through the news accounts, the daily conversations between the destroyermen, the court of inquiry, the court martial, national politics, the newspapers, and the historical accounts. Using the analogy of an archaeological dig, something new was occasionally discovered, sometimes underfoot, other times uncovered in the next valley. The newly found stuff was not always a missing bone—it was often an insight into the significance of the bones already on hand. In some cases, errors were made but not detected or acknowledged. Thus it has been impossible in this story to describe all the events, actions, decisions, and apparent facts that appeared. As a result, in the analysis of the disaster, I was impressed with the unnoticed events that might have put light on its virtual history; that is, why the disaster occurred, and the alternatives that were considered, discarded, ignored, or never seen. I was also puzzled by the occurrence of this disaster despite its minimal chance of happening.

A note by Hugh Trevor-Roper: At any given moment in history there are real alternatives ... How can one "*explain* what happened and *why*" if we only looked at what happened and never consider the alternatives ... It is only when we place ourselves before the alternatives of the past ... for a moment, as the men of the time lived, in its still fluid context and among the still unresolved problems, if we see those problems coming upon us ... that we can draw useful lesson from history.

A note by Sir Isaiah Berlin: No one will wish to deny that we do often argue among the best possible courses open to human beings ... and that historians ... do attempt to establish, as well as they are able, what these possibilities are ...

When an historian, in attempting to decide what occurred and why, rejects all the infinity of logically open possibilities, the vast majority of which are obviously absurd, and, like a detective, investigates only those possibilities which have at least some initial plausibility, it is this sense of what is plausible—what men being men could have done or been—that constitutes a sense of coherence within the patterns of life ...

A statement by David McCullough during an interview by Roger

Mudd in *Great Minds of History*: "The hardest thing to convey in writing history is that nothing ever had to happen the way it happened."

Insight

This section discusses alternative actions that the *Delphy* command could have considered, and presents a variety of the author's comments.

Maneuver Required to Get a Fix on Pt. Sur Light. Given the technical necessity of getting a fix on Pt. Sur, it is surprising that the *Delphy*'s command gave no order for a dual attempt. Option one could have been a message: "*Delphy* to *Lee*, attention Capt Morris. The visibility observations from the *Farragut*, *Kennedy,* and *Somers* indicate that a sharp pair of observers on your easternmost ship would have a good chance to see the Pt. Sur Light, and your navigator would be able to get a fix on that light. Request you make your best effort to get a fix." This option indicates the possibility of angling the easternmost ship toward the coast.

Option two could have been a message: "*Delphy* to *Kennedy*, Cdr Roper, Division 32 C. Request you take steps necessary for *Kennedy* to get a fix on the Pt. Sur Light, and report that fix to *Delphy*" (Illustrations **3, 11, 15.**)

Capt Morris Was an Excellent Division Commander. He was not yet, however, Watson's active deputy squadron commander. Capt Morris would have been encouraged by the above message to *S. P. Lee* asking for assistance in sighting Pt. Sur. Such an event could have moved him to become an active deputy. Later, when he knew his division was making less than 20 knots, he could have challenged Capt Watson's decision that the squadron's speed-made-good was 21 knots, an error that led to the turn-eastward decision. As it happened, Morris did not challenge the 21-knot decision. As the OOD put it, challenging Capt Watson was a losing bet.

Near 9 P. M., Capt Morris Knew That His Ship, *S. P. Lee*, Was About to Turn Eastward. It was *Lee*'s OOD, however, who saw *Delphy*'s turning point in its wake, signaled the *Lee*'s turn left, and alerted the *Young*, on its stern, with two long blasts of the ship's whistle. It was now critical for Morris to pass that signal down the column line, but he failed to do so. The *Lee* maneuvered, slewed hard to port, turned, and backed full. This saved the *Delphy*'s stern from being rammed by the *Lee,* and allowed *Lee*'s starboard side to hit the rocks at 8 knots. (The wrecked ships are shown in Illustration **17**; *Lee* and *Nicholas* are shown in Illustration **2**.)

Hunter Finds RC Problems Everywhere. Common sense was missing, however, when LCdr Hunter got upset at 2 P. M. while he was looking at two initial radio compass misreadings. These misreadings were due to *Delphy*'s weak source signal, and its location near the limit of the RC instrument's range. Hence, being upset with this misreading was an undue reaction. A normal reaction by the nearby USS *Corry* shows it held its course and within fifteen minutes had another set of satisfactory bearings in hand, and their course confirmed.

Hunter's Concern with RC Reliability Continued. For hours he would not make a request; then he would claim that the bearings were unreliable and that an excess of RC traffic prevented him from getting the bearings he wanted. The RC record (Appendix II) shows that this claim was without merit, as U. S. Navy and commercial ships got bearings as requested. The seagoing tug USS *Partridge*, under the command of Chief Boatswain J. A. Pierce, made frequent requests for RC bearings. He countermarched to Pt. Arguello and, at 10:00 P. M., reported, "Can hear Arguello sirens" (Illustration **13**).

Watson and His Friend Were Comfortable as the *Delphy* Steamed South. Watson had little contact with his division commanders, and they didn't contact him. Squadron 11 was headed for one of the great naval gambles of history. Many of history's great ocean ventures have entailed gambling with the fate of men and ships; some of those ventures failed despite the best of skill and effort. Squadron 11's best skill and effort, however, were not to be seen until after dark, in the fog, in the sea, and on the rocks.

Unexpected, Undetected Event. The *Delphy*'s late-afternoon locations were influenced by the onshore summer airflow that blew inland over the coastal lowlands. This, along with bad steering, moved *Delphy* into the shoal waters north of Pt. Arguello, and inside the 50-fathom depth contour shown in Illustration **28**.

Extenuating Circumstances. In February 2001, a group of civilians came aboard the submarine USS *Greenville* in Oahu for an offshore tour. Unfortunately, the tour had serious consequences, as the submerged submarine surfaced rapidly, striking and sinking a large Japanese fishing vessel.

The situation of Mr. Dooman, the civilian diplomat on the *Delphy*, was different. He was a quiet guest with valuable information to convey, yet he harmed the *Delphy*'s command all day and into the night, keeping Capt Watson's attention off the bridge and out of the navigation cabin. The circumstances of Dooman's trip indicate that it never should have happened at sea—it should have been undertaken a week later, on land.

Many Chief Executives Understand Their Strengths and Weaknesses. They choose and manage subordinates in a way that complements their own abilities. On this trip, Watson found it difficult to use the marvelous support available from his division commanders, but surprisingly, he found it easy to turn over the squadron's navigation to LCdr Hunter. As the CQM said, "Hunter will be fine, because Capt Watson will be nearby to overlook the operation without being burdened with detail." But something went wrong with this arrangement at the start, and something was wrong at the end, when Watson realized that Hunter was desperately trying to confirm the *Delphy*'s

DR-estimated position. Imagine, the captain and his navigator, a lieutenant commander, with a squadron of talent under command, did not know the ship's location, and at 8:35 P.M. were trying to calculate their most likely position, the position that would justify their decision to turn eastward in 25 minutes!

Much Has Been Written about the Historical Dangers of the Honda Area. The unseen underwater reefs of the shoal waters off the Lompoc coast are a hazard to marine traffic, especially during foggy or stormy conditions. On this summer evening in 1923, the Honda was no place for seagoing vessels plying its shoal waters after dark and in the fog. But the writings that blame the "Evil Jinns" and the "earthquakes off Japan" for this catastrophe are far removed from what actually caused the destroyer disaster that evening.

Trouble with the Radio Compass! In Squadron 11 there was no problem with the radio compass. There was, however, D. T. Hunter's serious problem with the radio compass, which the British invented during WW I, and which was welcomed in 1921 on its West Coast arrival at Pt. Arguello as an aid to navigate ships safely past Pt. Arguello and Pt. Conception. Squadron 11's problem was, as one navigator put it, "Hunter needs to be forced to train past his radio compass problem before he loses his ship." Instead, "Hunter was allowed to get away with instant anger whenever an RC was suspect." At the critical juncture on September 8, he was allowed to declare, without a technical reason, "This bearing is a misreading. Send me a reciprocal."

Coordination and Cooperation. Capt Watson minimized the ability of the division navigators to contribute to the success of the voyage and to safeguard their ships. Watson's plan that everyone just follow the *Delphy* discouraged cooperation among the squadron commanders and the squadron's excellent array of navigators.

Naval history shows that coordination is vital. Early in WW II, the U.S. Navy was faced with an aggressive U-boat campaign against

American shipping off the southeast coast of the United States. The U.S. suffered a great loss of seamen and tonnage in the first year and a half, and the U.S. Navy sank fewer than 40 U-boats. At the end of that period, the U.S. Navy's 10th Fleet launched a persistent and coordinated operation aimed at sinking U-boats. With that effort, the defense statistics improved, as about 80 U-boats were sunk in a half-year span.

Risk vs. Uncertainty. At 8:30 P.M. LCdr Hunter and Capt Watson did not know where they were. They had no way to meaningfully estimate the probability of success in turning eastward from their uncertain position. They did have a safe route west of San Miguel Island. They had no navigational foundation for making any other route choice. They had no basis for estimating the probability of success or failure in gambling and turning eastward from an uncertain position, so they gambled, and turned eastward (Illustration **28**).

Drinking and Drunkenness. Drinking was a suspected cause of error in Squadron 11. Capt Watson said, "There is no drinking on a destroyer. The ship is too small and everyone would quickly know if drinking occurred. Everyone is in close association, and one cannot conceal liquor from the others. Liquor was not on board any ship of Squadron 11." Nonetheless, something was awry with the Dooman-Watson afternoon visit.

Salvagers found the silver coin lost by the captain's guest, but no mention of the guest or his silver appears in the official record. Word was, however, "Mr. Dooman is worried about being called as a Watson defense witness in the court martial, because he was with the captain in his cabin when the *Delphy* struck the rocks."

The Great Maritime Wrecks of History. Studies of the great maritime losses of history indicate that there is a limit on our ability to fully understand why those seven destroyers went aground. To this day, for example, we do not fully understand the human fallibility that caused two of the great maritime wrecks of history: the loss of 1,500 people aboard the *Titanic* and the loss of 1,200 aboard the *Lusitania*. We still cannot answer all the navigation questions.

Missed Opportunities. Squadron 11's communications on the fateful day were cluttered. A typical view on the bridge was that the radio operators had to work at not talking to each other, and the general result was stifling.

Risk Compensation. This psychological phenomenon indicates that, when a given behavior now seems less risky than it did before, people will compensate by doing it in a riskier fashion. Hence, improve the highway and the safety of the average car, and people will drive faster.

In Squadron 11, it is possible that the advent of the radio compass led to a substantial increase in the squadron's confidence in their leader's decision-making ability, but did not actually have that effect on the leader. It could be part of the reason why two divisions followed the *Delphy*'s blind turn eastward.

Safety vs. Schedule. The voyage of Destroyer Squadrons 11 and 12 on this day off the California coast was all about "the priorities each squadron gave to safety and schedule." In Squadron 11, the safety priority was low and the speed-schedule priority was high. In Squadron 12, the safety priority was high, and the speed-schedule priority was low.

Chapter 9

Failure of the Destroyer Squadron 11 Command

Piloting is navigation based on frequent positions determined by reference to known geographical points, such as lighthouses, landmarks, and known maritime marks.

—Lt R. F. MacNally, USS *Kennedy*

Introduction

The priorities aboard USS *Delphy*, flagship of Destroyer Squadron 11, were clear on the day before the squadron's endurance run to San Diego. Capt Watson was commander of Destroyer Squadron 11. LCdr Hunter was the captain and Ltjg Blodgett was the navigator-executive officer. By the day of departure, however, additional new priorities were in place. Capt Watson had arranged to discuss the programs of the Japanese Navy with his guest, the diplomat, Mr. Dooman. Yet, the capable Capt Watson was confident he could juggle both priorities. LCdr Hunter's priorities now required he act as ship's navigator. Yet, the capable LCdr Hunter was confident he could juggle both priorities.

As the voyage took place, Capt Watson picked up another priority squadron responsibility as he made multiple decisions without consulting with or advising his division and ship commanders. Likewise LCdr Hunter's picked up another priority squadron responsibility as he made decision after decision without considering the views of the excellent navigators on the *Young* and *Kennedy*, and without seriously considering the views of his former navigator, Ltjg Lawrence Blodgett. This arrangement kept Capt Watson off the bridge, and later led him to wrongly conclude, "all's right with the squadrons's navigation." This arrangement also kept LCdr Hunter from coordinating with other squadron navigators, and later led him to wrongfully conclude that his ship was eight miles offshore, when in fact it was in shoal waters.

The Pre-voyage Conference

Capt Watson held the conference on the day before departure. He welcomed the division commanders, ship commanders, and LCdr Donald (the squadron's engineering officer), LCdr Lewis (the squadron's gunnery officer), and Lt Wild (the squadron's communications officer).

Holding a sheaf of papers in his hand, Capt Watson announced,

"This is RAdm Kittelle's order to test our cruising turbines," and passed a copy to each officer. "I will form the squadron off the San Francisco Lightship at 8:30 A.M. Saturday, on a southerly course in line of divisions. You will conduct tactical maneuvers and short-range battle practice. Destroyer Squadron 12 will proceed independently. The only part of the operation that may prove difficult is the matter of the standard speed specified. I am concerned because of the recent engineering casualties the squadron has suffered. I have high hopes for an excellent engineering record on this endurance test, and I now introduce our squadron's engineering officer."

LCdr Donald spoke: "I'm glad that the fuel and speed restrictions imposed for reasons of economy have been relaxed, and we can look forward to a high speed exercise that will closely simulate wartime conditions. The standard speed of 20 knots will crowd the ship's cruising turbines to the limit and, although the order for this endurance run has come without warning, it leaves little room for excuses. Keep in mind that we are no worse off than Squadron 12. If they can make the good run they say they will, we can make a better one. If we make good scores on this run, and keep pitching the rest of the year, I expect to see a big red "E" for excellence in engineering blossom on one of our smokestacks..."

Cdr Pye asked, "What will be our course after we clear Pt. Conception?" (Illustrations **3**, **10, 12** and **28**). "Will we go to the west of San Miguel Island or turn eastward into the Santa Barbara Chanel?" Capt Watson said, "I'll get back to you about that matter at a later date."

The conference ended. Capt Watson and the squadron staff officers left the wardroom. The remaining senior officers were annoyed at the lack of a discussion after the prepared talk, and the lack of any word about the radio schedule for contacting the *Delphy*. Cdr Roper was poised to ask what was the plan if they had engine problems and couldn't maintain the standard speed. Cdr Calhoun wanted to know the plan for coordinating the work of the flagship navigator and the division navigators. The senior-officer ship commanders were annoyed because they were accustomed to having a chance to speak. Now they realized that all of the important decisions had been made before the meeting started.

Cdr Herbert Roesch and Cdr Walter Seed left the meeting together. Seed said, "I don't feel comfortable when all of us gather in the *Melville*'s spacious wardroom, and we say nothing. I think something's up. Our captain is planning something special." Roesch replied, "All I feel is that Watson's ready to give orders, and I'm ready to request radio compass bearings."

The voyage started as planned. Watson waited till they passed Pigeon Pt., and then he found Hunter in the *Delphy*'s little navigation cabin. Watson said, "Listen, I want a smooth column-formation run to San Diego, and I don't want any commander ruining the endurance run for some dumb reason. So *Delphy* will refrain from broadcasting its estimated positions, and we will avoid contacting the ship commanders before we send our 8 P.M. position to RAdm Kittelle. After we clear Pt. Arguello, I will pick the next course. We will change to that course, and everyone will follow us." This was Capt Watson's announcement to his flagship commander of his intent to make a record-breaking endurance run without advice from his extraordinarily talented staff, the very officers who could make that endurance run a success.

Captain Watson's Special Orders

Saturday, September 8, 1923 was a typical late-summer day, and a safe day for the San Francisco-San Diego voyage. The U.S. Battle Fleet steamed southward. As Squadron 11 prepared to depart, Capt Watson reminded LCdr Hunter, "I want the squadron to make a superior showing on this test." After noon, Watson issued special orders to ensure that this would happen. They were: "The ships will go 20 knots, *Delphy* will navigate for the squadron, the division and ship commanders will not request RC (radio compass) bearings."

Watson's intent in issuing these orders was to ensure that the squadron would set a record, but the orders were flawed. They did not favor success because they came without an exchange of ship positions between *Delphy* and its ship commanders. They did not favor success because they came without: cooperation between the *Delphy*'s two navigators, help from the division commanders, and an understanding of the grave risk in changing course from an uncertain position, and an understanding of the risk in changing course without giving advance notice to the squadron.

These unfavorable conditions show Capt Watson's willingness to accept danger, his confidence of key support from his deputy, Capt Morris, and his confidence in an outstanding piece of navigation by LCdr Hunter. As the day developed, however, Watson would not receive the support he expected. Capt Morris would have an inkling that the evening course change would not be routine, but he would do nothing to clarify that routine.

Morris' division ship, *S. P. Lee,* would get the command's turn-eastward signal at the last moment, but Capt Morris would not send that signal down the line. The *Lee*'s helmsman would know that the ship in front of him had actually turned only when he saw the *Delphy*'s turning wake. The *Lee*'s bridge was then consumed with desperate steering and engine control to avoid ramming *Delphy*'s stern, getting past the *Delphy,* and maneuvering the *Lee* so as to crash its starboard side into the rocks.

Afternoon and Evening Aboard the *Delphy*

The first goal of the afternoon was to get a position fix on the Pt. Sur Light. Chief Cummings was on deck scanning for the escarpments that mark the start of the Pt. Sur coastline (Illustrations **3**, **11**, **14**). It was 2 P.M., and the OOD logged the ship's course, speed, and weather observations. The chief put his head into the navigation cabin and said, "It's a cool summer day, visibility three to four miles in fog, and a moderate northwest wind."

It was 2:30 P.M. and the OOD called out, "Propeller revolutions 222, magnetic compass heading 150 degrees." Navigator Hunter used these speed and direction data to estimate the distance *Delphy* had traveled during the last half hour, and he dead reckoned the ship forward to its DR-estimated 2:30 P.M. position. He told Blodgett, to plot and label that position on the chart (Illustration **3**), continue the DR until given new instructions, and alert the deck to notify them immediately if they spotted the Pt. Sur Light. Blodgett passed the word to Cummings who was steadily scanning the coast. Cummings soon reported, "I have not been able to recognize the escarpments that mark the start of the Sur coastline. I've not seen the Sur Light or heard its horns" (Illustrations **11** and **15**). Cummings returned to deck. Blodgett reported to Hunter, "We can't see Pt. Sur. I suggest we send message to *S. P. Lee*, who is closer to the coast—*Delphy* is seaward and cannot get a fix on Pt. Sur Light. Request you get your shoreward ship to scan the coast for the Light, and report to us at once." But Hunter took no action, because he believed that action would cause an unnecessary delay.

After a while, the downcast Blodgett joined Cummings on deck. "We just threw away our chance to get a fix and confirm our DR. We have barnacle growth on our bottom, we're not making 20 knots over the bottom. We're unduly confident in our direction over the bottom. I should have had the gyrocompass fixed when we were in San Francisco." Cummings looked at Blodgett. "I'm sorry we couldn't identify Pt. Sur. I've put another set of eyeballs on deck lookout, and I'll stay on deck and scan for the Piedras Blancas Light. Maybe we'll be lucky."

Blodgett continued, "We muffed it. Capt Watson should have ordered the *Lee*'s landward destroyer to make a serious effort to get a fix on Pt. Sur."

Later, Blodgett briefed Hunter on the best chance for the *Delphy* to get a fix on the Piedras Blancas Light. "You know, that light will be even farther away from us than Pt. Sur. But it's worth a try, because it sits on the seaward end of a promontory just north of San Simeon.

Our best bet is to put one ship on a course to close on the coast, until they get a fix." Cummings added, "Blancas is generally below the stratus deck at mid-afternoon, so I can frequently see it even when Pt. Sur is not visible." LCdr Hunter's response was simple: "There's a lot of coastline left. The afternoon visibility should improve. Keep an extra observer on deck. Look for something you can recognize."

Capt Watson was visiting with Mr. Dooman. It was an hour later when Capt Watson and LCdr Hunter met. Hunter said, "I think junior Blodgett is overly concerned with our routine navigation." Watson showed no interest in the subject, and returned to his quarters. Hunter talked to Chief Cummings. The chief said, "Blodgett's spent San Francisco time with Lt MacNally of the *Kennedy*. I think it would be worthwhile to have Blodgett ask MacNally for his latest estimated position."

Hunter remained quiet. Cummings returned to the deck and scanned the coast for a piece of terrain he could recognize. The extra eyeballs said, "Look for the Nipomo Dunes."

Capt Watson paid a short visit to the cabin during the late afternoon, and he noted that Hunter had confidence in the extended sequence of DR estimated positions. He noted Ltjg Blodgett was quiet and hesitant. He passed through the bridge, but he spent little time listening to the bridge talk and observing the helms steering problems. Everything seemed shipshape in the navigation cabin, and Capt Watson gave Hunter's DR line of estimated positions a vote of confidence, a vote Hunter mistook for a vote of technical approval. Approval from his captain, a man who had once been an excellent navigator, meant everything to LCdr Hunter, and he relied on that approval. Unfortunately, Watson was not navigating, and his vote was miles away from a technical approval.

As evening approached, neither Watson nor Hunter sensed the increasing danger. Instead, each went his own way. Watson visited with Mr. Dooman, and Hunter focused on achieving the performance schedule his captain wanted. Blodgett spoke to Cummings: "I've lost my clout. We are going DR all the way. I have no confidence in our propeller-count speed." Cummings was tired, and all he said was, "No more moaning." But Blodgett continued, "Did you recognize anything in the Dunes?" Cummings replied, "No, we saw lots of sand, but nothing specific I could recognize. Don't fuss, Hunter is a fine officer."

The casual afternoon ended when *Delphy* received three northwest RC bearings in a row between 6 and 7 P.M. Blodgett's reaction was swift: "We are heading straight toward Pt. Arguello. We need to verify our distance from shore. We need to take depth soundings."

Not impressed, Hunter said no and departed. Blodgett went to Cummings and gave him an earful: "Talking to Hunter is talking to a pair of deaf ears. I don't think he even remembers we started this DR line of positions at 11:30 A.M. with a fix on Pigeon Pt." The chief, looking skyward, replied, "Larry, that's enough griping. Tend to business."

The Isolated *Delphy* Command

The views of the *Delphy*'s officers and crew, signaled the fact that three officers aboard the Squadron 11 flagship, the *Delphy* command, were making their own way without contacting the rest the squadron. Not contacting the other navigators and commanders was a classic error.

LCdr Donald, the squadron's engineering officer, had convinced everyone that the trip to San Diego would be an important engineering test, so the word back to the ships was, "It will be a big day for the engineers." When Capt Watson's special orders were received, however, the senior commanders realized that Capt Watson had other plans. But those commanders received no hints from the *Delphy*'s leaders and had a tough time figuring out just what Watson's plan entailed.

They did not know that LCdr Hunter had taken over as *Delphy*'s navigator and had assigned his regular navigator to miscellaneous routine duty before the ship had left San Francisco. They did not know of the friction between the two men, and the junior officer had no spark to fight with the ship's commander. Hence it was now ordained that Hunter would navigate *Delphy* and it would lead the way.

Capt Watson's special orders took hold quickly, and Watson was soon *the* Squadron 11 decision maker, and LCdr Hunter was *the* Squadron 11 navigator. This arrangement was marked by a lack of communication within the squadron, and a set of restrictions on the freedom of the ship commanders. This put the division and ship commanders in a tenuous situation, and they became dependent on Capt Watson to give them the navigational information they needed to safeguard their ships. The issue became a serious problem when Watson failed to send his RC bearings or his estimated positions to any ship, and the ships' commanders failed to insist on receiving the information they needed, or take independent action.

The squadron commanders did not press Capt Watson, or take individual action because they did not suspect that something special needed doing. Thus they failed to ask *Delphy*: "What is your estimated time for clearing Pt. Conception? What is your intended course?" They failed to request permission to obtain an RC bearing or request an RC bearing of their own—as the *Stoddert*—or "Request you send me your 8 P.M. estimated position." Most ships did not use their own direction finders, or intercept some of the RC bearings to *Delphy* as did the *Nicholas.*

Despite this poor situation, awareness was high as the squadron moved southward. Each commander sensed a problem, because he did not know the spread between his estimated position and the *Delphy*'s. The few commanders who intercepted *Delphy*'s broadcast of its 8 P.M. DR-estimated position were surprised that their estimated position was quite different from *Delphy*'s. Nonetheless, they did not contact *Delphy*. They persisted in believing: "The squadron flagship's estimated position is superior to ours. It is based on navigational data we do not have."

Most of the ship commanders were aware of danger ahead, yet only a few saw a danger above the threshold required for them to take independent action to safeguard their ships. The *Nicholas,* commanded by LCdr Herbert Roesch, was an exception. Its radioman intercepted three of *Delphy*'s RC bearings: (326 deg at 2:26 P.M.), (320 deg at 6:40 P.M.), and (168 deg at 8:35 P.M.). The bridge of the *Nicholas* was shaken when it received that 168-deg bearing, which indicated that the *Delphy* was to the south of Pt. Arguello—an impossible location according to their nautical chart. But LCdr Roesch, on *Nicholas,* had three sharp commanders ahead of him in the column: Cdr Toaz on the *S. P. Lee,* Cdr Calhoun on the *Young,* and Cdr Davis on the *Woodbury,* so he did not voice his concerns to *Delphy.*

Several commanders were aware of a few clues that indicated the squadron's predicament, but they had difficulty in recognizing its genuine extent, and mustering the spirit required to challenge the highly respected squadron leader. Today this seems surprising, considering the array of talented and experienced captains, commanders, lieutenant commanders, and excellent navigators involved.

The *Delphy* had put a mild traditional face on a project that required an all-out squadron attempt. Hence *Delphy* was proceeding in ignorance of the above concerns. Capt Watson made the decisions, but was out of touch with his squadron's talent and the bridge of the *Delphy,* so he does not sense the squadron's operating difficulties nor feel the pressing need for him to verify Hunter's DR navigation. Capt Watson had confidence in LCdr Don Hunter's navigation, because Watson was not navigating and was not duplicating Hunter's navigation. His mind was fixed on an extraordinary and speedy test run to San Diego.

In the evening world around the *Delphy,* its navigation problem was evident in the lack of a position fix after 11:30 A.M.; the helmsman's steering difficulty; the three consecutive 320-deg RC bearings between 6 and 7 P.M. (indicating the ship was closing on the coast); the afternoon occurrence of summer onshore coastal winds, and the lack of a confirmed distance offshore. All these signs warranted, but did not demand, an exchange of estimated ship positions between LCdr Hunter on the *Delphy,* Cdr Calhoun on *S. P. Lee,* Cdr

Pye on *Farragut,* and Cdr Roper on *Kennedy*—but no such exchange occurred.

Capt Watson's attempt to set a record-breaking endurance run was motivated by opportunism and his misconception about the ease with which that run could be achieved. As the day ended, however, a crisis developed in the small navigation cabin, from which there was no downward, outward, or upward communication. Thus, the *Delphy* command proceeded, time and again, to act on false premises with consequences they could not foresee and from which they could not escape.

One by one, Commanders Calhoun, Pye, and Roper concluded, "*Delphy* knows its position because it is the only ship with all the navigational information. Its command is blocking the information flow, and we will get no hint of the next course until Watson chooses to tell us." Hence *Delphy* never learned that Cdr Roper's position was six miles closer to the coast than *Delphy*'s. Likewise, *Delphy* never got Cdr Calhoun's vital news that the *S. P. Lee*'s position was seven miles to the north of *Delphy*. Until the *Delphy* actually turned eastward, the squadron's ship commanders believed that *Delphy* would alert them as soon as they verified their estimated position and decided to change course.

The above events had a serious impact on Ltjg Blodgett, the displaced junior navigator, who cornered CQM Cummings on the forward deck and unburdened himself: "My recommendations turn into suggestions and disappear. If Hunter is at odds with my view, he just says no. If Watson is present when I recommend some action, Hunter gives me his quiet veto; he says nothing, and Watson avoids the question. The water is always 'too deep' when I ask for a depth sounding, and they only talk to each other about our next course. Hunter is still set on dead reckoning from that single fix we got before noon. We have isolated ourselves from the squadron and we never exchange our estimated position with anyone."

"Calm down, Larry," said Cummings. "They have their reasons, and Hunter will soon take care of the mess."

After Hunter sent his estimated 8 P.M. position to the admiral, he forgot to devote the next hour to an overriding concern for safety. He lost sight of the crucial question of his true location. He needed support from the squadron commanders, but he never asked for it, and they never offered. At that moment Squadron 11's future was up to the good judgment of the its entire command—every division commander, every ship commander, and every navigator.

Notwithstanding all this, Capt Edward Watson chose to rely solely on his chosen navigator, LCdr Donald Hunter, a man who did not understand that his RC bearings might be inaccurate for precision navigation, yet still be correct for determining the ship's passage of Pt. Arguello. [Part of Hunter's problem with the radio compass had merit—it was not on his ship, nor was it under his control.] But his critical, solitary, and late decision to assume an ordered reciprocal of an RC bearing was a clear-cut mistake.

LCdr Hunter Fails to Delay the Turn Eastward

At 8:59 P.M. ship commander and navigator LCdr Hunter was standing on the *Delphy*'s bridge, 8:39 and 8:58 P.M. RC bearings in his hand. They and three earlier bearings all indicated that *Delphy* was north of Pt. Arguello. The go-it-alone Capt Watson had left the bridge. There was neither OOD, nor navigator, nor helmsman, nor chief quartermaster who could give the order to turn eastward at 9 P.M. It was all up to Don T. Hunter, and he had doubts. His hopes for a southerly RC bearing were gone, and he spoke to Ens Morrow. "We have two bearings to justify delaying the turn eastward. We have a way out of this turn versus no-turn dilemma."

Hunter was ready to say. "Maintain course. Call Capt Watson to come to the bridge." But Hunter did not say anything.

Chapter 10

Dead Reckoning All the Way

One of the most action-packed places on any ship at sea is the bridge of a destroyer. Here, half a dozen operations may be going on at once, all of them parts of a tightly coordinated program. Signalman, navigator, talker, skipper—all destroyermen, regardless of rank or rating—must work as a team to meet the high performance standards set by the destroyer force as a whole.

—Capt William G. Schofield, USNR

Retrospect

Destroyer Squadron 11 had a group of ship captains who were also excellent navigators. This group included LCdr D. T. Hunter of the *Delphy,* Cdr William Calhoun of the *Young*, and Cdr L. P. Davis of the *Woodbury*. During gunnery practice, Cdr Davis doubled as gunnery officer, and when the trip to San Diego started, he had lent a hand to his executive and engineering officer. Cdr Davis was also his own navigator. Cdr Calhoun was an excellent navigator, and a commander who worked closely with his executive and navigator, Lt Eugene Herzinger. He realized that Cdr Calhoun was an unusual officer with battleship and submarine experience, and he was impressed when Cdr Calhoun said, "I lack experience in boats."

LCdr Hunter was an experienced navigator, a former navigation instructor at Annapolis, and an associate of Davis and Calhoun. Hunter, however, was the only one of this threesome who had problems with the radio compass, and the only one who believed in long-distance navigation by dead reckoning alone.

On this voyage, Hunter dead reckoned one position after another without concern about the reliability of the ship's compass heading and speed. This situation gradually worsened, because Hunter could not confirm the ship's indicated direction, as the gyrocompass was not working. He could not confirm the ship's indicated speed because he had no taffrail log to check the apparent speed determined by counting the ship's hourly propeller revolutions.

The situation that fostered *Delphy*'s day of navigational error was created in San Francisco when Hunter took over the regular navigator's position held by Ltjg Blodgett. Overall, it would have been wiser for Hunter to oversee Blodgett's work than to take his place.

Having Blodgett doing navigation routine would have encouraged Hunter to focus on special measures to ensure a fix on Pt. Sur, and to consistently compare *Delphy*'s DR-estimated position with the estimates of division flagships *S. P. Lee, Farragut,* and *Kennedy.* As the

Delphy moved south, Hunter made a major error: he assumed that Chief Cummings would be able to see and recognize the change in shoreline profile just north of Pt. Sur, when his line of sight would be perpendicular to the rocky coast. He also assumed that seeing that Sur coast profile would alert Cummings to recognize Pt. Sur itself (Illustration **15**), but when the fix on Pt. Sur was missed, Hunter should have put Blodgett to work. After all, the goal was to win the endurance run, not argue with the young Ltjg Blodgett, so why didn't Hunter let Blodgett use the RC and make a stab at a fix on Pt. Piedras Blancas, the next light to the south?

The answer lies in the original command decision to make a record-breaking endurance run and not slow down for any "dumb" reason. Thus, no plan was ever made for a safety measure, such as talking to another navigator. Instead, every thirty minutes, Hunter believed the latest shaky DR position estimate and remained oblivious of the dangerous combination easing *Delphy* into shoal waters: bad steering and afternoon onshore winds blowing over the coastal lowlands. He may have believed these factors were unimportant, but even so, it is still difficult to understand his hour-by-hour belief in *Delphy*'s estimated DR line of positions.

Capt Watson came by the navigation cabin, saw no need to be on the bridge in mid-afternoon, and departed. Hunter's mind was at ease. He was reasonably confident that the distance of eight miles offshore estimated by *Delphy*'s DR line of positions was correct, and he was very confident that the ship's plotted position on the line of positions was farther southeastward than shown in Illustration **28**.

To increase their chance of seeing the Pt. Piedras Blancas Light, Ltjg Blodgett suggested they get closer to the coast by angling toward it. He was unable to sell this opportunity to Hunter, however, because the maneuver would add extra distance. Hence *Delphy* maintained a heading of 150 deg true. CQM Cummings was diligent, and kept an extra observer on deck, but no special action was taken; no one went up to the crow's nest, and no one compared the *Delphy*'s position with that of another ship. CQM Cummings reported, "The coast is too distant, and it's hard to recognize anything." LCdr Hunter said, "The offshore distance of *Delphy*'s DR line of positions is correct. We may be moving southeastward faster than estimated."

Both conclusions were wrong.

Given Capt Watson's experience and leadership, his eminent family background, and his father's high hopes, it is not surprising that Watson decided to lead Destroyer Squadron 11 on a record-breaking endurance run. What is shocking, however, is the confused manner in which this noble attempt was made. It is about a captain confusing the power he held, by virtue of four gold stripes on his sleeves, with the power of the extraordinarily skilled men under his command.

Piloting Destroyers

A basic problem in navigating a 1923 destroyer was its long narrow construction and its tendency to roll and pitch. A look at the USS *Sumner* (Illustration **31)** helps picture this class of four-stackers: 1,200 tons of steel, 310 feet long at its waterline and 31 feet wide at its center, with a draft of 9 feet. Its complement was 122 men, and its designed SHP was 26,500, which when delivered to its two 9-foot diameter propellers rotating at more than 400 revolutions per hour could produce a speed over 30 knots. On this September day with brisk northwest and west-northwest winds, it was an ordeal to steer the *Delphy* southward. The OOD's steady call to the helmsman was "Mind your rudder."

Coastal navigation in the open ocean can be a relaxed process, but Squadron 11's coastal navigating skirted shoal waters. Since *Delphy* failed to get even one fix on a known geographical point, its situation by late afternoon was in question: as the OOD put it, "We don't know our location." Blodgett told Cummings, "Our confidence in our estimated position is decreasing from hour to hour." Cummings replied, "Say something useful."

Blodgett said, "Don Hunter has lost confidence in the RC bearings from the U.S. Navy Radio Compass Station." Cummings sounded dissatisfied. "Haven't you got a recommendation?"

Blodgett belted out his reply, "Hunter needs to call Commander Calhoun. Ask him to get his signal flags ready." But Hunter would not talk to Cdr Calhoun, nor would he allow junior navigator Blodgett to talk to Lt MacNally the "excellent navigator" on the *Kennedy.*

USS *McDermut*'s Success; USS *Delphy*'s Folly

Squadron 12 *McDermut*'s successful passage of Pt. Arguello is shown in Illustration **12**. The ship's passage of Pt. Arguello, clearing of Pt. Conception, and Capt Tomb's excellent judgment are confirmed by the entries in the ship's deck log, which also shows that *McDermut* slowed to 10 knots at one time, apparently to take a sounding. The RC bearings backed from (305 deg at 9:31 P.M.) to (240 deg at 10: 10 P.M.), and the navigator reported, "We are abeam Pt. Conception, and it is safe to turn into the Santa Barbara Channel."

Squadron 11 USS *Delphy*'s folly is shown on the map in Illustration **28**. This map is based on available data other than the ship's deck log, which was "lost." The map shows the 8, 8:30 and 9 P.M. DR-estimated line of positions. As shown in Illustration **28**, *Delphy*'s actual 9 P.M. position was just west of Pt. Pedernales, on the 320-deg RC bearing line from the RC station. On the other hand, the *Delphy*'s DR-estimated position is south-southwest of Pt. Arguello. LCdr Hunter was confident that his line of positions was accurate and that he was eight miles west of Pt. Arguello. He is obsessed, however, with *Delphy*'s exact place on that line. Hunter's estimates are wrong; he is practically on the coast, a few miles northwest of Pt. Arguello. He has blanked out serious question about the DR-estimated positions shown in Illustration **28,** and his judgment near 9 P.M. is "It is safe to turn eastward into the Santa Barbara Channel." At 8:35 P.M. Junior Navigator Blodgett pleads for a depth sounding. Hunter denies that request. Blodgett says, "I think we are landward of the 50-fathom depth contour (Illustration **28**). We're in shoal waters."

Watson and Hunter reply, "Not necessary. Water too deep. Sounding will just slow us down."

[Historical note: The pirate Blackbeard used hand soundings to save his ship from the British Navy in 1718. The soundings allowed him to navigate through the narrow inlets between the barrier islands off the coast of North Carolina.]

The Last Sixty-six Minutes

Ens Morrow came on the *Delphy*'s bridge as Officer of the Deck at 8 P.M. He logged, "It's dark, foggy, and the forward visibility is unknown. Looking over our stern, I can see the lights of the third ship in the column." About ten minutes later the radioman reported having intercepted an RC bearing sent to Cdr Roper's division. Morrow figured this would be the first in an important series, so he logged it with number, bearing, time, and addressee (#1, 326 deg at 8:11 P.M., addressed to *Stoddert*). The OOD called Hunter immediately and gave him the intercepted RC bearing. Hunter replied, "It's unlikely the *Stoddert* made this request on its own. The navigator on the *Kennedy* probably flashed his okay beforehand. Tell the radioman to request an RC bearing for *Delphy*."

Hunter's RC bearing arrived, (#2, 320 deg at 8:25 P.M., addressed to *Delphy)*. Hunter said, "We need to confirm this bearing. We have been steaming southeastward at 20 knots. By now, this bearing should have backed to a more westerly direction. This damn bearing is wrong. We should change our course toward the west and see if the next bearing confirms our known change in direction."

Another RC bearing was intercepted, (#3, 330 deg at 8:32 P.M., addressed to *Stoddert)*. Capt Watson was on hand, and the idea of stringing the squadron's ships on a short westward leg vanished.

Hunter ordered, "Request another RC bearing." Then he huddled with Capt Watson, and the two began a vigorous tête-à-tête. They manipulated *Delphy*'s navigation numbers and the unexpected, intercepted RC bearings sent to *Stoddert*. They strove to answer the question of what was the *Delphy*'s true position.

Ltjg Larry Blodgett pressed for a sounding at 8:35 P.M. "We must know whether the ship is inside or outside the 50-fathom depth contour on the navigation chart" (Illustration **28**).

Hunter and Watson talked little but soon agreed, "No need to slow down. No need for depth sounding; water here is too deep." Hunter ordered, "Get another RC bearing!"

Hunter's RC arrived. (#4, 333 deg at 8:39 P.M., addressed to *Delphy*). Hunter reacted, "They have sent us a misreading." He made no request for the RC station to confirm its transmission. He was steamed, and said, "Send this message to the RC. We are to the south of you. Send us a reciprocal." The RC replied with (Reciprocal 168 deg). Hunter and Watson pored over this reply, and concluded, "Our speed made good is 21 knots, not 20, and we are likely to be south of our last DR estimated position. That 168 deg reading from the RC station may be a bearing on the *Delphy*. If so, we should not delay our turn eastward. The longer we stay on this course the greater the risk of running into San Miguel Island." Capt Watson gave the order, "At 9 P.M. turn on a course of 095 deg true." Hunter passed on Watson's order, and ordered Ens Morrow to request another RC. As LCdr Hunter waited, he thought of the clues that supported a change to an eastward course. He said, "The *Delphy*'s speed made good is 21, not 20 knots. Our DR estimated line of positions is about right, because no one questioned the *Delphy*'s DR estimated 8 P.M. position that was sent to RAdm Kittelle."

Ens Morrow collared Chief Cummings. "What the hell is going on with the raft of RC requests from *Delphy* and *Kennedy*? Didn't *Kennedy* get our 8 P.M. position report to the admiral?" Cummings replied: "Yes, they got it. And, yes they are looking hard at the four RC bearings on hand, two *Kennedy* and two *Delphy*. They are asking, 'What is the *Delphy*'s problem? Why did *Delphy* demand a reciprocal after its 8:39 P.M. RC was received?'"

Hunter's RC arrived (#5, 323 deg at 8:58 P.M., addressed to *Delphy*). Lieutenant Commander Donald T. Hunter now had five RC bearings of record saying: "Your ship is to the northwest of the Pt. Arguello RC station." Two of those RC bearings were in his hand. The chance was nil for a sequence of five similar RC bearings to be error. The OOD thought the message implicit in those five RC bearings was clear: Don't turn eastward. Call for positions from the division leaders *S. P. Lee, Farragut,* and *Kennedy.* Talk to Cdr Calhoun on the *Young*.

Capt Watson's order came: "Turn on course 095 deg at 9 P.M., but it came without a cautionary companion order to slow ship speeds to eight knots and double the distance between the bow and stern of each ship.

At 9 P.M. USS *Delphy* turned eastward as ordered. Two divisions in the squadron column followed. The ships turned eastward at 20 knots into the fog, the dark, and the unknown.

At 9:06 P.M. the *Delphy* rammed the rocks at Pt. Pedernales, three miles northwest of the U. S. Navy Radio Compass Station, Pt. Arguello, California. By sunrise it was evident to everyone that seven Squadron 11 destroyers were stranded on the rocks.

The third division in the column, Cdr Roper's Division 32, did not turn eastward. It slowed, maneuvered ship by ship away from the coast, and took depth soundings. At 9:27 P.M. the division flagship, *Kennedy*, received an RC bearing of 0.5 deg, and at 9:37 P.M. the *Stoddert* received an RC bearing of 317 deg. The ships of Division 32 formed and safely moved south until midnight. They returned to the disaster site the next morning and aided in the rescue effort.

Opinions: Why This Disaster Happened

The underlying cause of this disaster was the embarrassing loss of the Destroyer Squadron 11's newest ship, the USS *Zeilin,* during the Presidential Review of the U. S. Battle Fleet Pacific on July 28, 1923 in the waters off Seattle. The *Zeilin* and two destroyers from Squadron 12, were honored to be escorts for the U. S. Navy's presidential transport, the *Henderson.*

On that morning, the *Zeilin* somehow got in front of the *Henderson* and got rammed broadside. In minutes the *Zeilin*'s crew was in the water, and a major rescue was under way. This was a most embarrassing event for the proud Capt E. H. Watson, Commander, Destroyer Squadron 11, and the squadron's reputation suffered. Watson decided that he and his squadron must recover their reputation as soon as an outstanding opportunity presented itself. That opportunity tuned out to be RAdm Kittelle's forthcoming order for the endurance run of his two squadrons from San Francisco to San Diego on September 8. Capt Watson decided Squadron 11 would show its stuff and beat Squadron 12 to San Diego by hours.

Watson was a most persuasive officer, and he developed a winning strategy for the endurance run victory. He convinced his flagship captain, LCdr D. T. Hunter of the *Delphy*, that the two of them could set a record-breaking time if they took full charge of the navigation, and led the squadron all the way. The key to success in that grand plan would be the *Delphy*'s firm control over the squadron's movement. Key to the strategy would be Hunter's takeover as the *Delphy*'s navigator, and continue as its skipper. Hunter would become the squadron's navigator. As the squadron passed Pt. Sur, and the squadron formed in column. *Delphy* would navigate and lead the column. Ship-to-ship talk would be minimal, and the squadron would hold a steady 20-knot speed.

Capt Watson made his first firm move during the pre-voyage conference. He gathered his officers in the large wardroom of the USS *Melville*. But he gave no hint of his grandplan, he answered no questions, and he discouraged any commander who was ready to discuss, let alone debate any part of the trip to San Diego.

Capt Watson's next move was to calm the eager navigators in the squadron. So he issued a set of orders which: prohibited each ship's navigator from requesting RC bearings from the navy's station at Pt. Arguello, required the 20-knot speed to be maintained, and signaled that LCdr Hunter would be the squadron's lead navigator. Hunter's response to this plan was to dead reckon the squadron from an initial fix at 11:30 in the morning. The end result was, at 8:30 P.M. the *Delphy*'s command, at the head of the squadron column, did not know where it was.

Ltjg Larry Blodgett's removal from his regular navigator's status allowed Watson and Hunter to negate, as necessary, Blodgett's suggestions. Blodgett's critical suggestion was made at 8:35 P.M. when he said: "We need to take a depth sounding to ensure we are not in shoal waters." The two leaders quashed this suggestion with, "Soundings are not necessary; they will just slow us down."

It was amazing that Capt Watson allowed LCdr Hunter to be the lead commander without a demonstrated proficiency in the use of RC bearings, to declare RC bearings to be void without technical reason, and to ignore the other squadron navigators.

The failure of the Squadron 11's navigation stands in contrast to the accurate navigation by the commander of Squadron 12. The Squadron 11 failure was highlighted by Capt Watson's lack of reliance on his outstanding division, ship, and navigation professionals. The official cause of this disaster was the errors of judgement and faulty navigation on the part of the Squadron 11 Commander, Captain Edward H. Watson, and the Commanding Officer, USS *Delphy*, Lieutenant Commander Donald T. Hunter.

The hidden crime committed at the U.S. Navy's court of inquiry would later be discovered to have been Watson and Hunter's studied silence as the court deliberated and pronounced Ltjg Lawrence Blodgett "Guilty."

Squadron 11 waited for the action of the U.S. Navy Court Martial, and the Squadron 11 commanders were pleased when the court promptly announced Ltjg Lawrence Blodgett "Not guilty." In hallway meetings, the Squadron 11 commanders agreed that a less than noble picture of the *Delphy*'s top officers emerged at the court martial of Watson and Hunter, when sworn statements—"We were not able to get RC bearings from the Navy's RC station because of their other traffic demands"—were later shown to be wrong.

At the conclusion of the court martial, it was clear that Watson desperately wanted to win the endurance run the way he planned it, but it was never clear why he didn't want an all-out squadron-wide effort. Several commanders were convinced that Capt Watson had kept his attempt to make a record-setting destroyer endurance run under wraps because he thought it was the only way to win.

These commanders agreed that the only thing certain at 8:58 P.M. was that the *Delphy*'s estimated position was most uncertain. Given that, how was it possible for Hunter and Watson to decide in good faith to turn the squadron, and give the order to turn without giving them any advance warning? [A few Squadron 11 officers agreed to meet and answer that question. The following is their informal answer.]

"We met yesterday. We imagined Capt Watson was with us. We asked him the question, and this is what we think he would have replied":

> Squadron 11 can make history today. We can make a record-breaking test run. It will require all of us to make a special effort to go a steady 20 knots, tend our engines, and pay sharp attention to our navigation. *Delphy* will lead and LCdr Hunter and I will work closely with Ltjg Blodgett. Each division commander will contact us every three hours starting at 1 P.M. During each contact we will tell him our latest estimated position, how it was determined, and give you our latest compass bearings. Each division will reciprocate. To avoid burdening the navy's Pt. Arguello radio compass station, I expect each division to confine itself to one RC request per hour.

PART THREE

The Courts Speak

Chapter 11

The Court of Inquiry

The court of inquiry convened in October 1923.
Its #9 Finding of Fact:

Delphy *disregarded all of the bearings received after 2000 except the 168 deg which had been given in accordance with the* Delphy's *request. 'Give us a reciprocal, we are to southward.' The* Delphy *was at the time of course change about 11.5 miles and 7 deg true from her dead reckoning position on which this change of course was based.*

—USN Court of Inquiry, *Twentieth Day Report*

Introduction

On September 11, Adm Robison, commander of the battle fleet, appointed the court of inquiry. The following editorial appeared in the *San Francisco Chronicle.*

> Naval regulations provide for the convening of such a Court on occurrence of any matter deemed serious enough to require a thorough investigation. No officer of the ill-fated squadron is on trial. The proceedings of a Court of Inquiry are to sift facts for the information of the convening authority, and to assist him in the performance of his administrative duties. Such a Court does not relieve the convening authority of responsibility for his administrative acts.

Naval instructions and procedures provide that the court of inquiry shall go thoroughly into the matter and include in its findings a full statement of the facts deemed to have been established. The court is further instructed to give its opinion as to whether or not any offenses have been committed or serious blame incurred. In other words, the court of inquiry affords the best means of collecting, sifting, and methodizing information for the purpose of enabling the convening authority to decide upon the possible necessity or expediency of further proceedings.

The court of inquiry convened on Saturday morning, September 22, 1923.

The president of the court was RAdm William V. Pratt, Commanding Officer, Battleship Division 4. Members were Capt George C. Day, Commanding Officer, Submarine Divisions, Pacific, and Capt David F. Sellers, Commanding Officer, Naval Training Station, San Diego.

The Judge Advocate was LCdr Leslie E. Bratton, commanding officer of the *Stoddert,* and the Assistant Judge Advocate was Lt Hardy B. Page, navigator of the *Paul Hamilton.*

Senior Counsel Capt T. T. Craven informed the court of the defense's serious problems. The commanding officer, division commanders, and most of the ship commanders involved in the incident were all under investigation. It was not possible for the defense counsels to obtain a complete picture of what had happened, and the specific role of each man involved, so the counsels could not properly guard the rights of the defendants. The court agreed, and adjourned until September 24 to give the defendants time to prepare themselves. Meanwhile, the newsmen made the most of Capt Watson's statement that he would assume full responsibility for the disaster at the court's next meeting.

The court of inquiry met; the judge's demeanor and the court's procedure followed navy tradition. The judges were highly qualified officers. They stayed in charge, they asked the hard questions; the prosecution advocates and defense counsels minded their manners. There were no histrionics.

The court of inquiry concluded its hearings on "October 12," and it issued a report with that date and the heading "Twentieth Day." The court also recognized a number of outstanding individual performances in—"Recommendations for Letters of Commendation." The Court Report was typewritten on legal-size paper starting with page 1022. It was signed by RAdm Pratt, President, and LCdr Bratton, Judge Advocate.

The court of inquiry's report contains: twenty-two "Finding of Facts," twelve "Opinions of the Court," and an Exhibit—"The Log of the Radio Compass Station at Pt. Arguello" (Appendix II).

The court's "Twentieth-Day Report" begins below with the heading "Findings of Facts." It is a true copy of the document in the National Archives, and has not been edited for style. It appears to have been typed on a manual typewriter. Please note: the court's report shows the ship's names without italics, and it uses A.M. and P.M., as well as the 24-hour clock.

Direct statements from the court's document are in quotation marks. As a few parts of the court's report were abbreviated, those are not in quotation marks. The author has used *italics* to call attention to a few passages of exceptional importance, placed a few supplementary remarks in brackets, and boldfaced the court's main headings. No change was made to the court's numbering system. The court's subheads have been boldfaced and indented.

The Court of Inquiry's Findings of Fact 1–3 are about Squadron 11. Findings 4–10 are about the *Delphy*, the leader of the destroyer column. Findings 11–12 are about the *S. P. Lee*, the 2nd ship in column. Findings 13–21 cover one ship at a time—the ships in the 3rd through 11th positions in the column. The 11th ship was the *Kennedy*, flagship of Division 32. Finding #22 covers the ships of Division 32, with column positions 12, 13, and 14, all of which turned safely westward.

The Squadron 11 ships (and their column positions before the stranding) were flagship *Delphy* (1st), Division 33, *S. P. Lee* (2nd), *Young* (3rd), *Woodbury* (4th), and *Nicholas* (5th), Division 31, *Farragut* (6th), *Fuller* (7th), *Percival* (8th), *Somers* (9th), *Chauncey* (10th), Division 32, *Kennedy* (11th), *Paul Hamilton* (12th), *Stoddert* (13th), and *Thompson* (14th).

The Court of Inquiry's "Finding of Facts"

1. "On 8 September 1923, Squadron Eleven, less the USS William Jones, USS Zeilin, USS Reno and USS Farquhar left San Francisco by divisions with orders to rendezvous off the San Francisco Light Vessel at 8:30 A.M. At 8:30 A.M. squadron took departure from light vessel steering various courses and speeds engaged in making practice runs in preparation for Short Range Battle Practice."

2. "At about 11:30 A.M. squadron passed Pigeon Pt. on port beam distant about 2 miles on course 160 deg. true, standard speed twenty knots. This was the last definite fix obtained before the grounding."

3. "At about 1430 the squadron changed course to 150 deg. true, Pt. Sur being approximately abeam but not sighted. Wind during afternoon was northwest, force 4–5, sea moderate and visibility at

least three miles ... At 1630 squadron formed column in following order: Squadron Leader, Division Thirty-three, Division Thirty-one, and Division Thirty-two ... The J. F. Burns dropped out of formation during the afternoon due to boiler trouble."

4. "At 2100 the Delphy changed course to 95 deg. true without previous signal to squadron. Signal was sent to next ship astern, S. P. Lee, giving the new course, after change of course was made."

5. "Delphy used a speed of 20 knots as the speed over the ground for computing dead reckoning positions. Consideration was given participated prevailing currents at this time of year, condition of ships bottom. Course of 150 deg. was used as safe course, the course recommended by sailing directions being 149 deg. true. *Delphy* was using a magnetic compass as gyro compass was out of commission due to needed repairs."

6. "Delphy received the following radio compass bearings from Pt. Arguello at 1415–167 deg. and 1426–162 deg. Ship was to northward and asked Pt. Arguello for reciprocal of bearing; at 1438–326 deg.; at 1813, 1832 and 1848–320 deg; at 2035–168 deg. (this bearing was a reciprocal of the bearing given at request of Delphy who stated, we are south of you, give us a reciprocal); at 2039–333 deg, at. 2058–323 deg. All bearings sent to Delphy indicated ship was to northward of Pt. Arguello except bearing of 168 deg. which was a reciprocal bearing asked for by the Delphy. No radio bearings received by Delphy were sent to ships of squadron."

7. "Delphy's 8:00 P.M. position was by dead reckoning as they did not consider they had obtained satisfactory radio bearings and did not therefore use them in computing their 8:00 P.M. position. Delphy's 8:00 P.M. position was sent to Commander Destroyer Squadrons Battle Fleet and to Commander Destroyer Squadron Twelve. Delphy's 8:00 P.M. position was not signaled to ships of the squadron. No 8:00 P.M. positions were asked for from ships of the squadron by the Squadron Commander or any Division Commander. Delphy's dead reckoning indicated ship would pass Pt. Arguello Light on port beam at 2025 distant 8¼ miles."

8. "Radio bearings received by Commander Destroyer Squadron Eleven were obviously in error when considered collectively for navigational purposes. Using times of separate bearings with distance run between. No definite fix can be accurately determined for the time of the respective bearings and therefore no definite error can be stated for bearings received. From navigational data available bearings were accurate within about ten degrees."

9. "Squadron Commander after consultation with the Commander and navigator of the Delphy determined upon a change to the left by considering the bearing 168 deg. (Reciprocal) and laying down various speeds to see where the ship would be on this line. It was considered that a speed of 21 knots had been made good and a course of 95 deg. true was determined upon as leading down the middle of the Santa Barbara Channel. It was not desired to pass too close to the unlighted islands to the south of the Santa Barbara Channel. Delphy disregarded all other bearings received after 2000 except the 168 deg. which had been given in accordance with the Delphy's request 'Give us the reciprocal, we are to the southward.' The Delphy was at the time of course change about 11.5 miles and 7 deg. true from her dead reckoning position on which this change of course was based."

10. "At about 2105 the Delphy ran head on at 20 knots speed on the mainland of the rocky coast at Pedernales Pt." No land, rocks or breakers were seen prior to grounding. There was a heavy bank of fog was lying over the coast, close in. Engine was backed full astern immediately but the ship did not move off rocks. Siren was sounded repeatedly. Squadron Commander directed radio signal be sent "9 turn" and "Keep clear to westward." Visual blinker signal sent by broadcast method, "Delphy aground." Megaphone used in attempt to warn ships astern."

11. Ship 2nd in column. "S. P. Lee obtained last definite off Pigeon Pt. at about 11:30, gyro compass checked with courses. Speed of 21 knots was used for dead reckoning. Intercepted only one radio bearing sent to Delphy at 1832 of 320 deg. true. This bearing checked with their D. R. position. Intercepted the Delphy 8:00 P.M. position

which was considered a fix determined by Delphy from bearings and all navigational data. Delphy's 8:00 P.M. position was about 3 miles WNW of S.P. Lee's D.R. position. Change of course made at 9:00 P.M. was considered a safe course for Santa Barbara Channel. Lee did not take any bearings with her direction finder nor did she ask Delphy for any bearings it might have from Arguello. Lee did not request permission to take bearings for herself."

12. Ship 2nd in column. "When the Delphy changed course at 2100 the S.P. Lee followed in column and received a signal giving the new course of 95 deg. true. This signal was not passed down the line. Shortly after change of course Division Commander and Commanding Officer on bridge Delphy was observed to apparently stop dead in water, grounding was realized; Lee observed Delphy apparently stop dead in the water. Lee's engines turned full speed astern with left rudder. Ship struck while making headway of about 8 knots on mainland and remained fast."

13. Ship 3rd in column. "USS Young obtained last definite fix on Pigeon Pt. at 11:32. Magnetic compass checked with courses. Speed of 19 3⁄10 knots was used for dead reckoning. Intercepted only one radio bearing sent to Delphy a 1813 of 320 deg. true. This bearing checked with D.R. position within about 2 miles. Intercepted Delphy's 8:00 P.M. position which was about seven miles ahead of Young D.R. position. This was considered as a fix determined by Delphy from all bearings and navigational data. Change of course at 9:02 was considered safe course for Santa Barbara Channel. No signal of change of course was received. Commanding Officer was notified of change of course, started to bridge, felt ship strike, was thrown to deck by again striking. Young turned over, starboard side down within about a minute and a half of first striking. She came to rest on her beam ends and about 100 yards off shore with her port side about two feet out of water. Men climbed and crawled to ship's port side remaining until ship abandoned."

14. "USS Woodbury, 4th ship in column obtained last definite fix at Pigeon Pt. At about 11:35. Magnetic compass checked course steered.

Speed of 20 knots until 1800 and then 19 knots used for D.R. Intercepted the three 320 deg. Radio bearings sent to Delphy at 1815, 1830 and 1845, all 320 deg. true. Bearing at 1830 ran through Woodbury D.R. position. Intercepted bearing sent to Delphy at 2039 of 333 deg. true. This was deemed in error due to bearing of 320, course steered and distance run. Presumed error in interception. Not considered for navigational purposes. Delphy's 8:00 P.M. position intercepted which was about 4 miles south of Woodbury's D.R. position. Reconciled this difference because of speed 19 knots was assumed from 1800. Woodbury followed the change of course to left, received no course signal. Course was safe to pass Point Conception by Woodbury's navigational position. Observed Lee sheer to port, Young to stop. Woodbury sheered to starboard, struck heavily amidships. Stopped, and reversed engines, but ship struck on small rocky island dead ahead almost immediately, and remained there. Crew abandoned ship to this rock that night. Ship held to rock by lines from ship."

15. "USS Nicholas, 5th ship in column obtained last definite fix at Pigeon Pt. At 11:34. Magnetic compass checked course steered. Speed of 20 knots was used for D. R. Intercepted radio bearing sent to Delphy at 1438 of 326 deg., also at 1840 of 320 deg. and 2035 of 168 deg. The last two not being reported to Commanding Officer and Navigator. D. R. position of Nicholas would put ship abeam of Point Arguello Light at 2030, distant eight miles. Nicholas did not intercept Delphy's 8:00 P.M. position. Nicholas made change of course to left following other ships in column. Confusion was noted ahead. Nicholas sheered to port. Engines were stopped and backed two-thirds with rudder left. Ship struck rock and disabled starboard engine, shaft separated at coupling. Ship grounded offshore from mainland and remained there. Since has worked inshore. Crew remained on board during night and abandoned ship on following day. After Nicholas struck rock it received signal from Delphy, "9-turn" and "keep clear to westward."

16. "USS Farragut, Division Flag, 31st Division, 6th ship in column, obtained last definite fix off Pigeon Point at 11:38. Magnetic

compass checked with courses steered. Speed of 20 knots used in D.R. though 19 also laid out on chart. Intercepted following radio bearings sent to Delphy; at 1813–320 deg. At 2035–168 deg., not known to be a reciprocal, at 2039–333 deg, at 2058–323 deg. Bearings could not be reconciled with D.R. which would put Farragut off beam of Pt. Arguello at 2050, distant 7 miles. Commanding officer was estimating navigational situation with bearings received. Did not use her own position finder. Did not ask Delphy for any other bearings she might have, or request permission to get bearings for herself. Officer of Deck reported head of column changing to left. Commanding officer came on bridge anticipating Arguello Light had been sighted.

When he saw change of course through about 40 deg. he became apprehensive; Division Commander and Commanding Officer viewed chart and navigation situation shown to Division Commander. Officer of Deck reported sirens ahead. Engines slowed to ⅔, immediately followed by order of Division Commander, stop, back full speed, gave right rudder to clear ship ahead. Backed until ship dead in water, heard cries of men in water from Young . Thought collision ahead. Observed rocks on starboard bow, backed full speed. Fuller observed astern, ahead ⅔ to avoid collision. Collided with Fuller about amidships starboard side at whaleboat davits, no material damage. Cleared, backed full speed, anchored in 15 fathoms of water, rocks observed close aboard in rift of fog. Dragged anchor backing, again anchored in 22 fathoms. Struck submerged rock while backing away after clearing Fuller. Leaks in fresh water tanks, secured boilers, remained at anchor overnight."

17. "USS Fuller, 7th ship in column, obtained last definite fix off Pigeon Point at 11:30 A.M. Gyro course checked course 1 deg. or 2 deg. to right of course signaled. Speed of 20 knots was used in D. R. No radio compass bearings were intercepted. Radio set sharp tuned and no interception can be obtained off the guarded wave lengths which were 310 and 1430. Radio bearings are sent out on 800. D.R. position of Fuller would pass Pt. Arguello at 2030, distant

8 miles. Fuller followed the speed signals of Farragut, Division Flag, next ship ahead, ⅔ ahead, stop, back ⅓. Tremor felt on Fuller, rang up full speed astern. Ships astern were closing up. Farragut and Fuller collided, cleared. A large hole was cut in steaming fireroom at time of grounding and boilers were secured; water rising rapidly, men secured and when they left firerooms were filling rapidly and water practically followed them up. Ship never got the full speed astern due to loss of power and was carried by sea onto the outlying rocks near the USS Woodbury. Ship was not abandoned until following morning."

18. "USS Percival, 8th ship in column, obtained last definite fix at Pigeon Pt. At 11:34 A.M.

Percival received no intercepted no radio bearings. Speed of 19.5 knots used for D.R. position placed the Percival abeam Pt. Arguello at 2045 distant 7¼ miles. Percival changed course at 2107 following the column. Confusion noted in ships ahead, thought there had been a collision, then observed Young on side from flash of searchlight. Ship backed out on reverse course 098 deg. true.

Farragut backed out ahead of Percival and directed she follow out and anchored in no less than 20 fathoms water. Anchored in 23 fathoms of water. Signal of '9-turn' and 'keep clear to westward' from Delphy was not received on bridge until after ship had backed out clear. Ship remained at anchor during night and sent ship's boats to stranded vessels next morning."

19. "USS Somers, 9th ship in column, obtained last definite fix on Pigeon Pt. at about 11:30.

Magnetic compass checked course steered. Speed of 19 knots used for D. R. Anticipated passing Pt. Arguello Light on port beam at about 2100 distant 7 miles. Only one radio compass bearing intercepted. It was reported by navigator to Commanding Officer; it was (a bearing that had been) sent to Delphy, received about 2100 and was 320 deg. In fact, this was a bearing sent to 12th Squadron. Commanding Officer treated it as a danger bearing. Somers changed course to left with rest of column. Signal of '9 turn' was received but not executed. Ships ahead showed stop lights, ⅓ speed ordered, hard right rudder, breakers ahead close aboard, full speed astern, ship struck twice before clearing, backed to westward, then turned on heel going outside 100 fathom curve. Ship remained underway all night. Came in following morning at daylight, anchored and sent ship's boats to aid stranded vessels."

20. "USS Chauncey, 10th ship in column, obtained last definite fix at Pigeon Pt. At 11:40 A.M. Magnetic compass checked with courses steered. Speed of 20 knots used for D.R. Expected to pass Pt. Arguello at 2030 distant 7¾ miles. No radio compass bearings were intercepted. Radio set sharp tuned. Chauncey made turn with column, observed confusion in ships ahead and ship slowed speed but continued ahead thinking it was a collision. Received signal '9 turn,' could not execute it as ships on both sides. Ship continued to forge ahead, passed Young overturned on side with men on it. Rocks were seen ahead. Backed emergency full speed astern. Ship struck astern while backing out, lost power and was carried by sea onto the mainland. Ship grounded to the right and further eastward from the Delphy. Anchors were dropped, ship was close to Young and crew of Young abandoned their ship to the Chauncey and thence to shore."

21. "The USS Kennedy, Division Flag 32nd Division, and eleventh ship in column, used course of 148 deg. true as course steered and speed of 19.7 knots for D.R. Intercepted following radio compass bearings sent to Delphy: at 1830–320 deg; at 2035–168 deg; at 2039–333 deg; at 2058–323 deg., also following intercepted bearings sent to USS Stoddert: 2012–326 deg. and 2032–330 deg. Kennedy anticipated picking up Pt. Arguello Light close aboard."

22. "Upon arriving at the turning point of the head of the column all ships of Division Thirty-two independently turned to the westward and maneuvered their ships to clear water. Division remained under way during the night cruising in formation in a thick fog endeavoring to locate the stranded vessels. Specific assignments were made to ships of the division to be prepared to render any assistance possible

to designated stranded vessels. Division anchored about daylight. A rift in the fog disclosed the stranded vessels about two miles distant at which time Division got under way, proceeded and anchored near scene of disaster awaiting further orders from Commander Destroyer Squadrons, Battle Fleet."

The Court's "Opinions"

Direct Cause of Disaster

1. "In the opinion of the court, the disaster which resulted in the stranding of seven destroyers on Pedernales Point, and the grounding of two others in the same vicinity is, in the first instance, directly attributable to bad errors of judgement and faulty navigation on the part of three officers attached to and serving on the USS Delphy, viz. the Squadron Commander, Captain Edward H. Watson, the Commanding Officer, Lieutenant Commander Donald T. Hunter and the Navigating Officer, Lieutenant (j.g.) Lawrence Francis Blodgett."

[The Court believed that Ltjg L. Blodgett was Delphy's navigator.]

Division into Periods

2. "Based on the testimony adduced, and to determine the degree of responsibility to be borne by the Squadron Commander, the Captain of the Delphy, the Navigating Officer of the Delphy, the Division Commanders of the 33rd and 31st Divisions, the Commanding Officers of the seven stranded ships and the Commanding Officers of the two ships which touched the ground, but which were not seriously damaged and also to determine upon other matters connected with the court's investigation, the court has found it fit to divide the period from the time of passing Pigeon Point abeam to the time when the last crews of the stranded ships were landed, into three periods, viz.

(a), 3. the period from passing Pigeon Pt. abeam to the time of the turn of the head of the Squadron to the left on a course of 95, which took place about 9:00 P.M. September 8, 1923.

(b), 4. the period from the time of the turn of the head of Squadron Column at about 9:00 P.M. to the time of the stranding of the last ship, viz. the Chauncey, in all a period of approximately six minutes.

(c), 5. the period which elapsed from the time of the stranding of the last ship, the Chauncey, at approximately 9:06, to the time on the following day, September 9th, when the crews of the Fuller and Nicholas, the last ships to land their crews on shore, were able to land them."

The Final Opinions:

Opinion considering radio;
Opinion concerning speed and soundings;
Opinion concerning the follow the leader doctrine;
Opinion concerning the various degrees of responsibility;
Opinion about unusual conditions at the time of the incident;
Opinion concerning the individual captains of the stranded ships.

Concerning Period "a" (defined in prior "Division into Periods")

3. "The D.R. course and the speed shown by revolutions were not made good, but the Squadron was during this time set in to the coast, and north of the D.R. position at 9:00 P.M. by a very appreciable amount... no unusual current conditions existed, but that this set to the north and east was caused by bad steering, together with a certain amount of current which, while not explicitly laid down in the Sailing Directions, may be expected at any time in any directions and should be guarded against by the careful navigator. During this period certain radio compass bearings were taken by the Delphy, but

the *fact that the bearings were not transmitted to the ships following, constitutes a neglect on the part of the Squadron Commander*, who should have seen that adequate information to insure the safe navigation was transmitted to them. However, upon not receiving adequate information to safeguard their own divisions, it then became the duty of the Division Commanders to ask for such information from the Squadron Commander, or take such independent action on their own part as would insure the safe navigation of their own units. Particularly did this duty devolve upon the second in command who should at all times possess himself of the requisite information to make him take over the commander of the entire unit and to conduct it in safety. To a lesser degree this comment applies to the next in command and to the captains of each individual destroyer. Period "A" was the critical period for upon the information possessed by each captain and each Division Commander depended his ability to make a correct and accurate judgement of what his action should be as he neared Pt. Arguello ... "The Court believes that too much stress was laid by all ships (but those in Division 32) upon the 6:30 radio bearing (to Delphy), because it checked with their D. R. positions, and the critical period following between 8 and 9, when stress should have be laid upon the receipt of radio bearings was neglected by all ships following the Delphy because (1) they placed too much confidence in the Delphy's 8:00 P.M. position, (2) because they placed too much confidence in the intercepted 6:30 radio compass bearing .... *The Delphy presents a curious case.* Confident in their own D. R. and discrediting the compass bearings because they were thought confusing, *the attitude of mind of the Squadron Commander, the Captain of the Delphy and the Navigator. ... was one of complete assurance at the very time when a doubtful situation had arisen* This situation arose between 8 and 9 and became particularly acute when the Delphy sent the signal 'We are to south of Pt. Arguello and asked for a reciprocal bearing.' The safe procedure at this time would have been to reduce speed, take soundings and proceed cautiously until further bearings had approximately fixed the position of the leader. This was not done and it indicated a state of confidence of mind of the leader which was naturally imparted to those following, who had not through their own individual efforts fixed the position of heir own ships. The result of the above procedure was that the Delphy, the 33rd and the 31st Divisions arrived at the turning point of 9:00 P.M., the Delphy with information inaccurately interpreted and the 33rd and 31st Divisions with insufficient information to enable them to quickly take appropriate and immediate action when such action was imperative."

Concerning Period "b" (defined in prior "Division into Periods")

4. "Had the responsible parties on the Delphy had not assumed her position through bad errors in judgement and misplaced confidence, to be south of Arguello, but had continued on the course 150 deg., it is the opinion of the Court that Arguello Light or its fog signal would have picked up ahead or very slightly on the port bow, a position which was not unsafe, as the squadron could have been maneuvered quickly to the to clear water westward. Particularly would this have been true had the speed of the squadron been reduced at 8:30 and soundings taken. The necessity of obtaining a fix at Arguello was apparent as the Squadron was to proceed through Santa Barbara Channel where fog might be expected at any time. This would have been good navigational procedure. Instead of this, *the Delphy without a proper fix turned sharply and blindly to the left to the course 95, at a speed 20, and at a distance from the shore… of less than 1½ miles from the reefs off Pedernales Pt.*"

"In sequence the 33rd and 31st divisions arrived at the turning point and made the turn with the Delphy. At this time or within the next minute or two, and only at this time could disaster have been avoided by the ships following the Delphy. It is doubtful whether the Delphy could have been saved by any action on the part of any of the following ships, for the Delphy up to this moment hd not indicated her intent to turn, her speed was too high, the officers responsible for her safety were too obsessed with the idea that they were south of Arguello Light, and the distance to the rocks was too short... But it is believed that had, at this time, the 33rd and 31st Divisions stood on, instead of turning to the left or had they turned sharply to the right, the 33rd and 31st Divisions would have been saved. This action on their part would not only have been good, but it was imperative, and it was necessary that it be made immediately and without delay. It is probable that this action would have been taken had those two divisions arrived at the turning point with all the information at hand then in possession of the Delphy, obtained by intercepting bearings, or if the method proved inadequate by directly asking the Delphy for this information, or failing in that by taking bearings themselves as was done in the 32nd Division, even though it was against the rules.

"In the opinion of the Court, no rules or regulations, no formal practice of guarding radio waves, may preclude... a commander from taking every navigational precaution to safeguard his own ship or division, as was done by the 32nd Division and in the 12th Squadron. He must risk every rebuke instead, and must at all times be prepared to take the initiative and to use individual judgement. The Squadron leader erred badly, very badly in judgement, but his errors must not be allowed to creep down the line even at the risk of a severe rebuke from the Senior in Command. The Senior may even welcome a suggestion which gives him a different point of view other than his own, particularly when he is in a doubtful or hazardous position himself. Having straightened out on the course 95, at speed 20, the position of the Delphy and the 33rd and 31st Division, like the Delphy was hopeless, the danger being greatest to those ships nearest the head of the column...

"Led by the Delphy straight for the bluff on Pedernales Point with the coast and reefs on the left hand, with the bluff ahead, and with an outlying island and sunken reefs on the right hand, neither a turn to the right or left could have saved these ships. The 33rd Division, like the Delphy, was doomed and crashed on the rocks and reefs to the right and left. Only by the promptness of action in backing... was the Division Commander of the 31st able to minimize the disaster to his division... Quick... action on the part of the captains of the Farragut, Somers and Percival alone save their ships... The Chauncey stood on and was stranded due to the Captains not knowing that the accident was stranding and not collision.

"Had the Squadron Commander sent a signal 'I am aground' instead of 'nine turn' and 'keep clear to westward' which conveyed inadequate information, it is possible the Chauncey might have been saved. At least the situation would have been clarified by the entire Squadron. The commander of Division 32, which Division was in the rear of the Column and therefore most favorably suited to avoid the disaster, was also by reason of more complete information better able to cope with the situation which developed immediately following the turn of the Squadron head at 9:00 P.M.

"By good judgement, good common sense, good navigational procedure, and by the good luck of being at the end of the column Division 32 turned individually to westward to safety. .... It is further the opinion of the Court that with the knowledge in the possession of the Division Commander of the 32nd Division, and of the other ships which was this, viz: that the Squadron had been very much inshore and to the northward, that had this division arrived at the turning point at 9:00 P.M., it would not have followed the Delphy in to sure destruction, and the present disaster would have been minimal. For his common sense and alertness the Commander of the 32nd is to be commended."

Concerning Period "c" (defined in prior "Division into Periods")

5. "Periods 'a' and 'b' reflect no credit upon the Navy. They were periods when (1) a grave error of judgement was committed by the Squadron Commander. (2) when a too blind faith on the part of the ships

following, was placed in the judgement of the Squadron Commander, (3) when too little initiative of the part of the ships following was displayed in determining their own positions was displayed.

"The disaster woke up Squadron 11. From that instant on the men of the Destroyer Force, Squadron Eleven, displayed a zeal, courage and coolness in the face of grave danger, which is a matter of pride to the Navy and should be to every American. From the Squadron Commander down to the humblest man on board there was perfect discipline and the highest traditions of the service were lived up to. Not a single case on any ship occurred where men of officers faltered in their duty, or failed to act calmly or cooly under orders. It is due to this perfect discipline that the loss of life was so small...

"Not a single attempt was made to abandon ship until the ship itself was a helpless wreck and then only when it became necessary to do so to save lives. Every precaution was taken and the work was done quietly, orderly and efficiently. Had this not been the case, it is probable that the loss of life would have been much greater due to confusion or a possible explosion of the boilers on some of the stranded ships.

"This part of the story reflects the highest honor upon the Navy; it is a story of coolness, calmness, bravery and discipline in the face of grave danger. The conduct and bearing of the Squadron Commander and that of all officers connected to with the disaster was at the time and has been since during the entire conduct of the Court of Inquiry beyond reproach and deserving of the highest praise. Recommendations follow for officers and men deserving special mention for conspicuous actions."

Considering Radio

6. "After considering carefully the testimony adduced the Court finds nothing which reflects upon the efficiency of the radio compass installation. A mass of confusing testimony has been brought forward to prove that the bearings may not be relied upon, but out of this tes-

timony shines the clear fact that it was not the compass bearings sent to the Delphy which were wrong, but the judgement of the men who interpreted these bearings and who used them wrongly. All the night of the 8th of September, the 32nd Division cruised to the north and south of the Arguello Light in heavy fog working their way through by the agency of the radio compass bearings and the use of the lead."

Concerning Speed and Soundings

7. "Up to 8:30 P.M. the speed of 20 knots on the course of 150 deg. true was not excessive. The weather conditions were not such as to make this speed dangerous from the point of view of seamanship and danger of collision with other ships. Destroyers handle better at this speed and current has less time to act on them and drive them from their set course. The H. F. Alexander ... was passed proceeding north at approximately the same speed of twenty knots. *After 08:30 speed should have been reduced in order to take soundings, and after 9:00 P.M., if it had been necessary to head into the land in order to get a fix off Arguello, the speed should have been reduced to a minimum until the light was sighted or heard, or an approximate fix obtained through the agency of compass bearings, checked with soundings.* Only so long as the course was parallel with the land and not too close, or away from the land was the speed of twenty knots a safe speed, but it was safe so long as it did parallel the land, or was away from the land until the fog shut in, when it should have been reduced."

Concerning the "Follow the Leader Doctrine"

8. "An attempt was made to show that the principle of follow the leader was so fundamentally part of the destroyer doctrine, that to depart from the practice was always a grave error ... unless the unit leaders had information ... which warranted their so doing. This is

no doubt true when the leader is right.... A departure from policy, plan... is rarely permissible, but in the tactical execution... much latitude must be allowed the subordinate. Not only must it be allowed, but the subordinate must take this initiative on his own responsibility when his judgement tells him this is the correct course to follow.... The Division Commanders and individual ship Captains are always charged with the safety of the unit under their command no matter who leads, unless it be in the presence of the enemy... No destroyer doctrine ever advocated the blind following of any leadership, on the contrary the primary and fundamentals are—loyalty to the plan and in this way loyalty to the leader if the plan be correct....

"Had Nelson at Cape St. Vincent blindly followed the leader, John Jervis would not have gained the victory which he did... Blindly following the leader or unreasoning adherence to set regulations is more in accordance with the practice of the past leaders who hesitated to depart from the line ahead, even when advantages would accrue from a departure from such practice.

"The plan on September 8 was to proceed to San Diego. The procedure was a movement in column formation. It mattered little so far as detail went how the plan was executed so long as it was effectively carried out and the tactical details of execution were not at variance with the policy of the leader or would cause him embarrassment. Nothing can replace the use of sound common sense on the part of the subordinates and if he is not furnished with sufficient information by his leader to absolutely safeguard his own unit or to effectively carry out the plan he must ask for it himself, and failing in this he must use every effort of his own to obtain it in order to better execute the general plan and by so doing aid the efforts of the leader. This is imperative and is believed to be much more in accord with destroyer and fleet doctrine than to blindly follow the leader. Through unknown or unforeseen circumstances the leader may frequently err, as was the case when Tryon gave the order which resulted in the collision of the Camperdown and Victoria, and the loss of the latter with great consequent loss of life."

[The Court's citation about Nelson is from the 1797 case where Admiral Lord Nelson acted against tradition and took an enormous chance when he failed to follow the Royal Navy's line-of-battle rule and pulled his ship, *Captain,* out of the line and made for the Spanish van. For this action his fleet commander, Admiral Jervis, could have cashiered Nelson from the service, but Nelson's action threw the Spaniards off balance and led to a British victory.]

Unusual Conditions at the Time of the Accident

9. "In reviewing the testimony, the Court is forced to the conclusion that no unusual conditions existed. It is true there was fog and that the lights which served as navigational aides were difficult to make. It would have been better practice to have made Pt. Sur and thus to have obtained a later fix before approaching Pt. Arguello which was to be turned at night... The price of good navigation is constant vigilance. The unusual is always to be guarded against and when the expected has not been eventualized, a doubtful situation always arises which must be guarded against by every precaution known to navigators, such as *the use and correct interpretation of compass bearings, and particularly by use of the lead and a proper reduction in speed. When you cannot see, you hear and feel, until you are sure.* The current on this coast are so variable and so unseasonable in their actions, that they cannot be relied upon definite and *no ship is safe when close to the coast unless it actually knows where it is. Dead Reckoning* alone *can never be relied upon. It is always the Captain who is sure in his own mind without the tangible evidence of safety in his possession, who loses his ship."*

Concerning the Various Degrees of Responsibility

10. "In the opinion of the Court there is nothing which will excuse the Squadron Commander, the Captain of the Delphy and the Navigating Officer from accepting full responsibility for the accident. Their responsibility is full and complete and the Court sees no extenuating circumstances."

11. "In the case of Division Commanders the Court finds that they must be responsible in a measure. It is true they were following in column, that they could not slow, they could not sound, that they could not without permission ask for compass bearings. But the fact remains that they did too blindly follow the judgement of the Squadron Commander, that they did place too much reliance on the 8:00 P.M. position of the Delphy, that they did place to much reliance upon the one bearing about 6:30 P.M. which unfortunately checked too closely with the dead reckoning position. Between the hours of eight and nine, the critical hours, they did not check on their own initiative the actual position of heir own units, and the result was catastrophe. It was possible to ask the Squadron Commander for information. It was possible to unguard the Battleship Wave and the Squadron Wave and thus to intercept the bearings sent to the Delphy. It was possible to ask to take bearings for themselves. It was possible to unguard the Battleship Wave and the Squadron Wave and use their own direction finders. The amount of traffic from Arguello between eight and nine was sufficient for them to have obtained a rough bearing, without interference to their leader, and thus to have obtained information which would serve to give them an approximately correct estimate of the situation when the Delphy turned shoreward at nine, and that might have enabled them to make a correct and accurate decision of their own at that time. The responsibility of the Division Commanders is much less than that of the Squadron Commander, the Captain and Navigator of the Delphy—but it is a responsibility nevertheless. Due to the subordinate position they held it was a responsibility which did not involve malfeasance,

but it does involve nonfeasance to a limited degree."

12. "Concerning the individual Captains of the stranded ships, their case is a peculiar one. They were not only following the Squadron leader, but they were also following their Division leader and in the case of the S.P. Lee and Farragut, the Division leaders were personally on board these ships. Their position was a trying one and there are many extenuating circumstances. They had two leaders whom they must go through before they could slow, take soundings, change course or even ask for radio bearings. They did attempt to intercept radio bearings, as was shown in the testimony, but unfortunately the two messages upon which most faith was laid were the two most misleading ones, viz. the Delphy's 8:00 P.M. position and the 6:30 compass bearing. They did not know that the Delphy's position was one by dead reckoning and not by fix. However, but to a lesser degree, the same responsibility which rests upon the shoulders of the Division Commanders rests upon them. In the period "A" up to the nine o'clock turn they were not in possession of the information necessary for them to take action radically out of the ordinary, which action was imperative at 9:00 or shortly after, if they were to save their ship. In other words it was necessary for them to take to take steps on their own initiative to obtain the information which they should and probably would have obtained had they been acting singly, but which they did not deem to be essential in the presence of their seniors. In this they erred and it was an error of judgement, for which they have a measure of responsibility similar, but less, than that resting on the shoulders of the Division Commanders. There is another aspect of the case. The traditions of the sea are strong, the ideals high, and the rules which seafaring men set for themselves are rigid and hard. Only by living up to the most rigid of standards may the lives of women and children entrusted to the care of seafaring men be safeguarded as far as human effort may make them safe. If a Captain loses his ship, he loses his command even when attending circumstances point almost entirely to his complete exoneration from blame. The Navy can do no less. Each

Captain that loses his ship must bear a responsibility due to that loss. Even though a court honorably acquits him of blame he must first assume the responsibility for the ship he commanded. Only by maintaining this standard can the high ideals and traditions of the Navy be preserved."

Recommendations for Court Martial

[The court of inquiry made a total of twenty-two recommendations. Recommendations #1 through #11 were *Recommendations for Court Martial*. The grouped order of presentation was: (#1, #7, #11) — (#2, #3) — (# 4, #5, #6, #8, #9, #10). Recommendations #12 through #21 were *Recommendations for Letters of Commendation*.]

The court recommended, in three separate paragraphs. that *Captain Edward H. Watson, U. S. Navy (Recommendation **1**), Lieutenant Commander Donald T. Hunter, U. S. Navy (Recommendation **7**) and Lieutenant (j.g.) L. F. Blodgett, U. S. Navy (Recommendation **11**), be brought to trial by General Court Martial on the following charges:*

I. Culpable inefficiency in the performance of duty, and

II. Through negligence suffering vessels of the Navy to be run upon rocks.

The specifications of the first charges should cover the offenses set forth in "Paragraph 10" (above) of the court of inqiry's opinion. The specifications of the second charge should cover the offenses set forth in "Paragraph 10" [concerning the various degrees of responsibility; as above] of the court's opinion.

*The court recommended in two separate paragraphs that two division commanders, Capt Robert Morris (Recommendation **2**), and Cdr William Pye (Recommendation **3**), be brought to trial on the charge:*

I. Through negligence suffering vessels of the U. S. Navy to be run upon the rocks.

The specifications of this charge should cover the charges set forth in "Paragraph 11" [concerning the various degrees of responsibility; as above] of the court's opinion.

The court also *recommended in six separate paragraphs that six ship captains—Cdr Louis Davis (Recommendation **4**), CdrWilliam Calhoun (Recommendation **5**), Cdr William Toaz (Recommendation **6**), LCdr Walter Seed (Recommendation **8**), LCdr Herbert Roesch (Recommendation **9**) and LCdr Richard Booth (Recommendation **10**). be brought to trial on the charge:*

I. Through negligence suffering a vessel of the U. S. Navy to be run upon the rocks.

That specifications of this charge should cover the offenses set forth in "Paragraph 12" (concerning the various degrees of responsibility; as above) of the court's opinion.

[The officers listened in disbelief, as they heard the court's decision to recommend Lieutenant Blodgett—the officer who was not the *Delphy*'s "navigator"—for court martial. They wondered how the legal counsels for Hunter and Blodgett perceived this unfair legal situation. Why Capt Watson and LCdr Hunter let this happen was never, to my knowledge, brought forth, but, days later, as the court martial progressed, Hunter finally came forward and said: "I was the navigator of the *Delphy*."]

Recommendations for Letters of Commendation

The names of each man recommended by the court for a Letter of Commendation, and the men recommended for commendation by RAdm Kittelle, are given in Chapter 4, ship-by-ship, at the end of each ship's story, near the story of their heroic actions. More than eighty men were cited for "displaying courage ... in the face of constant and imminent danger, for extraordinary heroism, for especially meritorious conduct, for meritorious conduct, and for certain specific personal acts."

Monetary Loss and Salvage

The court gave the names of the seven destroyers lost, stated a money loss of about $13.5 million, and $28 thousand damage to the two vessels that escaped. The story about patrolling the rescue sites and recovering the seamen's bodies is in Chapter 4. Salvage efforts are discussed in Chapter 13.

The court's report concluded with a list of the men who died and the men injured in the line of duty. In this book, however, that information is in Chapter 4, "Survival and Loss," to accompany the story of their deaths.

Chapter 12

The Court Martial

The court martial convened in November 1923.
Capt Watson testified for LCdr Hunter:
There was no apprehension of danger or the necessity of taking soundings. If the Delphy *had been where we had every right to think it was, a change was necessary to avoid San Miguel Island.*

—Capt Edward H. Watson, Commander, Destroyer Squadron 11

Introduction

Vice president Coolidge had become president by the time the court martial convened in November 1923. The tone of government in Washington was changing rapidly, and it was fortunate for the navy's welfare that Edwin Denby had been reappointed secretary of the navy. According to author J. T. Adams:

> Vice-President Coolidge was as yet little known when he took the oath of office in ... Vermont. Like Hughes and Hoover, Coolidge had been wholly unsmirched by the dirt of the Ohio Gang and other malefactors of the Harding regime.... Silent and with a mind that was singularly ordinary and commonplace, he nevertheless had a certain hard-bitten Yankee shrewdness and common sense which made him appear to many as a wise and safe leader ... closely identified with the national economic well being....

The findings of the court of inquiry and its recommendations were favorably received by Secretary of the Navy Edwin Denby and by Congress. The main goal of the new administration's economy-minded critics was focused, however, on finding people to blame for the loss of 15 million dollars' worth of government property, a senseless loss caused by driving seven new destroyers onto the coastal rocks of California. Secretary Denby's attitude was that the navy's prestige was already in peril from the oil scandal, and he must avoid action that looked even faintly like a cover-up. The court of inquiry's recommendations for court martial, however, spread a general gloom over the navy.

The court martial convened in early November. The title page, dated 1 November 1923, reads: "Record of Proceedings of a General Court Martial convened at Headquarters, 11th U. S. Naval District, San Diego, California, by order of the Commander-in-Chief, Battle Fleet, United States Navy. The Case of Edward H. Watson, Captain, U. S. Navy. The Record of Proceedings for Donald T. Hunter, Lieutenant Commander, U. S. Navy, 7 November 1923."

The nine members of the court martial:

VAdm H. A. Wiley, commanding, Battleship Divisions of the Battle Fleet, President

RAdm L. M. Nulton, commanding, Battleship Division 3

RAdm J. V. Chase, commanding, Fleet Battle Force

Capt DeWitt Blamer, Senior Member, Board of Inspection and Survey

Capt E. H. Campbell, commanding, Mare Island Navy Yard

Capt W. S. Crosley, commanding the *Idaho*

Capt S. E. Moses, Assistant Commandant, 12th Naval District

Cdr Leslie E. Bratton, Judge Advocate [commander of the *Stoddert*]

Lt Hardy B. Page, Assistant Judge Advocate [navigator of the *Paul Hamilton*]

Counsels for the defendants in the court martial:

Capt Thomas Craven and Cdr George Weyler for Capt Watson.

Cdr B. B. Wygant for LCdr Hunter.

Cdr Walter Anderson for, Capt Morris and Cdr Pye.

Cdr Henry N. Jensen for, Cdr Toaz, Cdr Davis, Cdr Calhoun, LCdr Roesch and Lt Blodgett.

Lt. Thomas Leovy for, Cdr Seed and Cdr Booth.

This summary is based on the documents cited and the sources given in the bibliography. It is not, however, a presentation of the actual record produced by the U. S. Navy Court Martial. Hence it is not a parallel chapter to Chapter 11, the court of inquiry's Twentieth Day Report, and the court of inquiry's Exhibit.

Trials on Charges of Culpable Inefficiency and Negligence

Captain Watson, Commander, Destroyer Squadron 11. LCdr Leslie Bratton, Judge Advocate, read the serious culpability charges as given by the court of inquiry. Capt Craven for the defense claimed that the circumstances that led up to the disaster involved an unexpected encounter, a difficulty in obtaining bearings at the radio-compass station because of congestion caused by the wreck of the *Cuba.* [This was a claim without merit, and was at odds with the court of inquiry's "Exhibit I."] Capt Craven said the change of course ordered "was not of itself considered dangerous." He cited Capt Watson's fine service record, and his courage in taking full responsibility.

Counsel Cdr Weyler said, "There were mitigating circumstances that could not be foreseen by Capt Watson." Capt Morris, commander Destroyer Division 33, Cdr Davis, commander of the *Woodbury*, and Cdr Calhoun, commander of the *Young,* appeared as defense witnesses. They said none of them had expected any danger. Capt Morris voiced his opinion: "I would have preferred to take soundings, but I never made any request to take them." He also said, "I would have preferred to slow down, because of the commercial traffic I expected to find in the Santa Barbara Channel."

The prosecutor, LCdr Leslie Bratton, argued that the fact that the squadron's vessels were wrecked indicated that Watson had been inefficient in the performance of his duty. "The radio bearings clearly indicated that the *Delphy* was north of Pt. Arguello and not in a position to safely turn eastward." Defense counsel Cdr Weyler maintained that Watson had heeded the bearings and given them every consideration. Weyler said, "Capt Watson made an erroneous judgement that had nothing to do with inefficiency in doing his duty." [Inefficiency—wanting in ability, incompetent—seven ships lost.] The court martial retired and deliberated, but *did not announce a verdict*. Custom indicated that this meant Capt Watson had been found guilty.

LCdr Hunter, Commanding Officer, Flagship *Delphy,* Squadron 11. Capt Watson was Hunter's star witness. He paid tribute to Hunter's navigational skill, and admitted that if the *Delphy* had slowed to 5 knots and taken soundings, the squadron could have been saved. But he reiterated that there was no apprehension of danger or the need to take soundings. The course, if made good, would have put *Delphy* in water too deep for soundings. Watson added, "If the *Delphy* had been where we had every reason to think it was, a change was necessary to avoid San Miguel Island."

The audience received the captain with mixed feelings. To one observer, "Watson was a diligent captain defending LCdr Hunter, his loyal subordinate, who had made a technical mistake while rushing to meet a deadline." To another, "Watson was a complacent captain falsely arguing that the disaster was due to mitigating circumstances, already heard and denied by the court of inquiry."

Counsel Cdr Weyler said Capt Watson "had heeded the bearings and given them every consideration... his mistake in judgement was made while all the facts were in mind." Watson's Counsel, Capt Craven, concluded, "The error of judgement made by Watson and Hunter was made by men who at the time were intent upon doing their full duty."

LCdr Hunter gave much the same testimony he had given at Watson's trial, and emphasized that "Capt Watson had at all times been informed of the navigational situation." LCdr Hunter admitted that: "He had disregarded the RC bearings, and contended without any explanatory support that the radio compass bearings had plainly been in error." There was a lot of discussion about the RC bearings, especially about the word "heed," which is defined as "to pay attention to, to listen to and consider." Both Capt Watson and LCdr Hunter "maintained they had indeed heeded the radio compass bearings, apparently because they had requested them, looked at them, and considered them—before ignoring them. Hunter's counsel, Cdr Wygant, said, "The results proved Hunter had made an error, because of the necessity for a quick decision."

The big surprise at the court martial came when Hunter stated, "I was responsible for the *Delphy*'s navigation. My navigator, Ltjg Blodgett, did nothing but routine work!"

The court retired and deliberated, but *did not announce its verdict*.

Ltjg Lawrence Blodgett, Navigator and Executive Officer of the USS *Delphy*. In view of the way Blodgett had been exposed by Hunter's "passivity during the Court of Inquiry," Hunter's admission was a surprise to the members of the court. They weighed this new evidence—never made to the court of inquiry—quickly and soberly. Blodgett's counsel, Cdr Henry Jensen, sensed the court had been profoundly affected by Hunter's declaration. Cdr Jensen stood up, faced the court, and calmly said, "I will call no witnesses." Surprisingly, but without noticeable effect on the court or the audience, Judge Advocate Leslie Bratton said, "The evidence shows that Blodgett was the Navigator, and that he had not performed his duty properly." The court retired, deliberated, returned, and announced a verdict: *not guilty and full acquittal*.

Trials on Charges of Negligence

Gloom prevailed over Squadron 11, and its ship commanders in particular, as the trial began. Having been immediately relieved of their commands, they thought they had already been prejudged. They also thought their chance of acquittal was remote, since the court of inquiry had said that they, as well as Capt Watson and the division commanders, were responsible for the disaster, even though they had only followed Watson's orders. The key question floating in the air was how all the ships' commanders and navigators could not have had the slightest feeling of present danger. The ship commanders' firm answer was that they believed that the squadron commander must have had assurance that his 8 P.M. position was accurate because of a fix and navigational data that they did not have. The officers who were tried are listed below in their normal column order. It seems there was little mention of the heroic conduct of these officers and their men during the disaster—Cdr William Calhoun and LCdr Walter Seed had both been recommended for citations by the court of inquiry and by Rear Admiral Kittelle.

Capt Robert Morris, Commander, Destroyer Division 33. Capt Morris' counsel, Capt Anderson, had Morris take the stand on his own behalf. Morris testified that, as soon as the danger became apparent, he personally blew warning whistles and did all he could to save the ships of his division. His military history was read into the court record. It contained highly complimentary statements about his ability and devotion to duty and included letters of commendation from Admiral Sims and Secretary of War Baker. After deliberating, the court announced a verdict of *not guilty and full acquittal,* with the caveat that it should not in any way be seen as a signal that lessened the general responsibility of division commanders for the safety of their ships. The verdict lifted the courtroom gloom.

Cdr William Toaz, Commander, Division 33 Flagship USS *S. P. Lee.* The case of Cdr Toaz proceeded much as had that of his division commander, Capt Morris, and the court heard much of the same testimony. The navigation procedure was discussed in detail, as were visibility and ship speed. But the court did not dwell on the *Lee*'s 21-knot speed made good, given in the court of inquiry's report—the identical, unduly high speed of the *Delphy* that appeared just before the turn eastward, a speed "different" from that used to get the *Lee*'s earlier positions. This matter was, in part, passed over because no deck logs were available to verify the hourly speeds actually recorded. The court deliberated and announced a verdict of *not guilty*.

Cdr William Calhoun, Commander, destroyer USS *Young*. Cdr Calhoun's trial was brief. Calhoun stated, "I navigated as carefully as I would have if I had been alone. I had every reason to believe

Delphy was doing likewise. I did everything I could have except those [things] which were forbidden—taking soundings and calling for radio compass bearings. The court deliberated, and Cdr Calhoun was found *not guilty*. Some of the gloom dispersed, and a hint of optimism appeared as the audience noted the shortness and favorable result of Calhoun's trial.

Cdr Louis Davis, Commander, destroyer USS *Woodbury*. Cdr Davis' trial proceeded in routine fashion. A highlight occurred when Davis was asked to give his definition of destroyer doctrine. He replied, "Doctrine is the unwritten understanding that develops between the officers of the force which enables them to keep constantly of one mind on matters of tactics and policy."

Davis made it clear that he had navigated as if he were alone, with the exceptions Calhoun had mentioned. He said he certainly would have taken soundings if he had been alone, and that he had been in column following both the Squadron 11 and Division 33 flagships. "I was confident the *Delphy* would never have continued at 20 knots if its officers had not known exactly the *Delphy's* position." The court deliberated and found Cdr Davis *not guilty*. This favorable result and the shortness of the trial dispersed most of the remaining gloom.

LCdr Herbert Roesch, Commander, destroyer USS *Nicholas*. LCdr Roesch's trial counsel was Cdr Jensen. Roesch's case opened with the testimony of the *Nicholas*' two radio operators, who said, "We intercepted three bearings." Unfortunately, they went on to say, "Our receiving set was not up-to-date, and we had difficulties. It was hard to guard the two waves we were supposed to guard, and intercept radio compass bearings on a third wave." The *Nicholas* had only two radio operators instead of the necessary three, and neither of them was able to intercept the *Delphy*'s 8 P.M. position.

The next witness was Ltjg H. F. Sasse, navigator and executive officer of the *Nicholas*. He explained the long process of navigating, laying out the courses on the chart, and plotting radio-compass bearings and the ship's positions. "Cdr Roesch was frequently on the bridge, checking his work, and standing watch as the deck officer. The navigational procedure was always the same, alone or in formation." After hearing other witnesses and final arguments by the defense and prosecution, the court deliberated for more than an hour, reconvened, but *did not announce its verdict*. This, by custom, meant a guilty verdict. The audience's optimism vanished.

It was not easy for them to understand the difference between the charges against Cdr Roesch and those against the other ships' officers, which justified a verdict of guilty for Roesch and a verdict of not guilty for the others. Perhaps Cdr Roesch's statement about the poor visibility, and the radiomen's testimony about intercepting three of *Delphy*'s radio-compass bearings—more than the other ships reported—suggested to the court that Roesch should have requested permission to take soundings, which might have started a line of questioning that could have saved his ship. Perhaps it was the fact that neither the defense nor the prosecution made any special effort to ensure that all the intercepted bearings were presented to the court.

Cdr William Pye, Commander, Destroyer Division 31. The prosecution witnesses were Cdr McClain (Commander, Division 31 flagship *Farragut*), Cdr Seed (Commander, *Fuller*), Cdr Booth (Commander, *Chauncey*). Fortunately, they all gave testimony favorable to the defense. Cdr McClain said, "Cdr Pye did everything possible to save his ships." Cdr Booth and Cdr Seed said, "Cdr Pye did not in any way contribute to the loss of the ships. Ltjg L. L. Hunter (Division 31 Acting Communications Officer) stated, "Cdr Pye was most interested in the navigation, and he was on the bridge practically all the time. Cdr Pye's conduct in the disaster was beyond reproach."

Capt James Tomb (Commander, Destroyer Squadron 12) testified that fleet regulations for the handling of divisions were developed for units of large ships. Tomb said, "The regulations were useful guides for destroyers, but not something anyone strictly followed." Under cross-examination, Capt Watson admitted, “Cdr Pye never failed to use proper initiative and he has already been commended for his conduct during the disaster.” Cdr Pye was impressive on the stand: “I had no warning of any danger ahead until the confusions and collisions ahead became evident. I never saw any red lights and I heard no whistle signals. All I saw was the *Young* on its side, the lights of two ships ahead, and the cries for help from the men on the *Young*. My concern was to save those men, for there was no warning that my ship was then in danger... I believe I did everything I could do under the circumstances... If the *Chauncey*, *Somers* and *Fuller* had received a signal from the *Delphy*—‘Ground ahead’ instead of ‘Nine turn’—I believe the entire 31st Division could have been saved.” The court deliberated Cdr Pye’s case and *announced a verdict of not guilty.*

LCdr Walter Seed (Commander, USS *Fuller*). Walter Seed testified firmly: “I did not take any soundings, because I could not do so at a speed of 20 knots. I was ready to request radio bearings, but did not do so because of the squadron’s order not to call for bearings from the RC Pt. Arguello station. I did not intercept any radio bearings because it would have been a violation of radio instructions to unguard one of the radio waves I was supposed to guard. I had every reason to believe that the *Delphy* must know what it was doing, or it would not have lead the squadron on a turn eastward at a speed of 20 knots under the prevailing poor visibility condition.” The court deliberated and *announced a verdict of not guilty.*

LCdr Richard Booth (Commander, USS *Chauncey*). The *Chauncey*’s executive officer and navigator, Lt C. V. Lee, testified, “I received the *Delphy*’s signal to ‘Nine turn’ just before I noted confusion ahead. I presumed there had been a collision and that the turn was to prevent other ships from being involved. When I saw the first sign of danger, rocks ahead, *Chauncey* had already started to turn, and it was to late to disengage, to back away. My ship could have backed away safely if we had received a signal ‘Ground ahead.’” Booth emphasized that he could have saved his vessel had the first signal been "Ground ahead." (Other commanders also voiced this view.) The radiomen testified that LCdr Booth had asked them to intercept radio bearings, but they were unable to do so while still guarding the two required wavelengths. The court deliberated and *announced a verdict of not guilty.*

Overview of the Testimony

The statements of prosecution and defense witnesses contained a variety of truths and claims. Some of the claims were apparently made with intent to create a false impression. Surprisingly, some of them had already been examined and denied by the court of inquiry. The essence of the main trial themes was:

Sense of danger. Most of the division and ship commanders were concerned about the lack of information from the *Delphy*—but they got no word about the intended new course, or time of course change. Hence they did not know in advance that the column would turn landward at 9:00 P.M. Although it may sound like balderdash, since the *Delphy* did not know where it was, Capt Watson seemingly had no apprehension of imminent danger. His complacent attitude as Hunter's witness appeared at odds with his earlier acceptance of responsibility for the disaster. Overall, there was an unwarranted sense in much of the squadron command that not seeing danger was similar to being safe. It never occurred to the squadron's commanders that *Delphy* would complete a turn eastward without sending notice of her intent beforehand. And they were amazed that even the *Delphy*'s flag signal that it was changing course—received by the *S. P. Lee, #2* in column—was never sent down the line. It was one sign of the basic squadron problem, a surprising lack of ship-to-ship communication, which received slight attention during the trial.

Cdr Walter Roper, Commander, Division 32, was the commander who felt uneasy with Capt Watson's constraints. His flagship, *Kennedy,* had an "exceptional navigator and two excellent OODs on duty." They felt free to talk to each other and to Cdr Roper, and they did. *Kennedy*'s navigator, Lt R. F. MacNally, and watch officers Ltjg Dalkowitz and Ltjg Wellborn, were the best in the business. They concluded: "The *Kennedy* will be close abeam Pt. Arguello near 9:00 P.M., maybe we should advise *Delphy* of our estimated position." Cdr Roper said, "Sounds like you know more than the captain. He's just trying to be sure he picks up the Arguello Light."

Cdr Walter Roper testified, "Ships do not make the speed shown by engine revolutions ... ships were yawing badly, and that tends to hold them back. I have noticed that destroyers never make the speed indicated by the turns on the propeller—never." When asked if he had intended to follow the leader around a change of course at 9 P.M. that night, he replied, "I wouldn't have followed the leader around a 65-degree turn. I don't believe in following the leader if the leading boy jumps off the barn." Roper's OODs thought the *Kennedy* should query *Delphy* about their 8 P.M. position.

The *Delphy*'s record reveals clear signs of danger, and a disregard for the problems it was causing by not advising its column of ships. For example, the *Young* intercepted *Delphy*'s 320 deg—1813 bearing, which agreed with *Young*'s position, but *Young* had no way of knowing that *Delphy* had ignored that bearing. The *Farragut* intercepted *Delphy*'s critical 168 deg—2035 "message," but *Farragut* had no way to detect that it was a "reciprocal" that *Delphy* had demanded.

Radio-compass bearings. Obeying Capt Watson's explicit order, the Squadron 11 commanders did not request bearings. That created a major problem, which came up in the testimony over and over again. The commanders said, "We had every reason to believe that the *Delphy* must have confidence in its estimated position because it had a recent fix. Otherwise, *Delphy* would have slowed due to its proximity to land, and the foggy condition." This confidence caused several diligent commanders to refrain from calling *Delphy* to ask for its radio-compass bearings. This confidence also discouraged commanders from calling *Delphy* and discussing the bearings they had intercepted.

Delphy did not use radio bearings to estimate its positions as it approached and "thought it passed Pt. Arguello." The record shows that every navigator knew, "RC bearings are accurate to within ten degrees, and therefore not suitable for precise navigation." They also knew, however, that precision was not required when the objective was to verify the ship's passing the Pt. Arguello RC.

The court of inquiry denied the specific claim that *Delphy* had a hard time obtaining needed radio bearings in a timely fashion. It surfaced again at the court martial, however, despite the written record in Appendix II, the Court of Inquiry's Exhibit, "Bearing Sheets: U. S. Naval Radio Compass Station, Pt. Arguello, Calif. Sept. 8, 1923," which shows that a number of navy and commercial ships obtained bearings promptly on request.

The defense's claim—that the Squadron 11 commander on the flagship *Delphy* could not obtain timely bearings because the RC station was jammed with evening traffic—was nonsense. *Partridge*, the navy tug commanded by Chief Boatswain's Mate Pierce, requested and received four RC bearings between 6:52 and 8:27 P. M. The assertion that *Delphy*'s ability to obtain RC bearings that evening was restricted by the demands from the destroyer *Reno* as it rescued the Cuba's survivors was untrue: *Reno*'s last request for a radio-compass bearing was at 11:40 A. M.

Squadron speed. *Delphy* never talked openly to the squadron about ship speed, even though the *Delphy* (1st in column) and the *Lee* (2nd) came up with the same "21 knot speed made good." The identical and unduly high 21-knot speed for those lead ships was peculiar, and related to the fact *Lee* had contact with *Delphy*, and had learned about the LCdr Hunter's decision—"21 knots is the speed made good." Hunter would have been better off if, instead of talking to the *Lee,* he had talked to the other division commanders.

Then, he would have found out that most of the squadron ships had average speed estimates *less than 20 knots*. [Their column position and average speed, from deck logs in the author's possession. were: 3rd, *Young* 19.3, 4th, *Woodbury* 20 until 1800, then 19, 6th, *Farragut* 20, but 19 laid out on chart, 8th, *Percival* 19.8, 9th, *Somers* 19, 11th, *Kennedy* 19.7, & 13th, *Stoddert* 19.1 knots.]

Depth soundings. Most of the commanders said they would have slowed and taken depth soundings if they had been alone. Under the existing circumstances—and specific orders fixing their speed at 20 knots—they could not take soundings. The failure of the *Delphy* command to take soundings, or see to it that a ship at the end of the column slowed and took soundings, was inexcusable.

The 8:00 P.M. radio message to RAdm Kittelle. No commander seriously considered that *Delphy* might have sent a dubious DR-estimated 8 P.M. position to the Commander, Destroyer Squadrons, based solely on dead reckoning from its before-noon fix on the Pigeon Pt. Lighthouse. They assumed (wrongly) that the DR-estimated 8 P.M. position must have been based on a fix, radio-compass bearings, and navigational information they did not have.

The testimony about *Delphy*'s radio transmission of its 8 P.M. "position" to Radm Kittelle on the *Melville* gives that "transmitted position in distance and direction from the *Delphy*'s "actual 8 P.M. position." Curiously, there was no mention of the wording in the original radio message to Kittelle, or the administrative objective for sending it. Hence it is hard to pin down whether *Delphy*'s message was qualified in any way. Did the message state, "This is a DR estimated position"—wording that might have caused the message to be routed to a knowledgeable commander who could have sensed a need for a follow-up inquiry?

The order to turn eastward at 9 P.M. As the trial developed, most of the squadron's commanders found it difficult to explain why Capt Watson had not informed them of his decision to turn the squadron eastward at 9 P.M. Most of the commanders found it hard to believe the order required them to blindly execute an eastward turn. They were shocked to find out—neither Hunter nor Watson had confidence in their flagship's dubious estimated D R position. Most of the commanders found it difficult to understand why LCdr Hunter's failed to delay the execution of the turn eastward at 9:00 P.M., while he was holding 8:39 and 8:58 P.M. RC bearings saying, "Your ship is **northwest** of the Pt. Arguello RC Station."

Who was the navigator of the *Delphy*? The commanders attending the court martial were visibly distressed when LCdr Hunter finally said: "I was the *Delphy*'s navigator." When informed, the court of inquiry's officers were dismayed to find out they had recommended Ltjg Blodgett for court martial, based on the assumptions that *Delphy*'s officers were telling the truth. Saddened at the lack of honest testimony by Watson and Hunter, the court-martial officers quickly conferred and soon announced Blodgett "not guilty."

Navy doctrine. This was largely a court of inquiry consideration. (An attempt was made to show that the follow-the-leader principle was a fundamental destroyer doctrine and that to depart from it was a grave error unless the unit leader had information that supported such a departure.) Capt Tomb, Commander, Destroyer Squadron 12, said, "The doctrine, follow the leader, was meant for large ships, not destroyers." Overall, the issues of policy, tactical doctrine, and allocation of responsibility appeared somewhat tangled to some officers, and they predicted their would be a change in Navy Regulations.

Mr. Dooman. There was no discussion or testimony given at the court martial about the presence of or the role played by the *Delphy*'s civilian passenger, Mr. Eugene H. Dooman. He is not mentioned in the court records, the deck logs, or the immediate accounts of the disaster. There is no knowledge of why there was zero information about Dooman at the trials, nor why he "remained faceless, and nameless" for years afterward.

The first published information about Mr. Dooman that I found was in Charles Hice's 1967 book, which includes a lengthy 1966 personal letter to Hice from Dooman in answer to Hice's earlier inquiry. Mr. Dooman's letter says, "I shall confine myself to answering your questions.

The Court Martial Verdicts, Punishments Given, and Public Reaction

Guilty of culpable inefficiency and negligence as charged: Capt Edward Watson and LCdr Donald Hunter.

Not guilty of culpable inefficiency and negligence: Ltjg Lawrence Blodgett.

Guilty of negligence as charged: LCdr H. O. Roesch.

Not guilty of negligence: Capt Morris, Cdr Pye, Cdr Davis, Cdr Calhoun, Cdr Toaz, LCdr Seed, and LCdr Booth.

The punishments were announced at the conclusion of the proceedings. The judge advocate was directed to record the following:

"The specification of the charge proved that the accused, Edward H. Watson, Captain USN, is of the charge guilty. The Court therefore sentences him to be placed at the foot of the Captain's List of present date, and there to remain until he has lost one hundred and fifty (150) numbers in his grade. In similar language the Court sentenced Donald T. Hunter, Lieutenant Commander, USN to lose one hundred (100) numbers in his grade of present date."

These sentences prevented any further promotion of these career officers. Both were released from arrest and returned to duty. The other officers were exonerated and returned to duty. Secretary Denby's disapproval of the court's not-guilty findings was ineffectual because he lacked legal authority to enforce it; however, a note was attached to each officer's personnel records.

Cdr Roesch's guilty verdict appeared unfair to the Commander-in-

Chief, Battle Fleet, Adm S. S. Robison, and he promptly disapproved the conviction.

The not-guilty verdicts for the other officers were recommended for disapproval by the Judge Advocate General and sent to Secretary of the Navy Edwin Denby, along with similar language about Adm Robison's set-aside ruling of Cdr Roesch's guilty verdict. In later action, Secretary Denby disapproved all the not-guilty verdicts, but those disapprovals did not result in any change of the court's and the admiral's action. The disapprovals were seen as the secretary's way of expressing his displeasure with those actions. A note of the disapproval was placed on each officer's official record.

Public reaction. According to Elwyn Overshiner, in *Course 095 to Eternity*:

> Despite the openness of the Court of Inquiry the American public remained dubious that all the information of the Pedernales smash-up had been revealed. Unfortunately, certain subsequent happenings did little to dispel the aura of a cover-up. *"The official record of the Findings of the Court of Inquiry disappeared from the Office of the Judge Advocate General in 1924."*

Overshiner also shows the content of an August 26, 1925 letter from Acting Judge Advocate General Leslie Bratton to the Chief Bureau of Navigation. It says that the record of the court of inquiry's proceedings had been taken to them as requested, during the last session of Congress, but only two of the three volumes had been returned. It asked the bureau to search their files for the missing volume. In a letter dated only five days later, Chief of Bureau W. R. Shoemaker says, "A thorough search had been made. The search shows that all the records were returned to the Offices of the JAG on June 10, 1924, and had not been seen since then."

The public impression was that the officers of the court martial were, in general, lenient in their judgment of the individual ship commanders because they had been ordered to follow their leader and not to request radio bearings. Additional support included the fact that the commanders had been given no navigational detail from their squadron leader and were discouraged from communicating with each other. The normally silent President Coolidge suggested that the court "had been most lenient."

[Stepping aside from the politics surrrounding the disaster, "most lenient" hardly seemed the best words for the president to have used about the ship commanders and Ltjg Blodgett. Also,it seemed a thoughtless comment, because it did not include a positive statement about the more than eighty heroes officially commended, such as Chief Boatswain's Mate Peterson, Machinist's Mate 1st Moon, the men in the engine rooms, the ship commander, the chiefs who swam through oily seas—and on and on—especially as the president had little personal or detailed knowledge about those men's heroic behavior during the rescue phase of the disaster. The the court of inquiry's and Radm Kittelle's recommendations for heroic individual actions and outstanding group performances are presented in Chapter 4. LCdr Hunter's detailed letter to Radm Kittelle recommends commendations be given to twenty-seven of the *Delphy*'s men.]

This partial quote is from *Military Misfortunes,* by military historians Cohen and Gooch, from the chapter entitled "What Can Be Done?—The Organizational Dimension of Strategy":

> Only through an appreciation of the ways in which military organizations work can we understand the failures which have puzzled those who experience them, those who observe them, and those who try to explain them.... For although in some cases the failures of a commander are manifest, in others they are either difficult to discern or impossible to explain simply by reference to flaws of character or intellect....The catastrophe... noted at the beginning of this

> book, stemmed in part from the failings of several men . . . But neither then nor earlier did they demonstrate any particular divergence from the norm of the organization that had educated them and promoted them.

Many of the Squadron 11 officers had illustrious careers through World War II. Some of them are presented in Chapter 13. One of Squadron 11's officers reached the rank of admiral, four reached the rank of vice admiral, and nine reached the rank of rear admiral.

Chapter 13

Aftermath

In 1923, the people at the memorial services for the men lost in the Destroyer Squadron 11 disaster were griefstricken for those lost, and overwhelmed with heartfelt thanks for those who survived.

Memorials of the Later Years

Fifty years after the disaster, July, 1973, the Anchor Monument and Plaque was placed on a concrete slab at the mesa's edge, just below the railroad's Honda section house, and surrounded with steel stanchions and chain. The plaque reads "Anchor from USS *Chauncey* raised by Vandenberg Aquailler Dive Club 28 July 1973." (Illustration **26** is a 1994 photo of the Anchor Monument and Plaque.)

By spring of 2000, the mesa in front of the monument had deteriorated. An agreement was reached between the U. S. Air Force, the U. S. Navy, and the Lompoc Historical Society. The Anchor Monument and its Plaque were transferred from the mesa site to the society, which has since placed the original anchor and plaque in its Lompoc Valley Historical Museum, Lompoc, CA. The museum is open to the public.

Fifty-two years after the disaster, April, 1975, The Naval Reserve Plaque was mounted on the concrete base of the Anchor Monument by the U. S. Naval Reserve Surface Division 11-45. Plans indicate that it will eventually be displayed in Lompoc. The plaque reads:

> The Honda Disaster. In these waters on September 8, 1923, twenty-three U. S. Navy sailors of Destroyer Squadron Eleven lost their lives when these seven destroyers ran aground: *Delphy*, *Fuller*, *S. P. Lee*, *Nicholas*, *Young*, *Woodbury*, *Chauncey*. U. S. Naval Reserve Surface Division, 11-45, Santa Barbara, April 1975.

Sixty years after, in September 1983, American Legion Proud Post 211 dedicated the Propeller Shaft Monument and Plaque in memory of the men lost in 1923, and placed it in the legion's courtyard in front of the their Lompoc headquarters. It includes one of the *Delphy*'s two-ton propellers, and a piece of its drive shaft, raised from the sea by the father-and-son diving team of Ernest and Carson Porter, of Atascadero. The Porter family donated the prop and shaft to

American Legion Post 211. (The monument and plaque are shown in Illustration **27**.)

The legion and the Lompoc community held a ceremony and dedicated the big twisted prop in memory of the men lost. Some 300 people attended. Speakers included Major General Jack Watkins, Commanding Officer, Vandenberg AFB, and Captain Gerald Fulk, of Port Hueneme, representing the secretary of the navy. The navy color guard was from Pt. Mugu. Ted Olsen, the son of the man who was the lighthouse keeper at Pt. Arguello in 1928, was a guest speaker. It was a special day for Casey M. Bass, a survivor of the tragedy and a man commended by the court of inquiry. A seaman on the *Fuller,* he was fifteen at the time of the disaster. The plaque at the Propeller and Shaft Memorial reads:

> "In Memory of the tragedy at Pt. Pedernales / Honda Point, 8 September 1923. USS *Delphy*, USS *S. P. Lee*, USS *Young,* USS *Woodbury,* USS *Nicholas, USS Fuller,* USS *Chauncey*. Dedicated 8 September, 1983 by the American Legion, William Proud Post 211. Monument donated by Ernest and Carson Porter.

Seventy-five years afterward, September 1998, services of worship and remembrance were held at Vandenberg AFB at the "Pt. Honda" site. The program included a responsive call to worship, invocation, reading of the scriptures, meditation by Lt Ronald P. Stake, CHC, USNR, Navy Hymn by Capt Patrick Genseal, USAF, roll call of those lost in the 1923 Tragedy, 21-gun salute, Taps, dropping of the wreath, and dismissal. The Lompoc Valley Historical Society presented a memorial plaque containing the names and ranks of the men who died. (Illustration **29** is Vance Newcomb's photograph of the memorial plaque, now on display in the society's museum.) The title and first paragraph read:

UNITED STATES NAVY

This plaque is dedicated to the memory of the 23 courageous sailors of U. S. Destroyer Squadron 11 who died in the service of their country when seven of their ships ran aground near Honda Point, California, on September 8, 1923.

One other memorable reminder of the disaster is the Porthole Cover, now in the society's museum. The porthole cover, in recent photograph by Janet Wilson, reads:

> *Delphy, Young, Chauncey, Woodbury, Nicholas, Fuller, S.P. Lee. Cover found by H. W. Anderson, a Lompoc diver, in 1969. Purchased from Louise Anderson and donated to the Museum by S. C. Wade. The cover is from one of seven destroyers wrecked at Pt. Pedernales on Sept. 8, 1923.*

The following "List of the Dead" was prepared from historical records on hand before the Memorial Plaque was dedicated. The twenty-three men honored are the same as those in Illustration **29**, with the addition of a hometown designation for each entry.

USS *Delphy*
James W.H. Conway, Fireman 3rd Class, Fort Omaha, NE
James T. Pearson, Fireman, 1st Class, Elk City, OK
Sofronio Dalida, Cabin Cook, Saipan Piaz, P.I.

USS *Young*
Ralph K. Buchanan, Chief Pharmacist's Mate, Sonoma, CA
Clitus A. Reddock, Radioman 1st Class, Ocean Beach, CA
Enrique Torres, Cabin Steward, Bulacin, P.I.
Ernest C. Harrison, Fireman 1st Class, Fort Neches, TX
Edward C. Kirby, Fireman 3rd Class, Charlotte, NC
Vern R. Van Schaack, Fireman 3rd Class, Fraser, IA
Hugh W. Skipper, Fireman 3rd Class, Newville, AL
August Zakrzewski, Fireman 2nd Class, Omaha, NE

John Young, Fireman 1st Class, Salt Lake City, UT
Henry T. Kirk, Fireman 3rd Class, East St. Louis, IL
Max H. Taylor, Engineman 2nd Class, Spokane, WA
Charles A. Salzer, Coxswain, New Orleans, LA
Ernest Jones, Cabin Cook, New Orleans, LA
James T. Martin, Seaman 1st Class, Dallas, TX
Everett W. Grady, Fireman 2nd Class, Gretna, NE
Gordon J. Overshiner, Fireman 3rd Class, San Jose, CA
Earl Duncan, Seaman 2nd Class, Rose, OK
Joseph J. Slimak, Fireman 3rd Class, Bridgeport, CT
Wade H. Morris, Fireman 3rd Class, Bluffdale, TX
Leo F. Rogers, Fireman, 3rd Class, North Baltimore, OH

After the 1998 memorial service, some history about the naming of the wrecked destroyers was provided by Harold Isbell, and published in the Lompoc Historical Society's *Legacy* (No. 80), edited by Vance Newcomb. All the destroyers were named for naval heroes who had distinguished themselves in action, and one for a secretary of the navy.

***Delphy*, No. 261,** was named in honor of Midshipman Richard Delphy, killed in action between the U. S. frigate *Argus* and the H. B. M. frigate *Pelican,* August 13, 1814.

***Chauncey*, No. 296,** was named in honor of Captain Isaac Chauncey, who distinguished himself in the *Constellation* and was in command of our naval forces on Lake Ontario.

***Fuller*, No. 297,** was named in honor of Captain Edward C. Fuller, U.S.M.C., who was killed in action on the Bois de Belleau on June 12, 1918.

***Woodbury*, No. 309,** was named in honor of Levi Woodbury, Secretary of the Navy 1831–34.

***S. P. Lee*, No. 310,** was named in honor of Rear Admiral Samuel P. Lee.

***Nicholas*, No. 311,** was named in honor of Major Samuel Nicholas, U.S.M.C., one of the first "Soldiers of the Sea" in the battle of

New Providence, West Indies, in April 1776.

***Young*, No. 312**, was named in honor of Captain John Young, who was lost at sea in 1781 in the sloop *Saratoga*.

A Bit of Post-1923 History about the 1923 Destroyers and Fighting Crews

At the start of World War II, Britain was desperate for ships to protect its supply convoys. Help came when fifty of these 1923 destroyer "four-stackers"—in prime condition—were turned over to the Canadians and British at a seaport in Nova Scotia. They fought in the Atlantic during World War II, and "hundreds of heavily laden convoys owed their survival" to the fighting crews of those ships, their guns, and their depth charges. Others fought in the Pacific. Their exemplary battle history is described in the book *Destroyers–60 Years,* by naval historian Capt William Schofield. According to Capt Schofield:

> The *Pillsbury* DD-227 (Illustration **20**) survived the Japanese attack on Cavite. In company with the U. S. gunboat *Asheville* and the Australian gunboat *Yarra*, it was ordered on March 1, 1942, to evacuate Tjilatjap. The three ships then made a desperate try to reach sanctuary in Australia. A Japanese force of three cruisers and two destroyers overtook them and sank them in the Indian Ocean.
>
> The USS *Borie* DD 215 was the squadron leader of seven destroyers which sped to Japan's aid after the Japanese earthquake of 1923. The heroic World War II incident about the *Borie* began in an Atlantic storm north of the Azores on the night of November 1, 1943. *Borie* drew an assignment, and went out to chase a U-boat. *Borie* then picked up a second U-boat on radar running close to the task group. By cold logic this was not a night to look for a fight. The sub was caught on the surface and driven below by gunfire and depth charges. Hours later *Borie* caught and engaged the second sub. The

> fight was vicious for an hour. Both vessels were hit. Both drove to attack. The *Borie* maneuvered, and rammed the sub abaft the conning tower. They disengaged and *Borie* managed to overtake the sub again and sink it with gunfire. *Borie* never recovered. Destroyers *Barry* DD 248 and *Goff* DD 247 moved to the rescue and saved all but twenty-seven men from the sunken *Borie*. This is the only single U. S. ship known to have sunk two U-boats in a single battle.

Captain Schofield also described heroic actions by the destroyers *Edsall* DD 219, *Stuart* DD 224, *Reuben James* DD 245, *Bainbridge* DD 246, *Whipple* DD 217, and *Pope* DD 225. He also wrote of the four-stacker class that preceded the flush-deck class, those with numbers lower than DD 186, some of which saw service in World War I.

The *Farragut*-class destroyers *Hull* DD 350 and *Monaghan* DD 354 were launched in 1935. They were 1400 tonners, larger than those of the previous flush-deck class, and had power plants of 42,800 S.H.P. The *Spence* DD-unk was a 2100 tonner built in 1942. According to A. B. Whipple's book, *Storm,* three of these ships were with the U. S. Battle Fleet in the Philippine Sea when it ran into Typhoon Cobra on December 17–18, 1944. These destroyers rolled "horrendously" and were "virtually unmaneuverable." All three were lost. Eighty men were picked out of the heaving seas, but 800 were gone. Details are given in Morison's *History of U. S. Naval Operations in World War II.*

There is limited history about the careers of the Squadron 11 ship commanders and the other heroic men after 1923. Most of the following is from the 1960 book, *Tragedy at Honda,* by the chroniclers Lockwood and Adamson. Fourteen of the Squadron 11 officers achieved flag rank:

"Four-star" Admiral W. L. Calhoun, Commander of the *Young*. During World War II he was charged with the logistic support of the Pacific Fleet, and naval shore-based establishments in the Pacific. He was retired in 1946 after 44 years of active service.

Vice Admiral W. S. Pye, Commander, Division 31. During WW II he served in the Office of Chief, Naval Operations. In 1936 he became Commander Battleships, Battle Force. Prior to Admiral Nimitz, VAdm Pye served as Acting Commander, U. S. Pacific Fleet. His active service ended in 1945.

Vice Admiral C. H. Cobb, commander, *Percival*
Vice Admiral R. H. Cruzen, engineering officer, *Delphy*
Vice Admiral C. C. Hartman, officer of the deck, *Farragut*
Rear Admiral L. E. Bratton, commander, *Stoddert*
Rear Admiral A. P. Mullinix, officer of the deck, *Delphy*
Rear Admiral F. L. Baker, communications officer, *Young*
Rear Admiral P. W. Steinhagen, engineering officer, *S. P. Lee*
Rear Admiral W. D. Wright, officer of the deck, *S. P. Lee*
Rear Admiral W. W. Juvenal, officer of the deck, *Woodbury*
Rear Admiral H. Ridout, officer of the deck, *Woodbury*
Rear Admiral L. L. Page, officer of the deck, *Chauncey*
Rear Admiral H. D. Power, officer of the deck, *Fuller*

Lieutenant Commander Walter D. Seed (Commander, *Fuller*) was commended in 1923 "for great bravery in swimming ... through a rough and turbulent sea in order to test the feasibility of and make arrangements for the salvage of his crew." After a few months' service Walter Seed was hospitalized, and was transferred, in August 1924, to the Retired List for reasons of ill health. We do not know if Cdr Seed's illness was related to his 1923 heroic swim in an oily sea.

Commander L. F. Davis (Commander, *Woodbury*) was commended in 1923 because he "displayed unusual decision and judgement in saving his entire crew." Cdr Davis was later promoted. Captain Davis served as executive officer of the battleship Colorado, Squadron commander of DesRon 1, and captain of the *Maryland*. He retired in 1940.

Lieutenant Commander R.H. Booth (Commander, *Chauncey*) was commended "for invaluable service in rescuing the crew of the *Young*. LCdr Booth was later promoted. Commander Booth served as instructor at the Naval Academy and the Naval War College. His seagoing assignments included commander of the *John D. Edwards* and executive officer of *Black Hawk*.

Late Letters About the 1923 Destroyer Disaster; Comments on the Salvage of the Wrecks

Long after the disaster occurred, Chronicler Hice received and published this letter from Cdr R.G. Sly USN (Ret.)

> I can understand that some of the survivors of the Honda thing being reluctant to discuss it ... some of them were very much at fault in this event: proven so by the Court Martial. Captain Watson was found guilty of several serious charges. I'm sure you could get it from the National Archives ... In 1923, I was attached to the *Young*. But most of us were guilty of some criminal negligence. It is not with bitterness that I say this, but it seems too many stories concerning Honda were written by officers whose interest doesn't seem to be fault finding, but rather to gloss over it with a "Gee, wasn't it too bad it had to happen to him and he about to be promoted to Admiral, too."

A letter dated 26 August 1925 says that the proceedings of the court of inquiry, containing radio-compass logs and ship deck logs, were passed directly from the Judge Advocate General (JAG) to the Chief of the Bureau of Navigation. A return letter dated 31 August 1925 from the Chief to JAG says: "They have made a search for the records, but no trace can be found of the Proceedings." In his book, Elwyn Overshiner asked this question: "What part, innocent or sinister, did this missing official material play in the Navy's greatest peacetime disaster?"

Trained professionals did everything imaginable in the process of saving themselves and each other. Yet, on the lead ships, it appears no one had a chance to snatch and save a few pages of the deck log. Officially, these deck logs are described as "lost"; some were recovered, however, and later described as "not able to be found."

The survivors had barely departed the disaster site on the Southern Pacific rescue trains when RAdm Kittelle issued salvage orders to navy work details, and to men from the Mare Island Navy Yard: "Without endangering life, endeavor to remove as many moveables such as money, records, confidential publications, sights, radio gear, instruments, torpedoes, ammunition, etc. as possible."

Capt Nutting, of the Navy Construction Corps, surveyed the ships, and recommended three prime objectives: recovery of classified publications, removal of dangerous ordinance, and obliteration of all traces of the wrecks. The navy hoped to "refloat" *Chauncey* and *S. P. Lee*, but optimism faded quickly when the first storm passed by.

Several salvage contracts were written—Flynn Salvage paid $1,650 for the hulls—but by February 1924 the contract with Flynn, to complete all salvage operations in six months and guarantee that no parts of the hulls would be visible after that time, was in trouble. Litigation developed immediately between Flynn and residents of Lompoc. The navy's concern grew as the contractor's ineptness and instability became known. The sad saga appeared to be near its end in December 1927, with a navy proposal to bomb or blow up the remains of the wrecks. In May 1930, Cdr Charles Brand wrote about what he saw when he inspected them at low tide: a few boilers and several sections of steel frame, here and there ... The salvage program was over. [Overshiner's book contains a documented chapter on salvage history.]

Radio Compass Improves; Navy Regulations Unchanged

Action was taken to "reverse" the measurement nature of the maritime radio compass, and a "radio beacon" was established at Pt. Arguello in 1925, so that ships equipped with the new "radio direction finder" could take their own bearings. The Pt. Arguello light was increased to 900,000 candlepower, and further improvement came in 1934, when the light's candlepower was again increased and a lighted buoy was anchored off Pt. Pedernales.

Few changes were made in the Navy Regulations after this disaster. "Penalties of the rocks, Universal Code of Military Justice" still contains the words, "Any person subject to this Chapter who willfully and wrongly hazards or suffers to be hazarded any vessel of the Armed Forces shall suffer death or such punishment as a court martial shall direct."

Navy doctrine has an important role in history, but in this disaster, "the destroyer doctrine of follow-the-leader" was not allowed as an excuse for losing a ship. "The doctrine did not die, however, nor can it ever be eliminated from the swift maneuvers of small fast ships in the heat of battle..."

The postscript at the end of the Lockwood and Adamson book, *Tragedy at Honda*, contains a discussion, *Honda in Retrospect*.

Bibliography

Adams, J. *The March of Democracy*. New York: Scribner & Sons, 1933.

Adams, R. "Seven Destroyers Wrecked on the Rocky Coast near Pt. Arguello." *Lompoc Record,* Lompoc, CA, 1923.

Bond, C. *A Fury from Hell*. Washington, D.C.: Smithsonian Publishing, 2000.

Bowditch, N. *Bowditch for Yachtsman: Piloting. Selected from American Practical Navigator*. New York, NY: David McKay Co.

Calhoun, S. *Crew Endurance Management*. Arlington, VA: Marine Safety Council, U.S.C.G. 2001.

California, State ARB. *Surface Wind Climatology*. Sacramento, CA: Air Resources Board, 1984.

California State Library. *U. S. Weather Bureau, Surface Weather Map, Sept. 8, 1923*

Casey, S. *Set Phasers on Stun*, Santa Barbara, CA: Agean Publishing, 1993.

Cohen, E.A. & Gooch J. *Military Misfortunes*. NY: Macmillan, 1990.

Cohen, Eliot. *Military Misfortunes in the Atlantic.* NY: Macmillan, 2002.

Dana, R. *Two Years Before the Mast*. Danbury, CT: Grolier Enterprises, 1909.

Duckworth, Spencer. *Storm in the Gulf of the Farallones: A Sailing Disaster (10–11 April 1982). National Weather Digest.* Washington, D.C., 1993.

Ferguson, N. *Virtual History: Alternatives and Counterfactuals.* New York: Basic Books, 1997.

Gawande, A. "When Good Doctors Go Bad." *The New Yorker,* 2000.

Gladwell, M. 2000. "The Art of Failure." *The New Yorker,* 2000.

Gladwell, M. "The Talent Myth." *The New Yorker,* 2002.

Hagan, K. *This People's Navy*. NY: The Free Press, Macmillan, 1991.

Heaney, Seamus. Poem, *Sophoclean.* Noted poet from Dublin, Ireland. *The New Yorker,* 2003.

Heneghan, C. ed. *Battle of the Atlantic*. Liverpool: Brodie Publishing, 1993.

Horton, R. "In the Danger Zone." *The New York Review of Books,* 2000.

Hice, C. *The Last Hours of Seven Four-Stackers*. Miamisburg, OH: The Ohioan Co., 1967.

Holland, F. *America's Lighthouses*. Miller, NY: Dover Publications, 1997.

Kiefer, J. B. and J. Myers. *Risk and the Passenger Vessel Industry.* Proceedings of the Marine Safety Council, Arlington, VA, 2002.

Knight, F. 1921. *Risk, Uncertainty and Profit.* Cornell University Press, Ithaca, NY.

Langguth, A. J. *Patriots, Men Who Started the American Revolution*. NY: Simon and Schuster, 1988.

Langley, R. *Practical Statistics*. New York, NY: Dover Publications, 1970.

Lilly, K. *Marine Weather Handbook*. Sausalito, CA: Paradise Cay Publishing, 1983.

Lockwood, C., and H. Adamson. *Tragedy at Honda.* Fresno, CA: Valley Publishers, 1960.

Lompoc Record, Sep. 14, 1923, and later.

Los Angeles Examiner, Sep. 10, 1923, and later.

Los Angeles Times, Sep 10, 1923, and later.

Maloney, E. *Chapman Piloting.* New York, NY: Hearst Marine Books, 1989.

Massing, M. "The Unnecessary Death of Beethavean Scotland." *The New Yorker,* 2001.

Maynard, H. *Industrial Engineering Handbook*. NY: McGraw Hill, 1963.

Miller, T. photograph of the *Sumner, DD 333*, at sea. Somerset, MA: Tin Can Sailors, Inc., 2003.

Moore, J. ed. *Jane's American Fighting Ships of the 20th Century*, NY: Mallard Press, 1991.

Moore, C. *Lusitania, An Epic Tragedy*, Walker, 2003.

Morison, S. E. *History of the United States Naval Operations in World War II. Vol. 13*. Liberation of the Philippines. Little, Brown, & Co.,

Boston, MA, 1975.

Mullaly, L. *Southern Pacific Lines in Los Angeles.* 1873-1996. Golden West Books, San Marino, CA, 2002.

Mullaly, L. Interviews with John Giorvas' son, Arthur, March 14, 1995; Darrel Brewer, May 5, 1995; and Ed Negus, July 6, 1995.

Morison, E. *History of Naval Operations in Wold War II.* Boston: Little, Brown and Co., 1962.

National Archives, U. S. Navy Court of Inquiry, San Diego, Oct. 1923. *Twentieth Day of Inquiry Into the Destroyer Losses at Pt. Pedernales on Sept. 8, 1923.*

National Archives, Exhibit at Court of Inquiry. *Bearing Sheet, U. S. Navy Radio Compass Station, Pt. Arguello, Sept. 8, 1923.*

National Archives, Military Reference Branch. *Deck Logs for Sept. 8, 1923 for Some of the Ships in the U. S. Battle Fleet Enroute to San Diego.* Washington, D.C.

Naval Historical Center, *The Navy Hymn,* Washington Navy Yard, Washington D.C.

Newcomb, Vance, ed. *Story of Marine Tragedy Written by Member of First Rescue Party,* The Lompoc Valley Historical Society, Qtr Bulletins 79–80, 1998.

Nova Teachers, "The Search for Longitude," Boston: WGBH Radio, 1998.

NYNEX Information Sources. *Nynex Boaters Directory,* Northern Calif. Ed., 1988.

Newspapers:

San Francisco Chronicle, Sept. 10-11, 1923, and later.

San Diego Sun, Sep. 14, 1923.

San Luis Obispo Tribune, Sept. 11, 1923, and later.

Santa Barbara Daily News. Sept.-Nov. 1923, and later.

Santa Barbara Morning Press, Sept.12, 1923, and later.

The Los Angeles Times, "Destroyers on the Rocks," Sept. 10, 1923.

The New York Times, Sept. 11, 1923.

Overshiner, E. *Course 095 to Eternity.* Arroyo Grande, CA: Helm Publishing, 1990.

Pritchett. P. *Resistance.* Dallas, TX: Pritchett and Associates, Inc., 1996.

Ramsay, D. *Lusitania, Saga and Myth,* Norton, 2003.

Reynolds, A., *Mariners Weather Log,* 1994. Admiralty List of Radio Signals, NODC, Washington, D.C.

Roberts, B. and R. Jones. *California Lighthouses.* Old Saybrook, CT: The Globe Pequot Press, 1998.

Roberts, J. A. *Climate of Pt. Conception to Morro Bay*. Meteorology Research, Altadena, CA: 1967.

Rousmaniere, J. *The Annapolis Book of Seamanship*. NY: Simon & Schuster, 1989.

San Francisco Chronicle. "Role of the Naval Court of Inquiry." September 12, 1923.

Santa Barbara Daily News. "Castaways at Honda." September 11, 1923.

Schock, R. "A Conversation with Chalmers Johnson." Berkeley, CA: California Alumni Association, *California Monthly,* 2000.

Schofield, W. *Destroyers-60 Years*. NY: Bonanza Books, 1959.

Silva, J. *Honda Left Turn 095.* Lompoc, CA: J. and M. Silva, 1986.

Sources for Railroad Rescue. Chapter 6, Southern Pacific: *Employees Timetable, Coast Division, No. 116, August 19, 1923.*

Railroad Gazette, May 17, 1907. *SP Bulletin,* October, November, 1923.

Stanton Center, 1992. *Fresnel First Order Lens at Pt. Sur Installed 1889.* Maritime Museum, Monterey, CA.

Stewart, D. *The Madness that Swept Miami,* Washington, D.C.: Smithsonian, 2001.

Sunday Oregonian, Sept. 9–10, 1923.

Suroweicki, J. 2002. *The Financial Page. Shredders Through the Ages.* The New Yorker. NY.

Taggart, D. V. *March to Precision Navigation*. Proceedings of the Marine Safety Council of the U. S. Coast Guard, Arlington, VA. 1952.

Thomas Bros. *California Maps and Road Atlas.* Irvine, CA: 1993.

Tobin, James. "*To Fly*." Washington, D.C.: Smithsonian, 2003.

U. S. Coast Guard. *Light List, Pacific Coast.* 1978.

U. S. Dept. of Commerce, Nautical Chart 18680 Pt. Sur to San Francisco.

U. S. Dept. of Commerce, Nautical Chart 18700, Pt. Conception to Pt. Sur.

U. S. Dept. of Commerce, Pilot Balloon Observations at San Diego for Sept. 7, 8, 9, 1923.

U. S. Dept. of Commerce, Surface Weather Observations for California

Stations for Sept. 1923.

Wernicke, R. *Big Sur*. Washington, D.C.: Smithsonian, 2000.

Whipple, A. *Storm*. Alexandria, VA: Time-Life Books, 1982.

Willshaw, F. Destroyer Archives NavSource, (www.navsource.org). USS *Sumner* DD-692, 2003.

Williams, K. *Measuring Response Readiness*. Proceedings of the Marine Safety Council of the U. S. Coast Guard, Arlington, VA., 2000.

Willshaw, Fred. Manager of Destroyer Archives NavSource (www.navsource.org). Help in obtaining USN photo of *Sumner* DD 333.

Woodland Daily Democrat, Sept. 10–11, 1923.

Worthylake, George, Table Bluff Light Station. *The Keeper's Log.* San Francisco, CA: United States Lighthouse Society, 2003.

Yett, Betty F. *West Coast Pilot*, Sausalito, CA: Paradise Cay Publishing, 1988.

Zadwick, Kenneth. President, Mare Island Historic Park Foundation. Vallejo CA: Tour of St. Peter's Chapel, information about destroyers built at Mare Island Navy Yard, 2002.

Glossary

Abeam– at right angles to the fore-and-aft line of a ship; a bearing of 90 degrees from starboard or 270 degrees from port.

Backing– a change of wind direction, with time, in a counterclockwise direction. A backing RC bearing is one that also changes in a counterclockwise direction.

Bearing angle– by a sighting compass oriented to a zero deg (north), reference is usually measured as the angle of your sighting, clockwise from 0 deg true north, through 90 deg east, 180 deg south, and 270 deg west.

Bearing bar– A bar with a vane at each end, designed to fit over a central pivot in the glass cover of a magnetic compass. Used for determining the compass bearings of a distant target.

Best estimated position– That position of a craft judged by the navigator to be the most accurate when the exact position is not known.

Characteristics of a light– The sequence and length of light and dark periods, and the color or colors by which a navigational light can be identified.

Chart– A map intended primarily for navigational use.

Circle of uncertainty– A circle within which a craft is considered to be located.

Coast pilot– A descriptive book for the use of mariners, containing information about coastal waters, harbor facilities, and channels, etc., of an area, particularly along the coasts of the United States.

Coast Piloting– Charting the movements of a vessel near a coast, by means of terrestrial reference points or known marine and anchored buoys.

Course– The intended horizontal direction of travel, usually measured from zero deg at the reference direction clockwise through 360 deg.

Course error– Angular difference between the course and the course made good.

Course made good– The direction to a point of arrival from a point of departure. After departure from a port, the course made good may be the direction of a navigational positional fix from the point of departure.

Course over the ground– The course made good over the ground.

Danger bearing– A maximum or minimum bearing of a point for safe passage past an off-lying danger, such as a group of reefs.

Dead Reckoning (DR) – Determination of ship's position by advancing a previous position or courses and distances, using the course steered and the estimated speed through the water.

Dead reckoning track– A series of dead-reckoning positions of a craft; a line of positions, based on successive DR-estimated positions. May involve an allowance for wind and current, course and speed, to estimate the speed made over the ground.

Deck log– The daily written record of the movements of the vessel with regard to its courses, speeds, positions, other navigational information, and important events that occurred aboard the vessel during each of the six daily watches. An entry is made for each watch and authenticated by the OOD of that particular watch. May include hourly observations of the sea, visibility, wind direction and speed. The daily log is countersigned by the ship's commander and navigator.

Estimated position– The probable position of a craft, determined from incomplete data or data of questionable accuracy.

Fathom– A unit of length equal to six feet, typically used to measure water depth.

Fix– A relatively accurate position determined by reference to known geographical points. It does not depend on any former estimate position.

Gyrocompass– A compass having one or more gyroscopes as its direction element, typically set to indicate true north.

Knot– A knot is one nautical mile per hour, about 1.15 statute miles per hour.

Nautical mile– A unit of distance equal to 1,852 meters (approximately 6,076 feet). A nautical mile is equal to about 1.15 statute miles.

Navigator– The ship's officer who navigates. He determines the ship's course, speed and location as required. The navigator indicates his approval of each ship's daily deck log by placing his signature on the final page of the log to the right of the Commanding Officer's signature.

Navigational foundation– Author's suggested definition: a measure of the underlying soundness of navigational procedures; an estimate of a vessel's movement or position based on the agreement between two sound procedures.

Agreement between a vessel's speed based on propeller revolutions, and a direct measurement of speed determined by timing the travel of a known distance—the distance between two position fixes, or the distance measured by towing a calibrated distance-traveled log.

Agreement between an estimated distance offshore of a verified line of position track, and depth soundings that conform to known depth contours on a nautical chart. Agreement with a position given by a nearby superior vessel that knows its latitude and longitude, or by a local vessel that is sure of its position by virtue of its local knowledge and recent sightings of specific local landmarks.

Officer of the Deck (OOD)– The naval officer on the bridge in charge of a four-hour watch. The OOD represents the commanding officer of the vessel for the assigned period, and is superior to all officers below the executive officer. An OOD is typically responsible for keeping the given navigational course, seeing that certain ship duties are performed on schedule, and signing the ship's deck log, which summarizes the activities of the watch.

Piloting– Navigation involving frequent or continuous determination of position, or line of position, relative to geographic points, to a high order of accuracy.

Radio Compass (RC) Bearing– In 1923 an RC bearing from a U. S. Navy Radio Compass Station was sent to a ship upon request and transmission of a source signal from the requesting ship. The bearing direction was the direction from the R C Station to the requesting ship. A (northwest, 315 degree) bearing meant the ship was to the northwest of the RC Station.

Rationalize– In 1923 an RC bearing could be "rationalized" while maintaining a speed of 20 knots. At *Delphy*'s location, it would have required a course change of about 45 deg to the west (without telling the RC station), holding that course for about 30 minutes, and then confirming the known course change by getting a new RC bearing that was consistent with the known change of direction.

Stadimeter–An instrument for determining the distance to an object of known height by measuring the angle subtended at the observer by the object.

Taffrail log – An instrument essentially consisting of a rotor towed through the water by a line attached to a distance-registering device secured at the taffrail.

Track – The horizontal component of the path followed or expected to be followed by a vessel or a storm center.

True course – Course relative to true north.

Wind direction – The direction from which the wind blows.

Appendix I

The Chain of Failure

I considered several approaches for analyzing this 1923 destroyer disaster. An approach designed to deal with battlefield conditions, multiple layers of command, and critical tasks has a nature and scale different from the one needed to analyze this peacetime tragedy. After much effort, the September 1923 records revealed a long and fragile sequence of minor, modest, and major failures—a "Chain of Failure,"—and I used this approach because it allowed me to track the host of failures that occurred:

- Actions taken that should not have been taken; and
- Actions not taken that should have been taken.

Each entry in the chain is a brief summary. The chain lists the failures that were detected; others may have occurred. A competent, attentive commander could and should have avoided the failures listed, and by so doing have prevented the disaster. (Navy documents are in Part III.)

In addition to the descriptive "class of failures," we considered "classes of mistakes" and "opportunities lost," such as a commander seeing an opportunity to query or inform the *Delphy* in a way that might have helped her navigator, but failing to do so because of the supposition that *Delphy* had all the navigational information—information unavailable to him.

Cdr Calhoun, commander of the *Young*, had "an estimated position about seven miles to the north of the *Delphy*'s estimated position." Calhoun could see *Delphy* close ahead, and had intercepted her transmission of her DR-estimated 8 P.M. position. Lt MacNally, navigator of the *Kennedy,* had an estimated position about six miles closer to shore than the *Delphy*'s DR estimate.

The failure sequence has a fragile nature. It might never have started had Capt Watson arranged Mr. Dooman's appointment for Monday in San Diego and spent most of his time on the bridge. The failure sequence could have been broken at the last minute had LCdr Hunter delayed executing the order to turn, called Capt Watson to the bridge, and said, "I have an RC bearing on our ship for 8:58 P.M. I have decided we cannot safely turn eastward, and I have delayed executing your order to turn to 095 deg at 9 P.M."

The chain is a haunting list of the alternatives faced and the decisions made by the squadron's officers. The timeline is approximate—the starting and ending times of single entries may be different. The first ten entries deal with some of the events that developed before *Delphy* passed Pt. Piedras Blancas; entries 11–22 deal with some of the events that developed south of Piedras Blancas until 8 P.M., and entries 23–38 deal with events after 8 P.M. until the *Delphy* became stranded.

The chain relies on the sources referenced, the appendices, the bibliography, the deck logs, and the documents in the author's possession. The numbers are for identification only. Specific USN responsibilities of the squadron, ship, and division commanders are in Part III.

1. Capt Watson's special order to maintain 20 knots failed to enhance RAdm Kittelle's order to test the cruising turbines. The usual interpretation of the admiral's order "to proceed at twenty knots" is that twenty knots is a desired speed, subject to decrease by the squadron commander's judgment of what's appropriate for the sea and general conditions encountered. Capt Watson's "main-

tain twenty knots" changed the intent of the original order from "desired" to "mandatory."

2. Capt Watson erred when he chose to spend most of Saturday visiting with his civilian friend Mr. Dooman. Hence he was seldom on the bridge, where the action is, ill prepared to solve the navigational crisis that developed that evening, and unable to see the futility of the last-minute manipulation of the uncertain navigational information.

3. At the squadron's pre-voyage conference, Capt Watson failed to answer Cdr Pye's question: "What course will the squadron follow after clearing Pt. Conception?" Watson said, "I will get back to you about that," but never did.

4. Ltjg Blodgett failed to get the ship's gyrocompass repaired while in port at San Francisco. The lack of a gyro meant that *Delphy* set the squadron's final course solely by magnetic compass.

[*Delphy*'s compass course appears to have been 2 degrees more landward than the *Kennedy*'s, as is evident in *Kennedy*'s deck log. Thus, *Delphy*'s true heading was more landward than indicated by her magnetic compass; thus she was more exposed to onshore winds.]

5. While in San Francisco, LCdr Hunter and Ltjg Blodgett failed to calibrate the *Delphy*'s propeller revolution count against a measured mile. The deck logs from the ships following *Delphy* showed their average speed was more than half a knot less than the *Delphy*'s indicated 20-knot speed.

[*Delphy* failed to detect that her true speed through the water was less than her indicated 20-knot speed; yet, without any supporting data, Hunter and Watson somehow estimated *Delphy*'s speed-made-good at 21 knots.]

6. LCdr Hunter made a mistake when he took over as navigator in addition to his job as ship commander. That action burdened Hunter and compromised his executive officer and regular navigator, Ltjg Blodgett, reducing Blodgett's status and his ability to influence the navigation.

7. Capt Watson issued "special orders" to the squadron's commanders that prohibited them from requesting radio compass bearings, forced them to maintain 20 knots, and caused them to accept the *Delphy*'s navigation. It denied those commanders the information they needed to safeguard their ships, and had nothing to do with fulfilling the admiral's order.

8-A. LCdr Hunter failed to plan ahead to get a fix on Pt. Sur. He should have planned to cope with the normal occurrence of variable fog. That plan should have noted that visibility might be restricted, and included a provision to have the easternmost destroyer steam close enough to the coast to get the required fix.

8-B. LCdr Hunter failed to get a fix on Pt. Sur.

9-A. Having missed a fix on Pt. Sur, LCdr Hunter failed to plan ahead for a fix on Pt. Piedras Blancas, the next lighthouse to the south. Well exposed and at a lower elevation, this light was usually easier to see than Pt. Sur. A plan should have been made to have the easternmost destroyer ease closer to the coast as it moved southward, and get a fix on Piedras Blancas. No plan was made.

9-B. The squadron failed to get a fix on the Pt. Piedras Blancas Light.

10. Having failed to obtain a fix on Sur and Piedras Blancas, Hunter failed to plan ahead for a future fix and for taking depth soundings before endeavoring to clear Pt. Arguello.

11. LCdr Hunter failed to verify the *Delphy*'s DR track by comparing his DR-estimated positions with those of other squadron ships. The record indicates that the ships were yawing and the steering was difficult. Along with an onshore wind as *Delphy* neared the coast, this caused her course to be more landward and slower than assumed by LCdr Hunter's dead reckoning. In addition, the compass on the *Kennedy* indicated that *Delphy*'s course was 2 degrees more landward than indicated by her magnetic compass.

[The *Delphy*'s deck log was "apparently lost." Hence we do not have the regular observations the crew logged for ship speed, visibility, and wind.]

12. Capt Watson failed to order the *Delphy*'s commander to transmit all his radio compass bearings and other nautical information to the division commanders. His inaction denied those commanders the information they needed to protect their ships.

13. The division commanders failed to request navigational information from the squadron commander. Lacking RC bearings and other information from the squadron commander, it became the duty of the division commanders to request that information before the *Delphy*'s 8 P.M. DR-estimated position was sent to the admiral.

[By virtue of his rank, command status, and his ship's #2 position in the column, Division commander Capt Morris did obtain certain information that the other division commanders did not receive, but he sent none of that information to the ships in his division.

With the approval of Division Commander Roper, LCdr Bratton of the *Stoddert* directly requested RC bearings to assure the safe navigation of Division 32. *Delphy* intercepted two of those RC bearings, but Hunter deemed them "wrong."]

14. Lacking RC information from their division commanders, it became the duty of the individual ship commanders to get RC bearings for themselves. It was also their duty to use their own direction finders.

[Only a few ship commanders made full use of their radio capability.]

15. LCdr Hunter failed to slow down and take depth soundings—information critical for estimating the ship's distance from shore. He failed to approve Ltjg Blodgett's important and timely recommendation that the *Delphy* take soundings.

[Hunter and Watson's rejected Blodgett's request to take a depth sounding with irrelevant remarks such as "Slowing down will ruin our engineering run," a statement that had nothing to do with the safety issue at hand, the water depth under the ship, and the ship's distance offshore.]

16. LCdr Hunter failed to recognize that the *Delphy* was headed directly at the Pt. Arguello RC station when he received three 320

deg RC bearings straddling 6:30 P.M. Then he failed to request radio compass bearings from 7–8 P.M., bearings that would have confirmed early on that *Delphy* was farther north than indicated by her DR-estimated positions.

[There was something odd about Hunter's ongoing decisions that the RC station's northwest bearings were wrong without requesting the RC operator confirm each suspected misreading. Hunter had the luxury of presuming that a single bearing might be a misreading. He knew, however, that the chance for misreadings two to five times in a row was nil, and he knew he had zero chance for a misreading of a west bearing, because such a misreading would imply that he was *on land to the east of the station.* Illustration **12**.]

17. Capt Watson failed to override LCdr Hunter's refusal to take soundings. Instead, he injected a careless opinion, "the water is too deep," an opinion that assumed the ship's DR position was correct—a fact not known. The failure to take soundings was a major mistake.

[As *Delphy* approached to pass Pt. Arguello, her DR navigation was dubious; Hunter should have grasped the critical need to verify the squadron's distance offshore. Watson's insistence that he could not slow to take soundings was flawed; he could have ordered the column's trailing destroyer to slow, take soundings, and advise the *Delphy*.]

18. Watson and Hunter—the Squadron 11 *Delphy* command—failed to conclude that it was crucial to get a position fix and confirm their DR-estimated 8 P.M. position before committing to that position and sending it to the admiral. Requests for position information should have been sent to commanders Calhoun, Pye, and Roper by 7:30 P.M.

19. Capt Watson failed to ask his division commanders for their latest DR-estimated positions before the *Delphy* finalized its 8 P.M. DR-estimated position. This failure denied the *Delphy* command vital information that it should have had before they estimated *Delphy*'s 8 P.M. DR position and transmitted it to RAdm Kittelle.

20. Capt Watson failed to send the *Delphy*'s projected 8 P.M. DR-estimated position to his division commanders before sending it to the admiral. This denied the divisions the opportunity to compare their estimated positions with the *Delphy*'s.

21. The *Delphy* command committed itself to *Delphy*'s DR-estimated 8 P.M. position, and sent that doubtful position to RAdm Kittelle without any assurance that it was a quality estimate of the ship's true location. Capt Watson's early approval of Hunter's questionable DR-estimated 8 P.M. position put Watson's reputation on the line before he had scrutinized Hunter's work or checked with the division commanders. This commitment caused immense problems, because it was near impossible to gracefully revise it before 9 P.M.

22. Cdr Calhoun failed to radio the *Delphy* upon intercepting her radio transmission of her 8 P.M. DR-estimated position and clearly state that the *Young*'s DR-estimated 8 P.M. position was 7 miles farther north than *Delphy*'s 8 P.M. DR-estimated position.

[Cdr Calhoun could see the *Delphy* about one-third of a mile ahead, but he assumed that *Delphy* had superior navigational information not in his possession.]

23. Ltjg Blodgett failed to use his own authority as junior navigator and EO to ask the second ship to his stern, the *Young,* for her estimated position.

24. LCdr Hunter erred when he rejected the two RC bearings sent to the *Stoddert* that he intercepted about 8:30 P.M., and the three RC bearings he requested and received during that period. [They showed the column was still northwest of Pt. Arguello, while Hunter's dead reckoning showed that *Delphy* was abeam of Pt. Arguello. Hunter never got a fix on Pt. Arguello, a fix on Pt. Conception, or a depth sounding to confirm it was safe to turn eastward.

Hunter later claimed he had difficulty getting RC bearings from 7 to 8 P.M., but the RC log shows this was incorrect. Between 7 and 8 P.M., the following nine ships obtained RC bearings: SS *Lakeshore,* USS *Selfridge,* USS *Melville,* SS *Arabian Prince,* USS *McDermut,* USS *Seattle,* USS *Partridge,* SS *Montebello,* and USS *Sloat.*]

25. Cdr Roper failed to radio the *Delphy* and advise them that *Kennedy*'s DR-estimated position was close to the coast and farther north than *Delphy*'s DR-estimated position. Cdr Roper explained to his lieutenants, who raised the question about *Delphy*'s safety, "The *Delphy* is steaming the coast near Pt. Arguello to be sure it gets a fix on the RC and the lighthouse."

26. Capt Morris carried special responsibility, since he was also the squadron's second in command, yet he failed to request the ships in his division to send him their estimated positions as they approached Pt. Arguello. This request would have revealed the difference between the estimated positions of the *Young* and the *S. P. Lee,* the 2nd and 3rd ships in the column.

27. Cdr Pye failed to press Watson for the answer to his pre-voyage conference question: "What course will the squadron take after it passes Pt. Conception?"

28. The *Delphy* command failed to recognize and confirm that *Delphy*'s DR line-of- positions track might be closer to the coast than shown on their DR chart for 8 and 8:30 P.M.

[*Delphy*'s DR track (Illustration **28**) showed her to be 8 miles offshore. Hunter made a major error as he approached Pt. Arguello: he fretted about the ship's NW–SE location on the overly extended DR line-of-positions track, but he never gave serious thought to the key question: "How reliable is that track's offshore distance?" This was a major error.]

29. LCdr Hunter erred in presuming the 8:25 P.M. RC he received was a misreading, and then demanding a reciprocal, which came in as 168 deg. This was a major error because the *Farragut* and other ships thought the 168-deg transmission might be a correct bearing. Hence it is likely that *Farragut* and others lost a chance to use the correct RC transmissions that they intercepted before and after 8:25 P.M.

[Hunter and Watson later used that reciprocal and their estimate that the *Delphy*'s speed-made-good was 21 knots to extend their estimated location by assuming that the 168-deg reciprocal track was a bearing (Illustration **28**). This speculation was without merit.]

30. Capt Watson and LCdr Hunter erred when they manipulated the "reciprocal" they ordered from the RC station, and their unverified ship speed data, to conclude that "21 knots was the speed-made-good."

[It is amazing that Capt Watson participated in the last-minute navigational manipulations used to turn the squadron eastward at 9 P.M. One explanation of why he approved this manipulation to support a turn eastward is that he did not know, nor sense the overall uncertainty surrounding the *Delphy*'s plotted DR estimated line of positions—a line of half-hourly estimates that started at 11:30 A.M. and was never confirmed by a single fix.]

31. LCdr Hunter failed to request the RC station to confirm their 8:25 P.M. bearing before he assumed it was a misreading. Hunter also failed to ask Watson for permission to have a squadron ship rationalize that northwest RC bearing before he presumed it was a reciprocal. Considering the risk involved in turning eastward without knowing where he was, it was foolish and dangerous for Hunter to proceed without calling the division commanders and asking for their latest estimated positions.

[An RC bearing could have been rationalized by a course change of about 45 deg to the west, holding that course for 30 minutes, then confirming that known course change by getting a new RC bearing and finding it consistent with the ship's known change of direction, a change unknown to the RC.]

32. Capt Watson and LCdr Hunter failed to assess all the available navigational evidence before Watson decided to change course to eastward 9 P.M. A call to the senior commanders would have shown that the average squadron speed was 19.4 knots and that *Delphy*'s magnetic compass was off 2 degrees.

[Watson left the bridge at 8:50 P.M., thinking there was still a margin of safety. Perhaps he believed that LCdr Hunter, the senior officer, navigator, and ship commander, would never execute the turn-eastward order if he had an 8:58 P.M. northwest RC bearing in his hand.]

33. Capt Watson made a major error when he failed to alert his division commanders of his final decision: "*Delphy* will change course to 095 degrees true at 9:00 P.M. Prepare your ship to follow in turn."

34. As soon as the *Delphy*'s 8:58 P.M. RC bearing arrived and showed that *Delphy*'s DR-estimated position was still to the northwest of Pt. Arguello, LCdr Hunter should have canceled the 9 P.M. turn eastward.

35. After canceling the turn, Hunter should have called Capt Watson to the bridge immediately, and requested that they get commanders Calhoun, Pye, and Roper on the radio and request their 9 P.M. estimated positions.

36. LCdr Hunter failed to signal "Slow the squadron's speed to ten knots," before turning eastward in poor visibility from an uncertain estimated position. Even if the *Delphy*'s DR-estimated 9 P.M. position had been valid, turning a destroyer squadron into the Santa Barbara Channel at a steady 20 knots was a dangerous speed, because of the expected increase in commercial and recreational traffic.

37. Capt Morris' *S. P. Lee* saw the *Delphy* turn, and received her 9 P.M. signal flag ordering "Turn to 095 degrees," but the *Lee* failed to pass that signal down the line.

38. After the *Delphy* hit the rocks, LCdr Hunter did not send a clear warning message to the squadron. The signal he sent, "Nine turn" and "Keep clear to the westward, " conveyed inadequate information. The signal "I am aground" would have clarified the situation for the squadron, and possibly saved the *Chauncey.*

Appendix II

Bearing Sheet, U. S. Naval Radio Compass Station, Point Arguello, California, September 8, 1923

Data from the Court of Inquiry's October 12, 1923 "Exhibit" in their report, "Twentieth Day"

Ship	Bearing	Time	Remarks
SS *Harvard*	320	0229	Good below 800
SS *W.S. Miller*	279	0235	"
SS *Harvard*	326	0229	"
SS *W.S. Miller*	257	0255	Good
USS *Corry*	279	0304	Weak
SS *Harvard*	312	0308	Good
SS *Harvard*	307.5	0320	Good
SS *Harvard*	286	0329	"
SS *C.A. Smith*	302	0352	Fair
USS *Corry*	158	0407	"
USS *Corry*	151	0425	"
SS *C.A. Smith*	299	0435	"
USS *Corry*	296	0439	"
USS *Corry*	288	0452	"
USS *Corry*	287	0502	Fair

Ship	Bearing	Time	Remarks
USS *Corry*	287	0522	Fair
USS *Corry*	267	0527	"
USS *Corry*	267	0544	"
USS *Hull*	284.5	0602	"
USS *Corry*	258.5	0606	"
SS *Ellobo*	304	0611	"
USS *Hull*	283.5	0616	"
USS *Corry*	234.5	0621	"
USS *Hull*	281.5	0625	"
USS *Corry*	215	0632	"
USS *Hull*	282.5	0634	"
SS *Ellobo*	300	0638	"
USS *Hull*	264.5	0645	"
USS *Hull*	258.5	0653	"
USS *Corry*	168	0705	"
USS *Hull*	211	0714	Fair
USS *Hull*	189	0721	"
USS *Hull*	177	0731	"
SS *Ellobo*	298	0744	"
SS *West Sequana*	166	0758	"
SS *Ellobo*	293	0809	"
SS *West Sequana*	179	0826	"
SS *West Sequana*	190	0900	"
USS *Sequoia*	172	0903	Weak, very
SS *West Sequana*	208	0930	Fair
SS *West Sequana*	220	1000	"
USS *Sequoia*	169.5	1013	Very weak
SS *West Sequana*	238	1033	Fair

Ship	**Bearing**	**Time**	**Remarks**
USS *Reno*	286.5	1100	Good
USS *Reno*	238	1119	"
USS *Reno*	215	1140	"
USS *Cuyama*	169.5	1213	Good
USS *Cuyama*	172.5	1230	"
USS *Partridge*	320	1401	Very Weak
Cdr DesRon 11	167	1415	Weak
USS *Partridge*	318.5	1421	Sigs weak
Cdr DesRon 11	162	1426	"
This ZNC is reciprocal of 162	326	1428	"
USS *Partridge*	312.5	1507	"
USS *Partridge*	311.5	1600	"
USS *Melville*	312.5	1610	"
USS *Seattle*	291.5	1616	Weak
USS *Melville*	312.5	1642	Good
USS Mc*Dermut*	320	1648	Weak
USS *Partridge*	307.5	1710	"
USS *Seattle*	285	1721	"
USS *McDermut*	324.5	1730	"
USS *Seattle*	282.5	1734	Good
USS *Melville*	310.5	1743	Good
USS *McDermut*	314	1805	Weak
ComDesRon 11	320	1813	Good
USS *Seattle*	264	1817	"
USS *Melville*	262	1820	"
USS *Seattle*	260	1827	"
ComDesRon 11	320	1832	"

Ship	Bearing	Time	Remarks
USS *Seattle*	257	1836	Good
USS *Seattle*	253	1843	"
ComDesRon 11	320	1848	"
USS *Partridge*	320	1852	"
SS *Lakeshore*	307.5	1909	"
USS *Selfridge*	356.5	1912	"
USS *Melville*	168.5	1918	"
SS *Arabian Prince*	191	1924	Weak
USS *McDermut*	324.5	1936	"
USS *Seattle*	228	1942	"
USS *Partridge*	307.5	1944	Good
SS *Montebello*	341	1959	"
USS *Sloat*	323	2002	"
SS *Lakeshore*	286	2008	"
USS *Stoddert*	326	2011	"
USS *Partridge*	326	2011	"
USS *Partridge*	284	2018	"
USS *Seattle*	218	2024	"
USS *Partridge*	280	2027	"
SS *Montebello*	334.5	2029	"
USS *Stoddert*	330	2032	"
ComDesRon 11	333	2039	"
USS *Partridge*	287.5	2043	"
SS *Arabian Prince*	203	2047	"
USS *Seattle*	207.5	2057	"
ComDesRon 11	323	2058	"
ComDesRon 12	320	2101	"
SS *Montebello*	301	2103	"

Ship	Bearing	Time	Remarks
USS *Partridge*	296.5	2105	Good
USS *J.F. Burns*	312.5	2116	"
ComDesRon 12	312.5	2119	"
USS *Partridge*	280.5	2122	"
USS *Kennedy*	0.5	2127	"
ComDesRon 12	305.5	2131	"
USS *Stoddert*	317	2137	"
ComDesDiv 32	303	2143	"
USS *Seattle*	200	2146	"
USS *Partridge*	210	2149	"
ComDesDiv 32	286.5	2152	"
USS *Seattle*	198	2157	"
ComDesRon 12	240	2203	"
USS *Partridge*	213	2214	"
SS *Arabian Prince*	212	2214	"
USS *Somers*	320	*2217*	"
USS *Partridge*	244.5	2221	"
ComDesRon 12	204.5	2223	Good
ComDesDiv 32	243.5	2228	"
ComDesRon 12	189.5	2238	"
USS *Partridge*	225	2244	"
ComDesDiv 32	234.5	2304	"
ComDesDiv 12	172	2307	"
SS *Richconcal*	156	2314	"
USS *Partridge*	174	2317	"
ComDesRon 12	158	2340	"
USS *Farragut*	323	2357	"
SS *Richconcal*	163	0002	"

Appendix III

Radio Compass Bearings for USS *Seattle* and USS *Corry* as they Passed Pt. Arguello

The two ships approached from the northwest and passed to the south on Sept. 8. The bearing of the *Seattle* backed about 90 deg in about 4 hours, and the bearing of the *Corry* backed about 100 deg in less than two hours, due to its greater speed.

USS* Seattle*, flagship, U. S. Battle Fleet Pacific

Bearing (degrees)	**Time** (24-hr.)
282	1734
264	1817
260	1827
257	1836
253	1843
228	1942
218	2024
207	2057
200	2146

USS Corry, *a Squadron 12 destroyer steaming alone*

Bearing (degrees)	**Time** (24-hr.)
273	0520
267	0527
267	0544
250	0606
234	0621
215	0632
168	0705

Appendix IV

Summertime Resultant Surface Winds, Based on the Historical Record from Two Coastal Stations Along Squadron 11's Route—San Francisco to Destroyer Rock

An afternoon onshore breeze over the California coast is the usual summer wind expected at stations along the California coast. The surface weather map for 8 Sept. 1923 (Illustration **7**) shows a typical summer pattern. Hence the long-term summer resultant surface winds provide a reasonable estimate of the resultant winds for such a summer day.

The climatological resultant daytime surface winds and latitudes for Fort Ord and Santa Maria are given below. Latitude reference lines are given on the map in Illustration **3**.

Time	**Fort Ord (36 deg 41')** (deg/mph)	**Santa Maria (34 deg 54')** (deg/mph)
7 A.M.	248/2.4	284/1.6
10 A.M.	275/6.6	301/6.7
1 P.M.	274/12.2	307/13.0
4 P.M.	270/12.0	305/13.2
7 P.M.*	259/9.1	306/8.5

* The above climatological 7 P.M. resultant winds (from 259–306 deg) indicate the wind was likely impacting the starboard side and giving the ship a shoreward push. This likely situation is consistent with the actual shoreward move of the *Delphy*, and the three 320-deg RC bearings it received between 6 and 7 P.M. (shown in Illustration **28**). Hence the *Delphy* commander, who was navigating by dead reckoning alone, had every reason to believe the RC bearings he received, which said the *Delphy* was heading for Pt. Arguello.

The above resultant winds show an adverse daytime summertime wind condition was likey for the Squadron 11 destroyers steaming 8 miles offshore on a course heading of 150 deg on 8 Sept 1923. In the case of those destroyers, a favorable resultant wind direction on the stern would have been 330 deg.

Appendix V

Deck Log Entries (9.8.23) for cruiser *Seattle*, tanker *Cuyama*, tug *Partridge*, and destroyers *Selfridge*, *Somers*, and *Stoddert*.

Data from power run of DesRon 12, *Sloat* and DesRon 11, *Reno*.

Seattle. 8 P.M. to Midnight. Steaming as before on course 156 true, 158 gyro, 138 per standard compass. Standard speed 13.0 knots. Obtaining radio compass bearings off Pt. Arguello at frequent intervals. Changed course to 90 degrees true. Richardson Rock bearing on chart 209 distant 27 miles, radio bearing brought forward from 9:57. (Pt Arguello 198). Burton Biggs, Ltjg USN.

Cuyama. 8 P.M. to Midnight. Steaming as before. 11:47 sighted Pt. Fermin Light bearing 90 true. Average steam 195#. Average RPM 91.0. J. J. Rochefort, Ltjg USN.

Partridge. 8 P.M. to Midnight. Steaming as before on course 135 deg. true. 9:45 received message fro ship asking for a bearing, then changed course following ship. At 9:52 started to countermarch, At 10:00 heard Arguello siren. Average steam 185 lbs. Average RPM 79.3. O. Eng, Boatswain, USN.

Selfridge. 8 P.M. to Midnight. Steaming as before on course 163 true., 143 PSC, making ⅔ standard speed. At 8:30 changed course to 193 true, standard speed 16 knots, At 8:32 changed course to 272 true, 252 PSC. Steaming on - pressure, making 5 knots. Stopped both engines. At 9:55 steamed on back pressure. Made turn of 360 degrees and resumed on course 272 true. Avg revolutions 69.l. R. S Dennett, Ensign USN

[On 9 Sept Mr. Dennett's ship will log the rescue of 12 men from the *Cuba*, wrecked on San Miguel Island.]

Somers. 8 P.M. to midnight. Steaming as before in column order of Divisions astern of USS *Delphy*, Divisions 33, 31, 32. Ships ahead seemed to be crowding up in confusion. Put rudder hard right and stopped. Went ⅓ speed ahead to clear USS *Percival*. At 9:10 ship ahead sounded siren and there seemed to be a collision as oil was seen to be burning on the water. At 9:11 sighted breakers close ahead on port hand. At 9:11 went astern ful speed on both engines . At 9: 12 bow hit rocks ahead and slipped off as ship gained sternway. Port propeller hit against rocks while going astern. Approximate location of grounding off Pt. Arguello. USS *Delphy* and ships of 33rd division appear to be aground. At 9:24 starboard engine astern ⅓ speed port. At 10:05 steadied on course 310 deg. true, 290 P. S. C. using engines only to keep steerageway. Taking soundings. At 10: 30 depth of water 26 fathoms. At 11:30 depth of water 41 fathoms. Foggy weather. Visibility during watch about 600 yards. Average steam pressure 250 lbs. Average RPM 112. J.P Womble, Ltjg

Stoddert. 8 P.M. to Midnight. Steaming as before in company with Destroyer Squadron Eleven, formation in column. USS *Delphy* leading. The fourteenth ship in column is a distance two hundred and fifty yards. Standard speed 20 knots, course 150 deg. true, 132 psc, visibility about (1½) miles. At 0900 *Delphy* changed course to left, followed by two van divisions. At 2107 received radio from, Commander Destroyer Squadron Eleven"Shove well off to left, nine turn." Also radio from Commander Destroyer Squadron Eleven, "Nine turn, keep clear to westward." At 2108 two-thirds speed immediately followed by stop. Changed course to westward to keep clear of all ships ahead and to get to seaward. KENNEDY was then on port bow. KENNEDY sounded backing signals. Backed until ship dead in water, took soundings and obtained 12 fathoms. Heard train on port quarter, immediately wen ahead two-thirds speed changing course to westward with hard right rudder. Changed standard speed to 15 knots, taking soundings. At 2126 stopped, no bottom obtained with hand lead 26 fathoms out. At 2129 on-third ahead on course 283 deg. true. At 2132 stopped. USS PAUL HAMILTON on starboard beam. Received signal from KENNEDY to form eighteen, course 270 deg. true, later picked up KENNEDY and THOMPSON. At 2150 formed with division. At 2157 two-thirds ahead. At 2204 one-third ahead. At 2205 stopped, commenced maneuvering to maintain position on KENNEDY, steaming on westerly courses. At 2221 stopped, lay to. At 2257 commenced steaming at various speeds and on easterly courses, standing in towards beach off Pt Arguello, to stand by stranded ships. Average steam 265, revolutions 112.1. J.H. Carter, Ensign US Navy.

Sloat. 8 P.M. to Midnight. Steaming as before on course 149 deg. true, in formation with **DesRon 12**, less, *Hull, Corry, Robert Smith,* and *Farenholt* . Standard speed 18 knots. *USS McDermut* guide. At 2001, changed to 154 deg. true. At 2010, changed course to 165 deg. true, and standard speed to 15 knots. At 2215 changed course to 128 deg. true. At 2215 changed standard speed to ten knots. W. A. Benoist, Ensign, U.S. Navy. [The 2215 entry shows DesRon 12 turning on a course of 128 deg, as shown in Illustration **12**, as it verifies it has passed Pt. Arguello It also shows DesRon 12 was in no hurry (due to fog).]

Reno. 8 a m. to 2 P.M. The destroyer *Reno* was alone and making a power run. Before 8 A.M. its speed increased from 8 knots to 19 knots and its average revolutions from 104 to 229. Here are *Reno*'s data during its 30–32-knot power run:

Time (24-hr.)	**Speed** *(knots)*	**Revolutions** (per hr.)
08	31	406
09	32	422
10	32	421
11	31	414
12	30	391
13	31	403
14	30	386

Appendix VI

Description of the Flush Deck Class* Destroyer, DD 186–347 series

Normal displacement: 1215 tons. First line DD.
Dimensions: 310 ft. at w/l, 314 ft. 4 in. (o.a.) × 30 ft, 11 in x 9 ft 4 in. mean draught.
Armament: 4-4 in, 50 cal, 1-3 in 23 cal, AA, 12 21 inch tubes in triple, deck mountings.
Oil fuel 375 tons.
Complement 122.
Designed S.H.P. 26,000-27,000 = 35 kts. Parsons. Westinghouse of Curtis turbines.
2 screws. 4 Normand, Yarrow, or White-Foster boilers.

Of these ships 36 were converted to fast transports in 1940–44; seven of these were lost and three damaged beyond repair. A further eight became light minelayers and 14 became seaplane tenders. In September 1940, 50 were transferred to the RN and RCN.

A photograph of the flush-decker destroyer* USS *Litchfield,* DD 336, is in Illustration **6**, and USS *Trever*, DD 339, in Illustration **4**.

---

* These destroyers are called the "Clemson Class" in some references.

These destroyers were built in the navy yard at Mare Island, CA. A U. S. Navy photograph of the USS *Sumner,* 333, (at sea) is in Illustration **25**. These photos show the detail of this great class of U. S. Navy destroyers.

The long, narrow construction of these destroyers made them prone to roll and difficult to steer on a constant course. The OOD frequently called, "Mind your rudder." Most of the ship had an actual width less than 31 ft. [This is a small distance—my sailboat was 31 ft long, 8 ft wide. The the tiller person could easily talk to the anchor person, and the navigator could reach from the navigation table to the coffeepot on the stove without moving either foot.]

The Farragut Class

With a huge stock of flush-deckers available, it was not until 1934 that the first of the eight-ship "Farragut" class was launched. At 1,400 tons, these vessels were larger than the flush-deckers, had a designed speed of 36.5 knots, and a "radius"of 6,000 miles.

Despite their increased displacement, these destroyers were still vulnerable, because they were impossible to maneuver in heavy seas and high winds, especially when their fuel load was light. In WW II, three 1,400-ton Farragut-class destroyers, built in 1934, were lost in 1944 during Typhoon Cobra in the East Philippine Sea. In his book, *Storm*, A. B. Whipple tells how those destroyers rolled to 90 degrees, and 850 sailors died when they went down. That loss accounted for most of the Pacific fleet's loss of life that day. One destroyer captain said, "The ship is unmaneuverable, I am stepping into the sea." Detail of this disaster is given in S. E. Morison's *History of United States Naval Operations in World War II.*

Appendix VII

A Tribute to the Navy Heroes and the Other Heroic Rescuers

This tribute to the hundreds of heroic acts that took place on that wet, cold, oily night in 1923 focuses on the citations recommended by the court of inquiry. Hence it allows us to sense the full impact of twelve heroic deeds. Choosing this limited number allows an opportunity to fully appreciate each one, a task that was near impossible in Chapter 4.

R. L. Rhodehamel, Machinist's Mate 1st Class, *for extraordinary heroism* in saving the lives of four shipmates at the risk of his own life after *(Delphy)* had stranded.

Commander William L. Calhoun, *for the coolness, intelligence and seamanlike ability* shown after the vessel under his command (*Young)* stranded, which action on his part was greatly responsible for the reduced loss of life on that occasion.

Chief Boatswain's Mate Arthur Peterson, *for extraordinary heroism* in swimming with a line from the *Young* to the *Chauncey* in a heavy and turbulent sea.

Lieutenant E. Z, Herzinger, *for especially meritorious conduct* in connection with saving the crew of the *Young* after the ship capsized.

G. C Ostergard, Machinist's Mate 1st Class, *for remaining at his post* in the engine room of the *Chauncey* until the water was above his waist.

Lieutenant Commander Walter D. Seed, *for great bravery in swimming a distance of about 75 yards* through a rough and turbulent sea in order to test the feasibility of and make arrangements for the salvage of his crew (*Fuller*).

Frank M. Moon, Machinist's Mate 1st Class, *for extraordinary heroism* in swimming with a line from the *Fuller* to a rock in a rough and turbulent sea in order to salvage the crew of that vessel. Valerus Vasvinder, Watertender 1st Class, Frank C. Colpits, Fireman First Class, George C. Lord, Fireman, Third Class, and James Moore, Fireman Third Class, *for meritorious conduct* in remaining at their post in the fire room of the *Fuller* until driven out by the inrush of rising water.

Commander W. G. Roper (*Kennedy*) *for his seamanlike ability and judgement* shown by him in handling the division under his command (DesDiv 32) on the night of the stranding of the 11th Squadron.

Seven ships were saved by the actions of their outstanding commanders and crews, and to some extent by the division's fortunate location in the column. All these ships were built in the Bethlehem Steel Yard in San Francisco. Here are the divisions, ships, and commanders.

(Div 31, Cdr Pye) *Farragut*, LCdr McClain; *Percival*, LCdr Cobb; *Somers*, Cdr Gaddis.

(Div 32, Cdr Roper). *Kennedy*, LCdr Bell; *Paul Hamilton,* LCdr McCauley; *Stoddert,* LCdr Bratton; *Thompson,* LCdr Symington.

The Civilian Rescue Leaders

Ron Adam, editor of the *Lompoc Record,* at the disaster site fourteen hours ahead of any other reporter.

C. L. Atkins, of Surf, wife of one of the telegraphers, who rushed to aid and feed the injured. She was on the train at 2 A. M. with all the eggs and milk she could find in Surf.

Glenn Baker, motor traffic officer; W. S. Bland, City Marshall. He summoned Clifford Smith and Adam to go to the section house at Honda. Bland and Baker crawled down the slippery cliff and talked to the ships' officers.

John Giorvas, SPRR track foreman, directed sustained rescue effort by the Honda railroad crew. Giorvas, who died in 1957, was posthumously recognized for his services by an act of the U. S. Congress on October 5, 1986.

G. T. Gunderson and Harry Seerey operated the track motor car out of Surf, and headed for Honda.

Farmers and nearby ranchers brought cable for, and aided the rescue work.

L. E. Heiges, M. D. and M. S. Kelliher, M. D. were the first and only doctors on the scene.

Lt Lee of the *Chauncey* was in command of the shore patrol left to defend the wrecks on the rocks. His letter of thanks for the people who gave aid to his men included:

The Red Cross of Lompoc; Ladies of the Auxiliary of the American Legion; Mrs. Stella White of the Lompoc Library; Mrs. J. T. Smith of Lompoc; Mrs. C. L. Atkins of Surf; William Sparks of Surf; John Giorvas and his men from the SPRR section quarters at Honda; Don Sudden; Mr. Olsen and the others of the Lighthouse Service, and the U. S. Navy Pt. Arguello RC Station.

W. J. Maes, SPRR General Foreman, authorized the intense rescue effort made by the SPRR.

Men at Pt. Arguello: George Olsen, Keeper, and A. A. Settles, Asst. Keeper, Pt. Arguello Light.

All the radiomen from the Navy RC Station, Pt. Arguello.

Noceti, Captain Giovanni, with his three partners: Nichola Ghio (who was in the crowsnest and spotted the men on the rocks), Giacomo Stagnaro and Fredrico Ghio—used their fishing boat, *Roma*, to rescue about 100 sailors from the rock where the *Woodbury* had run aground. [Now called Destroyer Rock.]

William Pittman, telegrapher at Surf, helped spread the alarm.

Rescue workers who used rope to pull sailors up the 100-ft cliff to the mesa. Many were badly bruised.

Road control men—on Monday, they "passed seven hundred machines" along the road to the coast.

Clifford Smith, first on scene with Bland and Adam.

SPRR section hands—quick to help sailors ashore and tend them. Also helped shore patrol.

Sudden, [Mrs.], nearby rancher, got the call from Pt. Arguello about the rescue; brought blankets. Sudden, Don, responded with his car, and drove rescued injured from the lighthouse to the railroad section house on the mesa.

Appendix VIII

The Mare Island Historic Park Foundation, St. Peter's Chapel, Vallejo, CA

The September 1923 destroyer disaster was keenly felt by the workers in the great naval shipyard at Mare Island, the relatives of those who were lost, and the relatives of those saved. The history of that shipyard began in January 1853. Plans for its closure were announced in 1996. The yard operated for 150 years, building canvas sailing ships, oil-powered steamships, destroyers, and nuclear-powered submarines.

My family and I sailed out of the marina just across the river from the gigantic cranes of the Mare Island Naval Shipyard, each gliding on its own railway track. All that is gone, but the Navy's former inter-denominational chapel, St. Peter's, is still in use. Tours are conducted by the staff of the Mare Island Historic Park Foundation.

Three destroyers built in this shipyard, USS *Trever,* USS *Litchfield,* and USS *Sumner,* are in Illustrations **4**, **6**, and **31**. About a dozen more were also built here.

A particularly serious loss occurred in WW II when three Farragut-class destroyers of Halsey's fleet went down with 900 men onboard in a typhoon in the East Philippine Sea.

A photograph of St. Peter's Chapel, taken in 2002 by Sacramento freelance photographer Janet D. Wilson, is in Illustration **30**. The chapel was built in 1901 as an interdenominational place of worship. The navy's link to St. Peter's ended in 1996 when the shipyard was closed, but tours and some community uses have continued. During a recent tour of St. Peter's, Kenneth Zadwick, of the Mare Island Historic Foundation, encouraged those in the tour group to protect the chapel's existence: "I want you to talk to your children and tell them about Mare Island's history."

A beautiful place to visit, the chapel is noted for its history and its twenty-nine stained-glass windows. A triptych in stained glass is dedicated to the naval heroes John Drake Sloat, David Glasgow Farragut, and Robert Field Stockton. (At one time, Capt Watson's father was Admiral Farragut's flag lieutenant.) New York Tiffany Studios made sixteen of the windows, each of which commemorates a person, a ship, or a battle. The windows were requested by Chaplain Adam McAlister, who was responsible for St. Peter's construction and who was stationed on the island at times from 1873 to 1916. The chapel also has twenty-five wooden tablets that are hung from its redwood roof. They honor naval heroes from President John F. Kennedy to the sailors who died in Samoa.

Over the years, services at St. Peter's in memory of the navy men and ships lost in 1923 were held and the Navy Hymn, written in 1860 by the Rev. William Whiting, was sung. It was. The first part of "Eternal Father, Strong to Save" is below, as obtained from the Naval Historical Center.

Eternal Father, strong to save,
Whose arm hath bound the restless wave,
Who bidd'st the mighty ocean deep,
Its own appointed limits keep:
Oh hear us when we cry to Thee
For those in peril on the sea.

Index

About the Author

Spencer Duckworth was born in Chicago, Illinois a few weeks before the destroyer disaster. He started at Elmhurst College, IL, in 1940, and later graduated from the University of Michigan.

He joined the U. S. Army Air Corps in 1942, and was commissioned a second lieutenant upon graduation from the Air Corps Advanced Meteorological Course at Chanute Field, IL.

He was discharged from the army in 1946, and worked as a meteorologist in the U. S. Weather Bureau's International Aviation Section at San Francisco Airport.

He joined the staff of Stanford University in 1951, and soon married Mary Elizabeth Wood. As a Research Associate at Stanford he was on the team that developed and successfully demonstrated the first atmospheric tracer system.

Two examples of his work are in the publications, *The Effect of Cities upon Horizontal and Vertical Temperature Gradients*—in the 1954 Bulletin of the American Meteorological Society, and in the formal report and presentation, *Comparative Travel of a Gas and an Aerosol*—at the 177th National Meeting of the AMS, and the Pacific Division of the AAAS in San Diego.

In 1960 Spencer joined the staff of the Bay Area Air Quality Management District as Chief, Air Analysis. He was part of the team that led the District's pioneer effort to control industrial sulfur dioxide by reducing source emissions and monitoring ground-level concentrations. In 1960 he was awarded the American Meteorological Society's designation as

Certified Consulting Meteorologist #20. One of his publications, *Air Analysis: The Standard Dosage-Area Product,* was published in 1967 in the Journal of the Air Pollution Control Association.

In 1967 he joined Metronics, a Palo Alto research company, as Chief, Environmental Engineering. Metronics was a leader in wind tunnel experiments to estimate the wind effects on large, tall structures before they were built. In 1969, at the request of Structural Engineer Edward Teal, Spencer presented the paper, *Wind Loadings on a Structural Model of the ARCO Twin Towers,* to a meeting of the Structural Engineers Association of Southern California.

Spencer started serious small-boat sailing in 1967, and his sailing improved with the purchase of a larger sailboat, and moves to the Berkeley Marina, the Vallejo Marina, and trips offshore to the north and south of San Francisco. During these years Spencer served on the Board of Directors of the Pacific Weather Analysis Corp., the first commercial company to use meteorological skills to select transpacific ship routes for the American Presidents Line.

In 1970 he joined the California Air Resources Board and helped develop and operate the Board's Division of Technical Services. In 1977 the State of California designated him as Registered Professional Engineer, Control Systems #1209. One of his major 1980 publications was *Effect of Meteorological and Other Factors on Air Quality Trends and Air Pollution Episodes*. In 1987 he retired from the California Air Resources Board as Chief, Aerometric Data Division.

From 1981 to 1996, Spencer held a U.S. Coast Guard License *"To Operate or Navigate Passenger Carrying Vessels of Not More than 100 Tons."* During that time he continued serious sailing on his oceangoing boat, the *Shenandoah IV.* In 1993 the North American Weather Association published Spencer's paper—*Storm in the Gulf of the Farallones, April 1982: A Sailing Disaster*—in the *National Weather Digest.*

The Duckworths are the proud parents of five children, four grandchildren, and five great-grandchildren. Mary and Spencer will celebrate their fifty-third wedding anniversary in 2005.